LIFE IN THE FRENCH FOREIGN LEGION

How to Join and What to Expect When You Get There

Evan McGorman

Hellgate Press

Central Point, Oregon

LIFE IN THE FRENCH FOREIGN LEGION

Hellgate Press
a division of PSI Research
P.O. Box 3727
Central Point, OR 97502-0032

(541) 245-6502
(541) 245-6505 *fax*
info@psi-research.com *e-mail*
www.psi-research.com/hellgate.htm

Editor: Kathy Marshbank
Book design: Constance C. Dickinson
Composition: Jan O. Olsson
Cover design: Mark Hannah

McGorman, Evan, 1967–
    Life in the French Foreign Legion : how to join and what to expect when you get there / Evan McGorman.
        p. cm.
    ISBN 1-55571-633-4 (pbk.)
        1. France. Armée. Légion étrangère. 2. France. Armée—Military life. 3. France. Armée—Recruiting, enlistment, etc. 4. McGorman, Evan, 1967– I. Title.
UA703.L5 M375 2000
355.3'52'0944--dc21

00-040992

Facing page: The *fouragère* is worn around the left shoulder on the dress uniforms of members of the *2ᵉ REP*.

Printed and bound in the United States of America
First edition 10 9 8 7 6 5 4 3 2 1

♻ *Printed on recycled paper when available.*

To the memory of Caporal-Chef Joseph Ofria,

with special thanks to
my mother, father, and brother for always
being there while I was "over there."

CONTENTS

PREFACE

In 1983, at fifteen, I learned from an article in a magazine that the French Foreign Legion still existed. From that moment on and for the next six years until I actually joined in 1989, I was consumed by the romantic images the French Foreign Legion conjures up.

There wasn't a day that went by in those six years that I didn't think about enlisting in its ranks and what the consequences of such an action might be. I thus embarked on a quest for information and knowledge about the Legion which ultimately proved rather fruitless and wanting. A couple of books and maybe a half dozen magazine articles was all I could manage to scrape together, and what little information there was only mentioned the history of the Legion or presented its affairs in a manner that revealed nothing of practical value to a potential recruit. While I was finally able to piece enough of the picture together to allow me to take the plunge, I still left with only a vague notion of what to expect.

While I was on my parachute course five months after joining, a friend of mine wrote me to say that he was toying with the idea of joining the Legion himself and wanted me to saturate him with as much information as I could to assist him in making a decision. I responded with a lengthy dissertation on what I'd so far learned, which wasn't much at the time, and was really only able to evince the need to be in exceptional physical condition before arriving. As it turned out my friend did not proceed, but this exchange planted a seed in my mind which gave rise to this book. I realized that no one really knows what they're getting into when they join the French Foreign Legion.

While working on this book I wrote to the Foreign Legion Recruiting Office in Aubagne to request some information on how to join the Legion. I didn't know how to contact the Legion before I joined and wanted to see what details they could provide someone interested in enlisting. All they sent me was a cover letter and a photocopy of a brochure. This information, though helpful, is far too succinct for someone wrestling with a decision of this magnitude.

It is due to this lack of available information that I decided to produce this publication, based on my own experiences, for those who may be seriously contemplating joining, and for the many for whom this subject is merely a curiosity. By no means do I wish to promote an exodus to the embrace of the Legion, but anyone who becomes preoccupied with joining will fare much better with some handy foresight. My intention is to provide such a person a solid basis from which he can make an informed decision. Throwing caution to the wind has a decided appeal in some circumstances, but the French Foreign Legion is not the place to experiment with this kind of approach.

Five years is a long time to commit to anything, and more so when your very existence may be at peril. The desertions that plague the Legion to this day reflect the myriad who went unprepared and unknowing. It is my hope that anyone who has ever dreamed about running away and joining the French Foreign Legion will be well served by the words that follow.

One final introductory note: I have several photos of the moments I experienced in the Legion and have included many of them, but with the eyes blacked out in order to impair recognition of the people in them. While it may not bother most to see their pictures gracing the pages of a book, there are those for whom it could be unsafe. The clearest example of this is a guy who had been affiliated somehow with the IRA (Irish Republican Army) and had actually faked his own death before joining the Legion. I am a strong advocate of the privacy of the individual and do not want problems befalling anyone because of my carelessness. Not on my watch, as the saying goes. For more information go to the website *www.ForeignLegionLife.com* or contact me at the e-mail address below.

mail@foreignlegionlife.com

Chapter 1

PRELIMINARIES

—

First let me say that I would not recommend joining the French Foreign Legion to anyone. Not only can it be an extremely hazardous occupation but the dozens of reasons I can and will present in one form or another all contribute to the one unfortunate truth of the whole experience: you will be disappointed in it. Unequivocally guaranteed.

Without exaggeration, nearly all of the people I served with were unfulfilled in their expectations of the whole affair, myself included. Except for the small number of men that genuinely find a better existence there and are willing to put up with its disillusioning reality, the vast majority grin and bear it or desert. While there are moments to be treasured, they are too few and far between to satisfy the yearnings that draw most men there in the first place.

But, disappointed though I was, I also believe that serving in the French Foreign Legion is an undertaking that is without equal. There isn't much on the planet that can compare to it. In fact, everything else seems very much an anti-climax after spending five years there. I haven't the slightest regret in having joined and, although I'm glad it's behind me now, I wouldn't have traded it for anything. In spite of its shortcomings, many have found it to be their beacon in stormy seas. So long as it offers a form of reprieve from personal and worldly woes, it will continue to attract and shelter men from all over the globe regardless of the reality.

1

Though I may paint a picture that is not all peaches and cream, the Legion is actually a half-decent organization that takes pretty good care of its members. All in all it could be a lot worse and undoubtedly was many years ago.

What Is the French Foreign Legion?

It is possible that you have heard of the French Foreign Legion but aren't exactly sure of what it is and what it does. The Foreign Legion is a French military unit of approximately 8,000 men that is merely a branch of the regular armed forces of France. What makes it unique is that it admits into its ranks strictly volunteers of nationalities foreign to France, although most of its officers are French. It is also renowned for accepting persons who are nothing less than outright criminals and providing them safe haven with the opportunity to reconcile with their past and have a second chance at life in return for five years of loyal service. Because of this the Legion is often inaccurately perceived as being a rogue mercenary outfit contrived of the most vile human beings found on earth.

While this may have been the case once upon a time it is hardly so now. But the aura of romance and mystique that has always surrounded the Legion continues to contribute to this misconception. A shroud of secrecy has constantly veiled the inner workings of the Legion due to its pledge to protect its members, which only adds fuel to the fire. Even today, obtaining worthwhile data about the modern Legion is a frustrating chore which does little to dispel false assumptions.

In 1831 King Louis Philippe authorized the formation of a Legion to be composed of foreigners for permanent service outside of France. Since that time the Legion has had a long and celebrated march through history and has been continuously involved in the unrelenting wars of France's colonial past. The traditional role of the Foreign Legion has been to maintain order in the overseas possessions of France, but it can be deployed anywhere it is needed. French colonial interests have greatly diminished over the years and, indeed, seven of the ten existing regiments now make their home in metropolitan France where once no Legion regiment was stationed.

Known for its austerity and discipline, deprivation and sacrifice, the French Foreign Legion is perhaps the most intriguing and famous fighting force in the world. Gone may be the days of camel trains, grueling marches in the Saharan deserts where to fall behind was to be left to die, and famous last stands where one fought to the death defending isolated forts against attacking hordes, but the sands of time have not eroded the impression many people seem to have of the Legion.

Today the Legion is as contemporary an infantry and light armored corps as you will find anywhere. It still upholds the conventions that made it what it is, even if these pillars of custom are slowly wearing away. Present day circumstances have relegated the Legion more to the role of a peace-time army but it still finds itself responding to the occasional crisis in Africa and around the world. Most recently it has been used in a peacekeeping function with the United Nations in Bosnia, Cambodia, and Kosovo, and in all probability will continue to fulfill duties of this nature in the years to come.

Before You Go

Before blundering headlong into uncharted territory, there are several areas of concern you are going to have to consider before arriving on the Legion's doorstep.

Of primary importance is your personal physical condition. You positively have to be in good physical shape. There's just no way around it. There is an endless glut of applicants for the Legion these days and they don't need a lot of reasons to reject you. I recently became privy to some statistics as quoted during a debate in the French National Assembly. In 1998 there were approximately 9,000 candidates who applied to the Legion at one of its recruiting centers. Of those 9,000, only 5,000 made it past the recruiting center to the more in-depth screening phase in Aubagne, from which only 900 were ultimately admitted into the Legion. This is only a 10 percent acceptance rate of those who apply.

If you are overweight, wear glasses, have poor teeth, high blood pressure, suffer from certain medical conditions, etc., your chances of simply getting past the recruiting center are slim to none. Be honest with yourself. Some problems such as high blood pressure or being overweight can be remedied before going. Ensure that they are. It would be a good idea to have a medical and dental check-up done of your own accord as it may save you a futile trip to France. The Legion does have quality doctors and dentists but they aren't there to correct your defects.

Assuming you have no real problems to speak of, your next most important concern is that you absolutely must, must, must be able to run. I can't stress that enough. If you can't run at least 10 kilometers (6 miles) at the drop of a hat at a firm, steady pace then you've got some work to do. This is vitally important. I've seen grown men reduced to whimpering babies because their bodies would not respond to the physical demands placed on them. Some physical minimums you should strive for are as follows:

- 30 pushups.
- 50 situps.
- Climb a 20 foot rope without using your feet.
- Run 8 kilometers (5 miles) with a 12 kilogram (26 pound) rucksack on your back in less than 1 hour. (The Legion is very fond of this one.)
- Complete 8 chinups with your palms away from you as you grip the bar.
- Also, try hiking long distances with 50 pounds or more on your back. You'll be doing lots of this.

It's true that most people are not at these standards when they arrive but you can make your life much easier and a lot less painful if you can meet or surpass them. You will not be turned away if you're outside these parameters — there's 16 weeks of basic training in Castelnaudary to get you up to snuff — but it's in your best interest to be within them.

The age range for joining is between 18 and 40 with parental consent required if you're 17, though I can't imagine anyone's parents consenting to their joining the Foreign Legion at 17 — or any other age.

It is unlikely you'll be allowed to join if you're married — or if they find out you're married. The Legion is primarily a single man's domain and doesn't leave much room for a wife or family, initially at least. Besides, the pay you receive as a fledgling *légionnaire* is hardly sufficient to support a family and the Legion is keenly aware of this. I did serve with one individual who kept the fact that he was married a secret then eventually moved his wife to the town in which he was stationed. He was then able to put in for leave most nights and, in essence, maintain a relatively normal existence with her. Although most people knew of this arrangement no one said anything since it was a done deal by then.

Neither will you be permitted to marry for the first five years of your contract once you've joined the Legion. You can't own a vehicle of any type including a bicycle, live off base in your own lodgings, have a bank account, come and go as you please, or do most things people in free societies take for granted. To qualify for these advantages you must complete your initial contract and stand on the five-year plateau before the gates of privilege finally open wide. Even after your initial contract the Legion will want to keep close tabs on you and regiment your life as much as possible if you decide to remain there. You will have to obtain permission if you want to get married, own a car, or have your own apartment. This may not sound too appealing if you don't think you should have to ask anyone's permission to do anything you want but those are the rules. If you don't think you can assent to the types of regulations the Legion imposes on its members, then you'd best not join. When you sign on with the Legion you need to understand that your obligations to it come first, and your own interests lag far behind in the dust.

This might seem rather obvious, but women are not allowed to join and it is highly improbable they will ever be permitted to do so. While several nations around the world are welcoming women into combat roles with a resulting decline in physical fitness standards, it is doubtful that the Legion will succumb to these pressures. Sorry ladies.

It is not necessary to speak French when you join but it's definitely to your advantage if you can manage a few phrases. Someone who speaks English is usually not too far away but this luxury is not always available to you and it's hard to function when you don't know what's going on around you. Sure, playing charades can be fun, but not when facing an ill-tempered *sergent* who's taken a sudden dislike to you and all you can do is stand there with the vacuous look of a bovine on your face. Don't worry though, you will learn.

You are going to need a valid passport, as you will have to enter France at your own expense in order to enlist. Check on possible visa requirements for your country of origin. You will have to surrender your passport when you arrive at the recruiting center. It will be returned to you if you are not accepted or at the termination of your initial contract. In actual fact, it is now possible to get it back after one year's service or less through a process called *rectification* but we'll cover that later. Make sure you both write down and memorize the serial number of your passport and its date of expiration. Having done this myself helped me get a new passport when I really needed one a few years after joining.

You may want to consider preparing a last will and testament before departing your country of origin. While none of us likes to think about this type of thing, it is best to plan for any eventuality. When you arrive at the Legion there will be several occasions where you are asked for information on next of kin in the event of your untimely demise. Make sure you bring a list of personal contacts with you.

Another concern is your banking arrangements and how you plan to manage any assets you may have while you're in the Legion. Are you going to maintain an account in your home country or close it before leaving? The Legion pays you an entire month's wage in cash once each month, but you can normally put it back into your Legion account or arrange to have it transferred to any account in the world. If you're hiding from your past you probably don't want to be transferring money to an account in your home country from France. You may want to go as far as opening an account in Switzerland, for example, before proceeding to join the Legion. Geneva is not too far away from the metropolitan regiments. If you have significant holdings in your home country you might wish to establish a power of attorney agreement with a trustworthy individual to administer your affairs while you're gone. My father was gracious enough to handle this for me while I was indulging my own interests in France.

Don't expect your friends and family to be thrilled with your visions of grandeur, glory, adventure, and romance when you finally break the news to them that you're going to join the French Foreign Legion. They'll understand only slightly less than you will exactly what you're getting into, even with the help of this book, so you can count on a fair amount of opposition. Be prepared for a deluge of opinions on your sanity and the lack thereof, but also for a flood of genuine concern and hand-wringing, which is not altogether unfounded. You're not exactly traipsing off to college. You may want to consider telling as few people as possible to avoid this onslaught of admonition, which will only undermine what you're trying to do. Although if you do waver under the convictions of others, you'll have to ask yourself if you are, in reality, ready to go through with this. I have known those who join first then let others know what they've done afterwards, but you might find that this isn't really fair to your relations. You're the only one who can make that decision.

If you've taken it upon yourself to develop a criminal record and don't know where to turn next, the Legion could very well be your means of redemption, but be forewarned; it is not the end-all cure-all it used to be. The days of "no questions asked" are a thing of the past, and you are thoroughly grilled once there. Minor infractions are usually overlooked. We all make mistakes, but if you're on the lam for a more serious crime such as murder, it won't endear you to the Legion's authorities.

The Legion can afford to be choosy these days and will opt for someone less potentially problematic than a serial chainsaw killer. Apparently, they do run a check on you through Interpol but what they are able to learn I really don't know. Nor am I completely sure they wouldn't turn you over to the proper authorities for a serious offense. For example, I doubt the Legion would have harbored Carlos the Jackal had he gone knocking on their door. Carlos the Jackal was an international terrorist who was responsible for several bombings in France and elsewhere. He was caught, tried, convicted, and sentenced to life in a French prison for his crimes. Once you have been accepted into the Legion though you are completely safe. I recall that one person I went through basic training with had let it be known he was in the Legion and it wasn't long before the French police came looking for him. The Legion merely denied he was there, had his name changed, and carried on as if nothing had happened.

Here's something else to think about. In speaking with several people over the years, many have said that joining the Legion is something they could visualize doing if they had a friend or someone else to join with. I would strongly advise against entertaining such a sentiment for a very good reason. If you find it necessary to lean on someone to embolden yourself into following through with this, you are definitely not mentally prepared to do so and have no business showing up at a recruiting center with another person in tow. Besides which, there is no guarantee that you would be together for long. Any delay or unforeseen circumstance for either of you at any stage of the selection process could quickly separate you. You could end up in different basic training *sections* and ultimately in different regiments. Not to mention the fact that one of you could be accepted while the other is found unsuitable. As it is, I don't think there are many who join in pairs or small groups. It is absolutely a one-man show. You have to be able to stand on your own two feet.

The single most important point you are going to have to ponder is whether or not you are fully 100 percent committed to spending five extremely long years of your life in the French Foreign Legion. If your heart and soul are not completely dedicated to this endeavor, you will be making a monumental mistake. Life in the Legion is trying enough without taking things at half measure. When I joined there was nothing on God's green earth I wanted to do more, but there were moments when even I contemplated desertion. It is something you genuinely have to want to do. Don't forget that you could be called upon to make the ultimate sacrifice or take a human life for a foreign government. When the

Gulf War started, the Legion regiments that were sent lost more than a few men to desertion. Take your time and think about this. Of course, when you're young, full of piss and vinegar, and absolutely lusting for some adventure, these minor details don't hold much water.

What to Take

In a nutshell, nothing you want to lose. You don't need a lot of excess baggage anyway. Everything you bring will be confiscated shortly after your arrival. Your passport, money, clothes, luggage, any books, electronic devices, knives, military gear, etc. is taken and put in temporary storage, your money in a temporary account. If you are accepted you will not see your belongings ever again except for your passport and money. If you are not accepted everything is returned and you can be on your merry way. I remember one guy who brought a leather jacket and tried to retrieve it at the end of four month's basic training. It had already gone missing. Myself, I tried to be clever by sewing a large sum of money in the seams of my jacket, thinking it might serve as an emergency fund or to be used at the end of my contract. I would have lost it had it not been discovered during the shakedown procedure. It was credited to my account. You will be allowed to keep the following:

- a French-English dictionary
- shaving gear, toilet articles, a towel
- cigarettes
- your watch
- your wallet and approximately 200 francs (about $50 U.S.). Don't take credit cards or a profusion of identification normally kept in your wallet
- an address book or personal contact list

Bring only a small amount of cash with the remainder of your money in travelers checks and memorize or hide the serial numbers; write them in pencil on random pages of your dictionary. This precaution may not be necessary but covering your ass is always worth the effort. Make sure you have enough to satisfy French customs officials that you can support yourself while visiting. Also, have a return or open-ended ticket for which ever mode of transportation you use to enter France. If you have previous military experience it doesn't hurt to bring a copy of your records to show what a fine prospect you are, but don't bring the originals.

Where to Join

Below are listed the various recruiting centers at which you can enlist.

94120 Fontenay-sous-Bois (Paris)
Fort de Nogent
Tel. 01 48 77 49 68

59000 Lille
La Citadelle
Tel. 03 28 36 08 72

44000 Nantes
Quartier Desgrées-du-Lou
rue Gambetta
Tel. 02 40 74 39 32

76038 Rouen cedex
Rue du Colonel – Trupel
Tel. 02 35 70 68 78

86000 Poitiers
Quartier Aboville
Tel. 05 49 41 31 16

57000 Metz
Quartier de-Lattre-de-Tassigny
Tel. 03 87 66 57 12

69007 Lyon
Quartier Général Frère
Tel. 04 78 58 40 21

66020 Perpignan
Caserne Mangin
8, rue François-Rabelais
Tel. 04 68 35 05 38

33000 Bordeaux
260, rue Pelleport
Tel. 05 56 92 99 64

21000 Dijon
Caserne Junot – 66, avenue du Drapeau
Tel. 03 80 73 54 86

67000 Strasbourg
Quartier Lecourbe – rue d'Ostende
Tel. 03 88 61 53 33

51000 Reims
Quartier Colbert
32 bis, avenue de la Paix
Tel. 03 26 88 42 50

13007 Marseille
La Malmousque – Chemin du Génie
Tel. 04 91 31 85 10

13400 Aubagne
Quartier Viénot
Tel. 04 42 18 82 57

64100 Bayonne
18, quai de Lesseps
Tel. 05 59 50 14 84

06300 Nice
Caserne Fillet – rue Sincaire
Tel. 04 93 80 59 06

31000 Toulouse
Caserne Pérignon
avenue Camille-Pujol
Tel. 05 61 54 21 95

On arrival in France you will, as a matter of course, have to pass through customs. If they ask, just tell them you're there on vacation and don't expect to be in the country longer than a month. You'll know by then if the Legion is going to accept you or not. Again, ensure you have adequate funds to reasonably support yourself. It is not necessary to tell them you're there to join the Legion, although if you do it shouldn't be detrimental. My own thinking on the matter was that it really wasn't their business that I was there to join the Legion. If I hadn't been accepted no one would have been the wiser and no harm would have been done.

After getting through customs you can do one of two things: Beeline it to the recruiting center or spend a few days taking that vacation you told the customs officials about. If you want to join in Paris, for example, the quickest and easiest way is to take a taxi from the airport or train station to Fort de Nogent, although the fare may end up being quite expensive. A cheaper alternative is to get a bus or train into the city, take the *Métro* to Château de Vincennes, and from there take a taxi the rest of the way. Fort de Nogent is just east of Château de Vincennes, which is located in eastern Paris.

Personally, I highly recommend a short visit in Paris. Not only is Paris a beautiful city but once you stroll through the gates of the Legion it could be a year or more before you are able to take leave. It also gives you a chance to get your second wind and make sure you really want to go through with this.

If you are in an undue hurry to join, don't be like one prospective hopeful who arrived one evening in Aubagne in the final days of my contract. An Irish fellow had jumped the perimeter fence to the base, found his way to our barracks and informed those he met that he wanted to join the Legion. Not only was this completely unnecessary but incredibly stupid as well. He was quite proud of the fact that he had entered the base sight unseen but I don't think he fully appreciated how fortunate he was that he didn't stop a bullet on the way in. The Legion doesn't advocate a shoot first and ask questions later policy, especially in mainland France in time of peace, but accidental shots have been fired by overzealous, tired guards on occasion in the heat of the moment. Luck of the Irish I guess. I believe they just removed him from base and told him to go join in Marseille, with an unceremonious kick in the seat of the pants, no doubt.

Even though I've listed the address for Aubagne in the "Where To Join" section, Aubagne does not conduct the initial processing of recruits. The nearest center where you can join is the Malmousque in Marseille. Neither will you benefit much by showing up at the gates of one of the regiments. They may be able to provide you with some information but you will still have to get yourself to one of the recruiting centers.

Chapter 2

FORT DE NOGENT

Y ou are unlikely to have many moments in your life that are as profound as when you first present yourself at the gates of the French Foreign Legion. For a pure, heart-pounding rush there can't be much else like it. My own heart was pounding like a jackhammer and I could barely breathe or draw spit. If someone had yelled "Boo!" I probably would have shit my pants. If at this point you decide that you may have bitten off just a wee bit more than you can chew, there's no shame in turning around and calling it quits. It took more than most people have just to get this far. There are opportunities to say the hell with it and ask to be released from your contract even after you've signed on the dotted line, but this gets harder and harder to do as you go along, and may ultimately lead to you attempting desertion if you discover that your heart's really not in it.

When you arrive at the gate, hand the guard a slip of paper on which you've already written: *Je veux m'engager à la Légion Étrangère* (I want to join the Foreign Legion). He'll let you in and have you wait while he summons someone to escort you further. Don't make the mistake of showing up around noon. The French take a two hour lunch break between noon and 2:00 P.M. and aren't the least bit interested in speeding up for a new recruit. Meanwhile, you're left wondering what diabolical schemes are being plotted against you.

Your recruiter will most likely be a *caporal-chef* which is a rank between corporal and sergeant. He'll take your passport and escort you to the main building. Once there you'll be given a preliminary search of your baggage but will still be allowed to keep everything, although I was relieved of a small pocket knife which I never saw again. You'll be given a receipt for your money and 200 francs of it to keep. You'll be asked to complete a series of questions from a sheet of paper pre-written in your own language. When this is finished, you'll be shown to a room and given a bunk and a locker to put your gear in. It's a good idea to bring a couple of padlocks for the lockers you will be using. You may not have anything worth stealing but things can go missing if you're not vigilant.

At some point you'll be issued an old work uniform to wear while you're there. Depending on the time of day you arrive you may be given a few chores to keep you occupied. Don't think for a moment you'll be lolling around on your bunk all day waiting for events to unfold. It is more than likely you'll be thrown into the kitchen to help with the great, never-ending, pot-scrubbing derby that is an integral part of life in the Legion. Unlike many armies, the French do not employ civilians to take care of this type of work, for better or for worse, so you will definitely be doing your fair share of it. It is at this time that you will become familiar with what is undoubtedly the single, most annoying, tedious, hateful word in the Legion vocabulary. That word is *corvée* (kor-vay). It means chore or duty and is usually of a menial nature. It is used to describe every type of cleaning or work-related detail and will be an everyday part of your life until you've been in long enough to have gained some rank and thus some immunity from it. As an example, *corvée cuisine* means kitchen duty.

Shortly after arriving in Fort de Nogent, you will be whisked away to a medical facility somewhere in Paris and given a precursory examination. Here, I believe, they are looking for obvious problems that may disqualify you. I remember one fellow recruit from Greece had bad eyesight and another from England was overweight. Neither were allowed to continue further. This is why I suggest having a medical exam done on your own before leaving for France. This is just the tip of the iceberg and more in-depth examinations will follow during the coming weeks.

The Contract

After completing the medical exam and returning to Fort de Nogent, you will be lined up with your fellow recruits and asked to sign a piece of paper. This will be your contract *(Acte D'Engagement)*. Yes, it happens that quickly. It is written in French so you probably will not be able to read or understand exactly what you're signing unless you get lucky and your recruiter speaks your language and can properly explain it to you. Fear not. You aren't being asked to sign away one of your kidneys. My own contract is shown below.

1ᵉ REGION MILITAIRE.

Place de PARIS

N° du registre : *1517/89*

Imprimé n° 311-6/4.

Instruction n° 2500/DEF/PMAT/
EG/B du 4 juillet 1978.

Format : 21 × 29,7.

(Recto.)

ACTE D'ENGAGEMENT
du nommé (1) H E N R Y, John
à titre étranger pour la légion étrangère.

L'an mil neuf cent Quatre Vingt Neufle Vingt Octobre

à   Onze   heures, s'est présenté devant nous (2) Capitaine   Officier Suppléant
Commissariat Arméé de Terre

M. (1)   âgé de   21   ans

exerçant la profession de Militaire   résidant à

canton de   département, pays (3)

fils de (4)   et de (4)   née

domiciliés à

Cheveux Chatains   Yeux Bleus   Sourcils Séparés

Menton Bifossette   Nez Droit   Dents C.M. 100%

Visage Ovale

Renseignements physionomiques supplémentaires :   Néant

Taille : 1,80 M   Poids : 77 Kgs

Marques particulières : Tatouage Epaule Gauche

lequel a déclaré vouloir s'engager pour servir à titre étranger dans la légion étrangère et, à cet effet, nous a présenté :   Médecin des Armées PAUME-GIBARD
                                 Médecin Adjoint de l'Infirmerie de
1° Un certificat délivré à la date du   20.10.1989   par (5) VINCENNES.
et constatant qu'il n'est atteint d'aucune infirmité, qu'il réunit la taille et autres conditions requises pour servir dans la légion étrangère.

2° Son bulletin de naissance, une déclaration d'identité (3) constatant qu'il est né le
à   et de Nationalité

3° L'autorisation de son représentant légal (6).

4° (7)

Après avoir reconnu la régularité des pièces produites, nous lui avons donné lecture (8) des articles 6, 7 et 13 du décret n° 77-789 du 1er juillet 1977 relatif aux militaires à titre étranger.

(Verso.)

Nous l'avons informé que :

1° Ses services compteront à partir de la date de signature, par lui, du présent contrat.

2° Le présent contrat comporte une période probatoire de six mois éventuellement renouvelable une fois par l'autorité militaire.
La période probatoire prend effet de la date de signature du présent contrat.

LE CONTRAT NE DEVENANT DEFINITIF QU'AU TERME DE LA PERIODE PROBA-TOIRE.

3° *Pendant la période probatoire initiale ce contrat pourra être dénoncé :*

31. Soit à la demande de l'engagé, agréée par l'autorité militaire, pour raison personnelle d'ordre social ou pour des difficultés notoires d'adaptation, exprimée jusqu'au terme du quatrième mois de service. Dans ce cas la décision définitive du commandement devra être signifiée avant la fin de la période probatoire initiale.

32. Soit à tout moment, par l'autorité militaire du fait :
— d'une inaptitude médicale pour une cause pré-existante à l'engagement ;
— d'une inaptitude à l'emploi ou à servir dans les rangs de la légion étrangère ;
— d'une inadaptation à la vie militaire.

4° *Pendant la période probatoire renouvelée ce contrat pourra être dénoncé* par l'autorité militaire pour inaptitude à l'emploi ou pour inadaptation à la vie militaire.

5° *A tout moment ce contrat pourra être résilié* dans les conditions fixées à l'article 32 de l'I.M. n° 2500/DEF/PMAT/EG/B modifiée du 4 juillet 1978 et notamment :
— sur demande agréée de l'engagé, pour raison personnelle impérieuse fondée sur des faits dûment reconnus et survenus depuis la signature de l'engagement ;
— d'office pour inaptitude physique ;
— par l'autorité militaire, pour insuffisance professionnelle ou par mesure disciplinaire.

« Après quoi le candidat a promis de servir avec honneur et fidélité pendant le temps, à partir de ce jour et s'est engagé, au cours de ce premier contrat, à ne pas se prévaloir de services ou de qualifications antérieurement détenues à titre français. »

Le contractant a promis également de servir dans les rangs de la légion étrangère partout où il conviendrait au gouvernement de l'envoyer et, après avoir eu lecture du présent acte, a signé avec nous.

Le commissaire de l'armée de terre
ou
l'officier suppléant,

John Henry

Période probatoire renouvelée le   pour une durée de six mois à compter du
conformément à la décision du commandant de la légion étrangère en date du   (3).
Contrat - annulé - dénoncé - résilié (3) pour   compter du   pour   (9) par décision du
n°   en date du   notifiée à l'intéressé le   .
Contrat devenu définitif le   (3).

Le commissaire de l'armée de terre
ou
l'officier suppléant,

———————

(1) Nom et prénoms de l'engagé.
(2) Nom du commissaire de l'armée de terre ou de l'officier suppléant et localité où il est en fonction.
(3) Rayer les mentions inutiles.
(4) Lorsque ces renseignements sont connus.
(5) Nom, grade et qualité de l'officier signataire du certificat.
(6) Si l'engagé est âgé de moins de 18 ans.
(7) Si l'engagé est français et n'a pas encore satisfait à ses obligations légales, autorisation du ministre permettant l'engagement à titre étranger.
(8) Si l'engagé ne connaît pas la langue française, il lui sera donné lecture dans sa langue, des clauses contenues dans l'acte.
(9) Indiquer le motif.

The first page basically lists a few of your personal details and physical characteristics. On the second page the terms and conditions are explained:

The recruit has been informed that:

1. His service begins as of the date of his signature on this contract.
2. This contract includes a six month probationary period eventually renewable by military authority.

   The probationary period takes effect as of the date of signature on this contract.

   THIS CONTRACT DOES NOT BECOME FINAL UNTIL THE TERMINATION OF THE PROBATIONARY PERIOD.
3. During the initial probationary period this contract can be terminated:
31. At the request of the recruit, agreed upon by military authority, for personal reasons or for notable difficulties in adaptation, expressed until the end of the fourth month of service. In this case the final decision of the commandment should be signified before the end of the initial probationary period.
32. At any time, by military authority by reason of:
    – medical unsuitability for a pre-existent cause at enlistment
    – unsuitability for employment or for serving in the ranks of the Foreign Legion
    – the inability to adapt to military life
4. During the renewed probationary period this contract can be terminated by military authority for employment unsuitability or for the inability to adapt to military life.
5. At any time this contract can be annulled as of the conditions fixed in article 32 … :
    – at the agreed upon request of the recruit for urgent personal reasons that have befallen him and been duly acknowledged since the signing of his contract
    – for reasons of physical unsuitability
    – by military authority for professional insufficiency or as a disciplinary measure

"After which the candidate has promised to serve with honor and fidelity [-smudged-] as of this day and has pledged in the course of this first contract to not prevail upon service or qualifications previously held by French right."

The contractee has equally promised to serve in the ranks of the Foreign Legion everywhere that the government deems it necessary to send him and, after having been informed of this present act, has signed with us.

Here you sign your John Henry and are now a proud member of the French Foreign Legion; for the moment at least. You still have to get through Aubagne. On looking over the contract I couldn't find where it says for how long you are signing. I think it may be under the part that got smudged but believe me, you are making a five year commitment here.

As you can see, the doors have not irrevocably closed behind you for five years the moment you put pen to paper. Years ago the Legion may have had you unyieldingly in their clutches to do with as they pleased but this is no longer the case. At the same time, don't expect to join then be released at your convenience, especially as time wears on. After investing a lot of time, money, and effort on you they won't necessarily be charitable in accommodating someone who enlisted on a whim. Generally speaking though, you can more or less decide to leave without too much trouble up until you commence basic training in Castelnaudary. It usually takes three weeks to a month to reach this stage. After that, the process becomes increasingly difficult but not impossible. A fellow I knew in my regiment was constantly in trouble and in jail for one thing or another and finally took the initiative and asked to be released from his contract. He wasn't able to adapt to life in the Legion and all that it demands, so they let him go without a lot of contention.

Once this auspicious occasion is complete you will be biding your time (scrubbing pots) until you are shipped off to Aubagne to begin the next phase of your adventure. If I remember correctly there are two weekly departures from Fort de Nogent.

Chapter 3

AUBAGNE

⎯

After being in Fort de Nogent for a few days, you and your fellow recruits will be loaded on a bus late one evening, taken to the train station, and sent on an overnight trip through France to Aubagne. It is roughly an eight hour journey and you likely won't sleep much. They don't splurge on sleeping berths for you and you'll probably be too excited to sleep anyway. A recruiter will accompany your group and will pick up more recruits as the train stops in other cities throughout the night. You will transfer trains in Marseille and arrive in Aubagne bright and early in time for breakfast.

Aubagne is the official headquarters and administrative hub of the Legion. This is where your life in the Legion begins once you've completed the selection process, and ends upon the termination of your contract. You will be spending approximately three weeks here undergoing security checks, medical examinations, aptitude tests, interviews, working on various labor details, and just waiting for time to pass. The hardest part about Aubagne is all the waiting around that you do.

Inauguration

A few hours after arriving, I believe it was the same day, your group will be herded to a room along with all your luggage. Here you will have to strip down to your underwear while your belongings are catalogued and put in a duffel bag for temporary storage. You will only be allowed to retain the items I previously mentioned. Once again, if the Legion accepts you into its ranks, your belongings will be disposed of unless you decide before your probationary period is up that you've had enough. At any rate, who wants to put on musty old clothing that's been sitting in a duffel bag for five years? You will have ample opportunity to accumulate new duds. If you aren't accepted your belongings are returned to you. When this is finished you are given a work uniform, a gym suit, boots, sneakers, and a small haversack for the rest of your things. At some point you are also given a few toilet articles such as shaving gear, soap, toothpaste and toothbrush even if you did bring your own. Do not bring an electric razor with you. I can't quite remember but I don't think you're allowed to keep them. If you've never shaved with a blade you may want to get into the habit of doing so before leaving for France.

You will find that the sleeping quarters here are much more crowded than at Fort de Nogent with most rooms being equipped with bunk-beds for roughly 18 recruits. Keep a close eye on the few belongings that you do have. Never leave your wallet or money unattended. When you have a shower, take it with you. Try and find a piece of plastic to wrap it in. Don't lend anything of yours to anyone unless you don't care whether or not you get it back. People come and go rapidly at Aubagne, so you could easily have something go missing. Follow these little guidelines everywhere you go in the Legion. While the majority of people are trustworthy enough, the Legion inevitably attracts those of dubious character who cannot be trusted. There are bad apples in every barrel and you will definitely discover this as you go along.

While you are in Aubagne and the recruiting center you will not be permitted to phone or write or have any contact with the outside world and you certainly can't leave the camp at night. You can expect a spartan existence from the time you walk through the Legion's gates until you've passed through basic training and into one of the regiments. Simple pleasures like acquiring a package of cigarettes or getting a can of Coke or a chocolate bar suddenly become a test of your resolve. If you're a smoker you'd better be prepared for periods when you may not be able to get your fix. You're not required to abstain completely but things are much less readily available to you. You're not allowed into the *foyer* every night to obtain these luxuries.

You're going to be rubbing elbows with a wide range of interesting characters. The Legion is truly the melting pot of the world and has probably had a representative from every country on the planet at one time or another. You won't even be able to communicate with a great many of them. Most of your fellow hopefuls will be down to earth and have their heads on straight, like yourself, but you will also be in the company of many criminal minds, fly-by-night dreamers, kooks, and loonies from whom you should definitely try and keep your distance. It's not that they're dangerous, as such, but you don't want their aberrations or thought processes to rub off on you. I've seen cases where large numbers of people jumped on a collective bandwagon even when they didn't know each other before coming to the Legion. Many have thrown in the towel before really getting started after being wrongly influenced by someone else's hysteria. When I was there, a group of about 25 or 30 of us who spoke English gathered together every time there was a break in the daily activities. Of that group, I can only think of three of us who ultimately were accepted and completed a full five years in the Legion. The rest were either weeded out at Aubagne or deserted one by one within two years. Keep to yourself, remain firm in your determination, and you'll do okay. Don't let any of this scare you. Believe it or not, most of the people you will meet in the Legion are pretty good fellows.

You'll find that everyone tends to band together according to their nationality or common language. This natural proclivity has led to these groupings being referred to as the "English Mafia" or the "Portuguese Mafia." This is strictly a colloquial term used in a facetious manner and is not meant to suggest the presence of organized criminal activity within the ranks of the Legion. Any type of crime that is committed is usually carried out by a lone individual. There are no organized extortionist mobs or sophisticated crime rings in the Legion.

Every morning and afternoon after you've eaten there will be a general assembly or *rassemblement* where you will be assigned to either a phase of your screening process or to duties to keep you gainfully employed at some productive enterprise. They will call out everyone's name one at a time and break you off into groups. Pay close attention and listen carefully for your name. At any given time there are well over a hundred recruits assembled and recognizing your own name is not easy when it's spoken by a foreign tongue. You don't want to wind up picking grapes in Puyloubier when you're supposed to be having a medical exam.

The screening process usually begins with more medical examinations. You will be spending long hours sitting in your underwear awaiting your turn to be poked and prodded. These exams are more detailed and will likely unearth any impediment not discovered while you were at the recruiting center. Unfortunately, I do not know exactly what their criteria is for whether you pass or fail but basically they will be looking for any reason you will not be able to perform duties of a highly physical nature and whether or not you may potentially become a burden or liability to them.

The Gestapo

After being in Aubagne a few days you will probably have started hearing about a shady entity called the "Gestapo," if this term is still in use. It is jargon that refers to a branch of the Legion concerned with its internal security. Be prepared for some lengthy rap sessions on you and your background.

They will interview you in your own language and gather more information on just about everything. Expect more questions on your personal statistics, your family, are you single, married, divorced, any dependents, which country and city you're from, what you were doing before you came to the Legion, your employment history and reasons for prolonged unemployment, your education and any special skills you may possess, if you've ever been convicted of a crime, taken drugs, are wanted by police in your own country, previous military experience and whether you were honorably discharged and so forth. Be ready for anything.

If you have done a misdeed or been involved in some regrettable circumstance in your life, honesty is probably your best policy here. Isn't it always? But, although I don't advocate bending the truth, you may want to selectively embellish certain minor details. As an example, I knew someone who had joined at 35 and told the Gestapo that he had been arrested for drug possession when he was 19. No problem, he was allowed to join. A couple of years later when he wanted to pursue a medical path within the Legion they checked his files at Aubagne, found this blemish committed 18 years earlier in the folly of youth, and was not permitted to follow this course of action. What I'm saying is that even though they may run a check on you through Interpol, from which I doubt they are able to glean much, their main source of information is you and what you ultimately decide to tell them. Don't cut your own throat needlessly. At the same time be diligent enough not to get caught in a lie as this will not help your case and may prevent you from being accepted. I'll leave this to your discretion.

Changing Your Name

It is during these discussions that it will be decided whether or not they deem it prudent to change your name based on what you've told them. If you're running from a situation you'd just as soon forget and have informed them of such, they will take the appropriate measures to protect your identity and, in effect, help you vanish. Your new name will be based on your nationality. If, for example, you're American they won't try hiding you by giving you a French name. It will be another name of American origin. The initials of your new name will correspond with the initials of the name you're relinquishing. For example if your name is John Smith your new name might be Jason Simmonds. Your date of birth will also be displaced by one month. Any changes that are made relate to your former identity to help you in remembering the details of your new one. This is not necessarily a mandatory procedure and many people keep their own names through the entire duration of their contract. You will notice a lot of recruits who come from France itself. I had always thought the French couldn't join the Legion but all that happens is that their names and countries of origin are changed. You wouldn't believe how many Swiss, Belgians, and Canadians there are in the Legion.

Aptitude Tests

Once you've sweated it out with the Gestapo, the next major undertaking will be a series of tests in your own language to determine your aptitude and I.Q. You're even given a test in Morse code to see how well you pick that up. Take these tests seriously. They will be used as a gauge to ascertain what you are capable of accomplishing and what career paths you are allowed to follow as you progress in the Legion. There are specialist courses available to you later on that take these scores into consideration. The end result will be a score out of 20, called your *niveau général* or general level, that is attached to your files for the remainder of your time in the Legion. My own score was 17 and I've seen them as high as 20 and as low as 4. I remember a fellow, I believe was from Morocco, who broke down crying after these tests. I'm not entirely sure why but I don't think he was able to fully understand the questions that were asked and when time was up he'd barely completed any, thus ensuring he did not remain in the Legion.

Acceptance

As the days pass you will be able to gauge your progress by way of a colored tab they give you to wear. In your first week you'll be given one in yellow, the second week in green and the third in red. Once you're wearing that red tab you've pretty much got it made and it's just a matter of wrapping up the last few details. If they take you off at some point and shave your head right down to the coconut, things are probably starting to move in your favor as well. At the very worst you get a free haircut out of the deal.

Another indicator of your progress is when you're given your serial number or *matricule*. It is a six digit number and must be memorized and recited in French under the watchful gaze of a member of the *cadre* before you leave Aubagne.

One of the final things that will take place in Aubagne is you being interviewed about why a strapping young fellow such as yourself would want to join the French Foreign Legion. Almost like a regular job interview. While there is no right or wrong answer to this, try to prepare a statement in advance that will properly convey why you want to be there. Half-cocked, fanciful notions may reflect the fact that you aren't really sure of what you're doing there. Make every attempt to give the impression that you are serious in what you are doing and have every intention of seeing this thing through to the end, even if you don't.

You'll know for sure that you're bound for Castelnaudary and 16 weeks of basic training when they take you to a supply depot on base and issue your *paquetage* or gear. It contains everything you will need in the months to come including the famed *képi blanc* which you won't be permitted to wear until you've earned the privilege. Representatives of your training *cadre* will also arrive at this time from Castelnaudary and assume control of the 30 or 40 of you who have made it through the selection process. Be ready for a slow gearing up or introduction of things to come such as a surprise morning jog that leaves you gasping like a fish out of water. You've had fair warning to be in shape before you get here. There isn't anything in the way of a physical regimen incorporated into the selection phase nor is there much chance to exercise in Aubagne, so you'd better be prepared before arriving.

Before embarking for Castel you'll be given an exclusive tour of the Legion's prestigious museum located on base. Enjoy it while you can. There aren't many chances to witness the memorabilia stored there. Of note is the famous wooden hand of *Capitaine* Danjou who was killed at Camerone, Mexico in 1863. You will also be formally addressed at the museum by an officer who will offer some sage words of wisdom, advice, and luck, of which you'll probably understand little, then that will be that. You're off to Castel.

Chapter 4

CASTELNAUDARY

—

Another train ride of about four hours will take you to Castel-naudary, the principal training facility of the Foreign Legion. The *quartier Capitaine* Danjou is the name of the ultra-modern Legion camp at Castel and has only recently been in use since they stopped using the *quartier* Lapasset, located in the town itself. The *quartier Capitaine* Danjou is three or four kilometers (2.5 miles) east of town. It is here you are molded into a shining example of man-hood. I recall arriving on either a Friday or Saturday then spending the weekend being assigned rooms, bunks and lockers, stowing our gear away, and just generally getting organized.

Orientation

Your group of recruits will be put in a *section* (usually 30 men) in one of the recruit training companies. Each company has a color associated with it which is indicated by a colored piece of cloth called a *foulard*, worn on the left shoulder of your combat uniform. The T-shirt of your sports gear also reflects this color. This is a common practice throughout all the regiments in the Legion.

You will be sharing a room with six or eight fellow recruits and a cor-poral, or *caporal*, who is in charge of that room and is a member of the training staff. A corporal in the Legion is not the equivalent rank found in British or American armies. A Legion *caporal* is closer to a sergeant in the British or American rank structure in terms of the authority he wields, and is obeyed as such. Don't ever try and get smart with one. It can be a trying circumstance having this kind of authority figure constantly in your midst as you can never entirely relax, but that's the way it's done.

You may notice before long that your *section* might have a *caporal* who is not fully-fledged in this rank but still has the same authority and responsibility as a regular *caporal*. This rank is something they call a *foot-foot caporal* and is still regarded as a normal *caporal*. They ask someone who has recently completed their basic training exceptionally well if they would like to remain in Castel as a member of the training staff instead of being immediately posted to one of the regiments. They are given the privilege of assuming the rank of *caporal* after a scant four months in the Legion with the advantage of becoming a full *caporal* after completing their tenure, which may last for several basic training courses. This is definitely a short-cut to becoming a *caporal*, as it can take two or three years or longer before your regiment sends you on your *caporal*'s course. Accepting this offer is probably more advantageous for those who have previous military experience in other armies and choose not to claw their way tooth and nail up through the ranks again. The downside of this, and I hope you'll heed my warning, is that *foot-foot caporals* are regarded with disdain once they are eventually assigned to a regiment and have a difficult time commanding the full respect they may have merited. No one likes someone who has taken the easy route when everyone else does it the hard way. One of the *foot-foots* in my basic training *section* had been a lieutenant in the Portuguese army and so had chosen this path, but had to endure a significant amount of contempt after arriving in the regiment. Even years later when he had proven his worth and all this should have been just an unpleasant memory, he was still required to withstand the inevitable scorn when this subject came up. I would strongly suggest you not accept any offer of this kind unless you have big shoulders and are willing to brave the derision of your peers and superiors. I'm not entirely sure why they even have *foot-foot caporals*. I think it is partially due to the fact that there are absolutely no volunteers from the regiments to be a *caporal* in any training unit at Castel.

Your *section* will normally have three or four *caporals* as training staff who take turns at being the *caporal du jour,* or corporal of the day. The *caporal du jour* is responsible for the coordination and organization of the numerous activities your *section* goes through in the course of a day. He oversees roll call in the morning, at night, and throughout the day, and ensures he knows the exact whereabouts of every member of the *section* at any given time, gets everyone assembled for all three daily meals, assigns *corvée* duties for the day, presents the *section* to the *sergent du jour* at the morning and afternoon assemblies, and carries out all orders issued by his *section* commander concerning the *section* on that day. Any questions, problems or concerns you may have on any given day are addressed to the *caporal du jour.*

Each company has a central nucleus known as the *semaine,* which is an office that controls the daily routine activities of the company. It is headed by either a *sergent* or *caporal-chef* with a *caporal* as a second in command and often has a *légionnaire* at intervals throughout the day to run errands. The name of it denotes the length of time the *sergent* and *caporal* are on duty there which is to say for one week, 24 hours a day. For each activity that is directed by the *semaine* a whistle is blown by the *caporal* with the name of the activity yelled out just prior to its commencement. For example, at 5:00 A.M. the *caporal de semaine* will blow the whistle and yell *réveille!*, which means wake up! At 5:30 A.M. he whistles *appel!*, and everyone assembles for roll call. This procedure takes place all day long. Some of the things you can expect to hear are *corvée compagnie!* (cleaning chores at the company level — thrice daily), *rassemblement!* (assembly for morning and afternoon parades or any reason necessary), *soupe!* (lunch or dinner time), *solde!* (pay), and *extinction des feux* (lights out). Any other activity or situation that arises is given to the *semaine* to coordinate.

We used to joke that this whole process was like having your hand held all day long and that we couldn't even be trusted to wake up or go to lunch on our own. It does serve a purpose though, particularly due to the language barrier and doesn't give you an excuse for missing anything vitally important; like getting fed or paid or knowing when bedtime is.

You will be paid each month while in Castel but you won't receive your entire remuneration. They will provide you with roughly 500 francs every month and retain the balance in your account, which will later be transferred to your combat regiment. You won't have many occasions in which to spend it anyway, as trips to the *foyer* are infrequent. It's enough to keep you in cigarettes and a few other goodies and that's about all. I'll talk more about your pay later on.

A phrase that you will soon become familiar with at Castel is *rendre compte*. Translated literally it means "to give back the count" but simply means to "report back." Any time you are given a task or duty of any nature by a superior, you are expected to *rend compte* at its completion. For example, if you spend all day in the mess hall on duty and drag your weary butt back to the barracks at night, you'd better make sure you *rend compte* to your *caporal du jour* and the *semaine* to let them know you're back before you do anything else. This seemingly insignificant little procedure is considered extremely important and failure to do so will bring down a firestorm of fury on you. Make sure you don't forget it.

Our first week at Castel was actually spent waiting for another compliment of recruits to arrive from Aubagne and join our *section* as there weren't enough of us to warrant starting the training. While awaiting this secondary group, a dozen of us were selected to take a driving course and be trained on several of the vehicles the Legion uses. Each *section* uses its own recruits as drivers so there is an immediate need to get some people trained. There is an excellent facility located on base for this purpose.

It was during this course that it really hit home as to what being in the Foreign Legion is all about. You're suddenly thrust into a situation where you're being instructed in French and are required to competently learn what you're being taught in a big hurry. When an instructor is yelling at you to push in the clutch and you're grabbing at the windshield wipers, hoping you're doing what he's asking, you'll know the true meaning of stress. Equally difficult is the classroom instruction, where an instructor prattles on at length with you desperately trying to absorb the material in preparation for the unavoidable test. As daunting as all of this seems, it is surprising how quickly you can learn.

Admittedly, during the written test that was a multiple choice questionnaire shown on a slide projector, we did receive some help from one instructor who surreptitiously pointed to all the answers. The answers were either A, B, or C and this instructor would indicate the answer with a pointer while asking aloud if the answer was "A, B, or C," pointing to the answer as he asked it. I'm not sure if anyone else noticed what he was doing, but to this day I find it quite amusing.

Following the arrival of the next batch of recruits a week later, we were reorganized and paired with a French-speaking partner or *binôme*. An interesting bit of Legion trivia is that approximately 50 percent of all members are from France or other French-speaking nations and the Legion puts this fact to very good use. Your *binôme* is responsible for helping you learn French as much as possible and for making sure you know what's going on at any given time. He's a bit like a constant guardian who's tail can be rapidly in a sling if you've done or not done something that can be traced back to him. Even though it's not easy communicating at first, you can usually make yourselves understood and get through things without a lot of fuss. Do try and get along with him — he's there to help. Unfortunately, not everyone is compatible with their *binôme* and fights sometimes ensue as a result.

Not long after everyone was settled, we were once again addressed by one of the officers of the base. His message was translated for everyone in their own languages by other Legionnaires. The one point he made that still sticks in my mind was his statement that "we are not here to make martyrs of you," which I found reassuring considering the "fight to the death" mentality that has been a part of Legion yore. In the late 1800s, *Général* de Negrier uttered his prophetic phrase in reference to having troops sent to Indochina, "You Legionnaires are soldiers in order to die and I am sending you where you can die," which does nothing to give you any peace of mind. Thankfully enough this sort of callous disregard for the welfare of its men is no longer an attitude the Legion upholds, though neither is France presently caught up in a costly war.

Yet another medical examination takes place during the first couple of weeks in Castel. What they're trying to find that wasn't covered at Aubagne I don't know, but if you've made it this far you won't have anything to worry about. I do seem to remember receiving several inoculations at this time.

The Farm

The training program begins with a month-long excursion to what is called "the farm," which is literally a rustic old French farmhouse out in the country. The Legion has several of these lodgings for training and each company has its own farm to use. The niceties found on base at Castel such as heated living quarters, hot water for showers and shaving, toilets, and decent food are not present here, so it serves well as an initiation into the rigors of life in the Legion. Our sleeping quarters were extremely crowded. We utilized triple-tiered bunks to accommodate everyone and had to share a tiny locker with our *binômes*. Make every attempt to claim a bottom bunk in this situation so as to save yourself a balancing act when you try to prepare your bed or go to sleep.

Each day begins with a wake up call at 5:00 A.M. Roll call is soon after to make sure no one has deserted in the night. Breakfast is a token offering of bread and coffee. There is a general cleaning of the quarters then everyone assembles for the colors ceremony or raising of the flag. This is usually followed by physical activity of some sort such as a lengthy jog, then a quick shower — hot on a lucky day — and a morning of training. Lunch is spread out over two hours followed by more training in the afternoon. There's a break for supper, then an evening class. You might have some free time in the evening to do some studying. Lights out is at 10:30 P.M., preceded by another roll call to ensure everyone is present. You may be called on to do guard duty throughout the night. The days are long, filled with activity, and the going is tough since there is a lot to learn and you won't fully understand the language at this time.

The meals are prepared by the recruits with the supervision of one of the *caporals*. Most of the time it simply involves heating up large tins of canned food and doesn't require much culinary expertise. Unfortunately, this trend of substandard food preparation is prevalent not only here and at Castel, but in the other regiments in their mess halls as well. The food is average at its optimum. A mess tin overflowing with slime-green spinach does not exactly excite the palate. Each meal, except breakfast, is begun with the singing of *Le Boudin* while on the farm. This should be the first song you learn:

Tiens, voilà du boudin,	Well, there's sausage,
voilà du boudin,	there's sausage,
voilà du boudin	there's sausage
Pour les Alsaciens, les Suisses,	For the Alsatians, the Swiss
et les Lorrains	and the Lorrainers
Pour les Belges, il n'y en a plus, pour	For the Belgians there's none left, for
les Belges, il n'y en a plus	the Belgians there's none left
Ce sont des tireurs au cul.	They are idlers. Idlers.
Tireurs au cul	

It's an appropriate ditty to be singing before you eat considering it's the only one I've ever heard of where anyone sings about sausage. When you get your first taste of blood sausage you'll definitely be wondering why the hell you're singing about it though. It's a thoroughly disgusting repast.

Another aspect of mealtime is the word *popotier*. Loosely translated it means server. The officers and NCOs of your *section* eat apart from the rest of you and are served by one of the recruits. You will have your turn at this undesirable task. This is a custom that occurs everywhere in the Legion, not just during training. What makes it one of those pain-in-the-ass traditions is that it's expected in almost all situations. Imagine setting up a table and chairs in the middle of a march so the *cadre* can be formally served while the rest of you plunk down on your arses to eat. Bloody ridiculous. This doesn't always happen, but you'll see it often enough or variations of the same theme. Once is far too many.

They will try to beguile you into believing how much of an honor it is to serve the *cadre,* but it's really only a ploy to justify the whole laughable premise. There was a *caporal-chef* who worked in the NCO's mess at Aubagne who'd been stuck there for eleven years, if I have my facts straight, who must have somehow bought into this theory. Unfortunately for him, he'd long since realized that he had erred in his reasonings and spent most of his 12 to 16 hour days whining and wallowing in self pity about how miserable his life was.

Your training will cover a wide array of material which includes basic drill and maneuvering, weapons, tactics, first aid, camouflage, rank structure, singing, French lessons, and Legion history and traditions, among other things. Most of it is pretty much a standard syllabus that could be utilized by any army. Two major differences will be the time devoted to language classes and learning a meager amount of French, and the time spent singing.

Speaking French

It is, at times, surprising how well the Legion's wheels turn considering the formidable language barrier that is an inherent part of life here. You're given a smattering of formal classroom instruction during which, at best, you will learn the basic rudiments of the language. This consists of learning a few elementary nouns, verbs, and grammatical rules through a lot of robot-like repetition with the assistance of your *binôme*, but will hardly leave you proficient in French. This will happen largely of its own accord through osmosis and being immersed in it day in, day out and will take some time. Before I joined the Legion I had taken six years of French in school and could hardly piece together enough words to make myself understood, but after being continually exposed to it every day, it wasn't long before things fell into place. It really depends on the effort you put forth in trying to learn. I knew one fellow from Romania who didn't know a lick of French before he joined but was speaking impressively after seven months. Another person I served with from Japan could barely manage a few grunts and mumbles on a good day after having been in almost three years. Though granted, in his case there was the additional problem of having to learn a completely new alphabet system as well, but others have done it. There are still others who can barely make themselves understood after five years and only learn what is required to get by.

One possible counter-productive factor in being motivated to learn is that the Legion is actually quite tolerant and understanding of any inability you may display in handling the intricacies of speaking the language. As long as you're able to understand and be understood everyone is happy. You're not expected to become fluent, but don't ever think you can get away with playing dumb anytime it suits you. This is an unwise practice and can easily incur the wrath of one of your superiors and lead to a highly explosive situation. There is almost always a way of being able to understand what is going on even if something has to be translated for you. You're still required to be able to function in the language and do your job. You're of little use otherwise. When the Gulf War started it was found that the *légionnaires* who were still fairly new to their regiments and not yet adept in French were more of a hindrance than an asset. With even a modest effort there's no reason you shouldn't be comfortably apt in speaking and understanding French within a year.

There is an unwritten rule throughout the Legion that you speak French until the work day is done whereupon you may converse in your own language with others of your mutual tongue at your leisure. This does not always happen by any stretch of the imagination. Most people of the same nationality/language tend to flock together during the course of the day and will naturally want to speak to each other in their own tongue. Speaking French during the day is an ideal opportunity to learn the language, but what is hard to take at times is someone continually badgering you to speak French. This does become a sore point occasionally and can create a seething resentment. While it may be polite and courteous to speak in a common language so that everyone can understand what you're saying, this doesn't always happen, nor is it a realistic expectation to think that it will. Most people are understanding enough of this fact, but be prepared to do many, many pushups defending your point of view when it doesn't coincide with that of one of your superiors.

The great melange of different languages all clustered together in one environment can, from time to time, create rather humorous circumstances.

I knew a fellow *légionnaire* from Romania who was permanently endowed with an extremely unfortunate misnomer for a last name. In French it translated into "fart bum" and the poor fellow carried this stigma with him through all his time in the Legion. He would have had no idea that his name would translate in such a regrettable manner when he joined and really, they should have changed his name in Aubagne, but someone probably thought it would make a good joke and left it alone. I'll leave it to you to figure out what his name was. It'll be good practice in learning some French.

A now semi-famous incident occurred at Castel with a newly ordained *foot-foot caporal* who was still learning French. He had been told to return the *section*'s binoculars or *jumelles* to the armory but misunderstood the order and paraded the entire *section* to the armory with their *gamelles* or mess tins. Suffice to say he was the target of a lot of good-natured ridicule for some time afterwards.

During a march in France our unit stopped for a break in a village that had a small store selling honey, so a few people decided to buy a jar to put on their bread ration. One fellow, thinking this was a good idea, bought a jar and was about to spread some on his bread when he realized he'd purchased a jar of varnish instead of honey. A good laugh was had by all.

Singing and Marching

Singing is a tradition deeply ingrained into the lifestyle of the Legion. The farm will probably be the place you are first taught a few of the many songs you will learn. Time permitting you may learn four to six songs during your stay there.

One of the *caporals* on your training staff will guide your *section* through a song in the classroom by projecting the words on an overhead projector then singing it while all of you listen. After a couple of repetitions the whole *section* will then participate and go through it several times. It takes awhile, but eventually it will come together. Once everyone can sing from memory you will be taught how to march in time to the song by marching in place at first, then by going outside and trodding up and down the road. You can bet you'll be spending long hours dedicated to this task. It is a perfect time filler since there is always a new song to learn and old ones can always be improved. It is also an excellent way of developing cohesion and unity within your *section*, especially when used as a form of punishment.

Recruits singing after receiving their *képis blancs.*

One of the truly awesome, spine-tingling, early experiences of your first days in Castel will be the singing you hear from the other units on base. Every day at noon and in the evening the respective companies assemble in block formation and slow march their way to the mess hall, singing one of the many Legion songs as they go. When it's done right it is nothing short of fantastic. I remember our first evening in Castel when these companies came marching out of the foggy darkness, singing as they slowly advanced. It was absolutely unforgettable. The chills and goose bumps are automatic. There is, in fact, a requirement that if you're in the vicinity of a unit that is singing you must stand at attention until it passes by, and rightly so.

The Legion actually publishes its own song book called a *carnet de chant* filled with dozens of melodies. Most of the songs are in French but a few are in German as a result of the heavy German presence in the Legion after World War II and their subsequent involvement in Indochina in the early 1950s. You will probably notice a common theme of death and defeat running through many of these songs which reflects the loss that is suffered by any army in times of war, but which also denotes the rather dismal fighting record France has displayed since the glory days of

Napoleon. It's not the most encouraging or inspiring subject to be singing about especially when you are now a part of whatever is to come.

Learning how to march in the Legion is a chore and a half. The rate at which you march in formation is roughly 88 paces per minute which is probably slower than you would normally walk if you were strolling down the street. The gait in most other armies averages about 120 paces per minute. It really takes getting used to as everything feels like it's in slow motion and it's a real battle trying to keep your body under control at this slow speed. The pace is supposed to signify the somberness of death and is also acknowledged as a sign of respect. When used in conjunction with one of the Legion's songs it really creates an impressive, stirring effect.

Code of Honor

One of the major endeavors you will undertake while on the farm is learning the Legionnaire's Code Of Honor (*Code d'Honneur du Légionnaire*). It is in French and will have to be thoroughly memorized for the ceremony in which you receive and are allowed to wear the *képi blanc* for the first time. Below are the seven parts to the Code of Honor, followed by the English translation:

1. *Légionnaire, tu es un volontaire servant la **France** avec **honneur** et **fidélité**.*
2. *Chaque légionnaire est ton **frère d'arme** quelle que soit sa nationalité, sa race, sa religion. Tu lui manifestes toujours la **solidarité** étroite qui doit unir les membres d'une même famille.*
3. *Respecteux des traditions, attaché à tes **chefs**, la **discipline** et la **camaradarie** sont ta force, le **courage** et la **loyauté** tes vertus.*
4. *Fier de ton état de **légionnaire**, tu le montres dans ta **tenue** toujours élégante, ton **comportement** toujours digne mais **modeste**, ton casernement toujours net.*
5. *Soldat d'élite, tu t'entraînes avec **rigueur**, tu entretiens ton **arme** comme ton bien le plus précieux, tu as le souci constant de ta forme physique.*
6. *La mission est **sacrée**, tu l'exécutes jusqu'au bout, a tout prix.*
7. *Au combat, tu agis sans passion et sans haine, tu **respectes** les ennemis **vaincus**, tu n'abandonnes jamais ni tes **morts**, ni tes **blessés**, ni tes **armes**.*

1. Legionnaire, you are a volunteer serving **France** with **honor** and **fidelity**.
2. Every legionnaire is your **brother-in-arms** regardless of his nationality, race, or religion. You will demonstrate this by the strict **solidarity** which must always unite members of the same family.
3. Respectful of traditions, devoted to your **leaders, discipline** and **comradeship** are your strengths, **courage** and **loyalty** your virtues.
4. Proud of your status as **legionnaire**, you display this in your **uniform** which is always impeccable, your **behavior** always dignified but modest, your living quarters always clean.
5. An elite soldier, you will train **rigorously**, you will maintain your **weapon** as your most precious possession, you are constantly concerned with your physical form.
6. A mission is **sacred**, you will carry it out until the end, at all costs.
7. In combat, you will act without passion and without hate, you will **respect** the **vanquished** enemy, you will never abandon your **dead** or **wounded**, nor surrender your **arms**.

The *Képi Blanc*

Before the *képi blanc* ceremony takes place, about a month into your training, you will have to complete a march as a *section* over a period of two days that will cover roughly 50 kilometers (30 miles). It is probable you will have done a couple of shorter marches beforehand in preparation. This distance may not sound like it's very long but rest assured it is, especially when the officer leading the march has basically nothing in his rucksack while all of you are packing substantial loads of anywhere from 40 to 60 pounds and are pushed to the limit in trying to keep up. This weight may not seem like a lot either but you can believe it gets heavier and heavier.

On our first day of the march we started in the late afternoon, comfortably covered approximately 15 kilometers (9 miles) and went to sleep in pretty good spirits. The next day we completed the other 35 kilometers (22 miles) which became more and more of an ordeal as the day wore on. It had turned out to be especially hot and it wasn't that long before some of us began falling further and further behind. It reached a point, as it often does on these marches, where those of us who were stronger were required to carry the rucksacks of those who were lagging behind and thus be saddled with twice as much weight. It also got to where everyone had run out of water and ended up finishing the march in a pitiful state, frothing at the mouth like rabid dogs with our tongues hanging out. It's funny how 35 kilometers doesn't seem like much when you've already done 15 until you actually attempt it. When you're not conditioned for this type of physical effort it can really take its toll.

In essence you don't really do a whole lot to earn the right to wear a *képi*. Other than the march, memorizing the Code of Honor, and having gone through about a month's training there's not that much asked of you, but they aren't just given away. It is earned more by virtue of the passage of time than by any great trial or tribulation although this could be debated, particularly by those who came close to collapse on the march. A month of basic training in the Legion could hardly be construed as a walk in the park.

The ceremony itself typically takes place at sunset although ours was at daybreak. Your *section* will assemble with *képis* in hand, ready to be worn. On cue you will recite the Code of Honor as a *section*, then, at the

The commanding officer of the *4ᵉ RE* pins the regimental insignia on a new recruit who has just donned his *képi blanc* for the first time.

command of your *section* officer, will don your *képis* with a flourish, sing *Le Boudin,* and so complete one of the very proud moments in your life. For myself the *képi blanc* was and is the ultimate symbol of the French Foreign Legion and to be standing there wearing one was special indeed. The colonel of the regiment was present and pinned the regimental insignia on each of us. One exceptionally nice thing they did for us was to have a photographer on hand for the festivities who took dozens of photos which we were later able to purchase. I mention this in extreme gratitude as I still have photos of this occasion. I'm not sure if this is done at every ceremony or whether we just got lucky, but it was a thoughtful thing to do and much appreciated.

New recruits pose as a *section* in front of the farm house after the *képi blanc* ceremony. *Caporals* and *légionnaires* are the only ranks that wear a white *képi* in the Legion. *Caporal-chefs* also wear a white *képi* but the chin strap and black band across the front are gold colored. All other ranks wear a black *képi* with a gold seven-flamed grenade on the front.

Rank, Saluting, and Addressing Superiors

Identifying rank is another important element you will learn while on the farm. Rank structure and insignia in the Legion are slightly different from that of the regular French army but you are only taught the Legion's. It is likely that you will interact with regular French forces in the future but you needn't be concerned about it at this time. On the next page is a list of the composition of the Legion's ranks and their equivalents in the British and U.S. armies:

Foreign Legion	British Army	U.S. Army
Maréchal de France	Field Marshal	General of the Army
Général d'Armee	General	General
Général de Corps d'Armee	Lieutenant General	Lieutenant General
Général de Division	Major General	Major General
Général de Brigade	Brigadier	Brigadier General
Colonel	Colonel	Colonel
Lieutenant-colonel	Lieutenant Colonel	Lieutenant Colonel
Commandant	Major	Major
Capitaine	Captain	Captain
Lieutenant	Lieutenant	First Lieutenant
Sous-lieutenant	Second Lieutenant	Second Lieutenant
Aspirant	—	—
Major	—	—
Adjudant-chef	Warrant Officer 1	Chief Warrant Off.
Adjudant	Warrant Officer 2	Warrant Off. Jnr Grd
—	—	First Sergeant
Sergent-chef	Staff Sergeant	Master Sergeant
—	—	Sergeant First Class
Sergent	Sergeant	Sergeant
Caporal-chef	—	—
Caporal	Corporal	Corporal
Légionnaire première classe	Lance Corporal	Private First Class
Légionnaire	Private	Private

You will undoubtedly remark that whereas in other armies only officers are saluted, in the French military all ranks from *sergent* and upwards are saluted by any subordinate rank. The French believe that once
you attain the status of being a *sergent* you are automatically superior to
those of a lesser rank and are hailed as such. It makes for a lot of arm
flapping throughout the day. Although, once you have acknowledged a
superior for the day there is no further need to salute him on that same
day. It can be a bit of a headache keeping track of who you have and
haven't saluted. The salute itself is similar to the British salute where
the palm of the right hand faces forward as the fingertips touch the tem-
ple. The major difference is that when the French finish the salute they
audibly slap the side of their right leg. If you're not wearing a beret or
other headgear just slapping your leg and raising your head a bit is considered appropriate.

The rank of *caporal-chef* has its own unique status. On the climb up the ladder in attaining ever higher ranks, anyone not interested in the responsibilities of becoming a non-commissioned officer (NCO) and continually advancing upwards can side-step onto this level and settle into a comfortable existence without being compelled to achieve greater heights. As well, anyone found unsuitable in becoming an NCO is nudged into this rank. You won't become a *caporal-chef* before the end of your first contract, but you will automatically be given it not long thereafter if you decide to stay in the Legion. This doesn't mean you can never be an NCO but it does give you the right to savor a number of privileges not available to *caporals* and *légionnaires* until you decide or have the opportunity to become one. *Caporal-chefs* no longer do *corvée* or anything related to it, can live off base, own a vehicle, get married, don't do certain guard duties, have their own dining hall, have their own drinking mess, can wear civilian clothes on base after hours, and enjoy the respect of both their superiors and subordinates to name a few. There is a light at the end of the tunnel after the hardships of being a *caporal* and *légionnaire*.

La présentation is another thing you will learn and routinely use. It is a conventional method of presenting yourself to a superior and is employed every time you are to speak to one of them in a formal setting or any time it is judged appropriate to be used. As an example, you might be summoned to your company commander's office. You knock, enter when called, close the door behind you all the while keeping your gaze fixed on the eyes of the captain, come to attention a few feet in front of him, salute slowly and properly, remove either your beret or *képi* with your left hand and say the following:

Engagé volontaire Smith,	Volunteer recruit Smith,
Deux mois de service,	Two month's service,
Première compagnie,	First company,
Section de Lieutenant Rousse,	Lieutenant Rousse's *section,*
À vos ordres mon Capitaine.	At your command, Sir.

After which the captain should say:

Met toi au repos.	Stand at ease.

To which you respond:

Je me met au repos à vos ordres,	I stand at ease at your command, Sir.
mon Capitaine.	

Whereupon you commence the discourse on whatever matter brought you there. Once your conversation is finished the captain will say:

Tu peux disposé.   You may leave.

You then come to attention, replace your beret or *képi* and say:

Je peux disposé à vos ordres,   I may leave at your command, Sir.
  mon Capitaine.

You would then salute, do an about turn, and exit from whence you came.

This might seem like a lot of trouble to go to just to have a discussion with your superior but the entire process is taken quite seriously and must be learned flawlessly. A variation of the presentation will have to be learned once you are posted to your regiment but it is essentially always the same. You will have to be proficient at this before you return to Castel and begin guard duties there. In a non-formal setting should you wish to speak to a superior, the least you would do is approach him, come to attention, salute if you're wearing headgear and say:

Engagé volontaire Smith à vos ordres mon Lieutenant.

Whereupon you would await acknowledgement and continue from there.

Introduction to Desertion

You will have noticed while on the farm that your training staff is constantly counting the members of your *section* throughout the day, with good reason. With desertions the way they are in the Legion everyone's whereabouts is known and accounted for at every moment of the day. The farm is an open environment compared to Castel where there is a fence to negotiate if you decide to take flight, so appropriate measures are taken to ensure your continued presence. I will discuss desertion in more detail a bit later on. I'm referring to it here because we did wake up one morning and find that three of our fellow recruits had flown the coup in the night. Unfortunately, or maybe fortunately, for them they were picked up at a train station within 36 hours wearing just their Legion gym gear. They had decided they didn't want to play anymore and were attempting to reach Spain without money, passports, proper clothing, or much food, and this in late November. Very foolish. Apparently, one of the three had been an alcoholic and was not having an easy time of things. So, the military police brought them back to the farm, paraded them around for awhile to make examples of them, reinforcing their resolve to desert even more I'm sure, then hauled them off to Castel for a stint in the lockup there.

As it was, this did not deter two Germans from vanishing in the night not long afterwards, one of them being our *foot-foot caporal*. One and possibly both had been from Berlin and had deserted a few days after the Berlin wall came down. I guess they got to missing the mother country. They were not caught as I'm certain the *caporal* had sufficient resources to get them home, and as far as I know they were not heard from again. Anyway, you can see what a real problem this is; and it's just the beginning.

Not long after you've earned your *képis* your *section* will bid adieu to the life of deprivation you've been leading on the farm and return to the relative comfort of Castel to continue training and carry out necessary duties there. Our farm at Raissac was only about 20 kilometers (12.5 miles) from Castel so don't be surprised if a leisurely march is incorporated into the return trip. This is not the last you will see of the farm. You can expect to return in the following weeks for more instruction and the final tests that will accompany the end of your training.

Guard and Service Duties

The Legion does not utilize civilian help for the same chores other armies employ them for, such as working in the kitchen, so it falls on each company to furnish this manpower on a rotating basis. These chores and duties are usually provided for one week at a time during what is called a *semaine de service* (service week). This procedure is followed in all the regiments and is a traditional part of life in the Legion.

Tradition aside, the *semaine de service* is a royal pain in the behind. It's not a bad concept, as such, but the real disadvantage is more apparent in the combat regiments. All activities in the company are suspended while everyone is scattered hither and yon performing these tasks. Because one company is always on service, the prospect of organizing any type of training exercise at a regimental level is rare. This and the fact that a regiment regularly has at least one company overseas somewhere means that most training is done on a company level at best. In the five years I was in the Legion our regiment was only involved in one training exercise of any magnitude that included the whole regiment.

Also, on the odd occasion where an entire regiment is deployed some-where, it is common to leave one company behind to mind the fort. This happened to my company in late 1990 when there was an insurrec-tion in Chad and the whole regiment except us was sent. We were not happy campers.

Neither have I mentioned that most of the duties are extremely te-dious and make for a day that never seems to end. I've done shifts in the kitchen where you scrub pots and wash dishes for a solid ten to twelve hours and still aren't finished when they finally let you go.

The most important function you will perform, and by far the most stressful, is guard duty on your regimental base. Guard duty in the Le-gion is taken extremely seriously whether it's protecting a small bivouac on a routine march somewhere in France or watching over your com-rades during a crisis deep in the heart of Africa. Your introduction to it will come after you have earned your *képi blanc,* as you are required to wear it while guarding the base during the day. The tension associated with this responsibility stems from a couple of things. During the day you must wear your parade uniform while on guard duty and it has to be absolutely impeccable. It must be ironed to perfection without the slight-est blemish and it is possible to spend many frustrating hours trying to get it up to standard. There are 15 creases that have to be ironed into your shirt which is a maddening task at any time. The *chef de poste* which is the *sergent* in charge of your guard unit will pass inspection on it to guarantee that you've done an immaculate job. The other stress re-lated event involved with guard duty is the presentation to and inspec-tion by the Commanding Officer *(Chef de Corps)* of the regiment. This occurs every day of the week except weekends and is never missed. I'll go into this in a moment.

Your guard detail will consist of at least six *légionnaires,* depending on the duties to be conducted, a *caporal* as a second in command, and a *sergent* in charge of the detail. You will probably be paired with your *binôme* and be on duty together at the same time. The length of the shift is 24 hours, during which you rotate between being at a post for two hours at a time with four hours rest in between.

After relieving the previous guard detail at roughly 7:00 A.M., two *légionnaires* will take up positions at the main entrance to the base and perform access control duties while the rest of the detail installs them-selves in the guard hut. Even though you may be on your four hours of repose, you can be called at any moment to carry out any necessary duty. Shortly after installing, the available *légionnaires* and a bugle player, led by the *sergent* will perform the colors ceremony. Everyone marches out to the flagstaff and, following a set course of conduct, raises the French flag. A similar procedure is followed in the evening to lower the flag. This happens every day without fail.

Around 9:00 A.M. the guard detail will assemble in front of the guard hut and make ready for the presentation to the *Chef de Corps.* While the presentation is going on all traffic in and out of the base is halted. It is during these proceedings that the level of tension begins to escalate. Your *sergent* is responsible for ensuring that everything comes off without a hitch and you can be sure you'll hear about it if you don't do your part properly. Shit rolls downhill.

When the *Chef de Corps* arrives the *sergent* calls everyone to attention and the bugler sounds a salute. The *Chef de Corps* will then stop in front of every member of the detachment who, one by one, presents themselves to him in a similar fashion as previously mentioned. He is usually accompanied by your *section* commander and will normally engage you in friendly chit chat, all the while assessing the overall performance of you and the other members of your group, which he will bring up with your *section* commander later on. You may not even entirely understand what he is saying to you, but this is of little import at this time. It's of greater significance that you are able to demonstrate that which you've already been taught by competently presenting yourself. This explains the presence of your *section* commander whose tail is ultimately on the line. Ordinarily, there aren't any repercussions to speak of for anything that may have been bungled as you are, after all, still in training. It's when you get to your combat regiment that mistakes have greater consequence. In any event, you will be greatly relieved when the *Chef de Corps* is finished with you and moves on to the next person.

Why does the most important man in the regiment take time from his daily schedule to engage in this procedure and not leave it to someone of lesser rank? Because guard duty is taken so seriously there is simply no better way to guarantee that the highest possible standards are adhered to, and that no lapse occurs in maintaining this level of discipline and professionalism.

In the evening you change out of parade attire into your combat uniform. You sleep in uniform with your boots on in order to immediately respond to any situation. A compliment of reinforcements will arrive to shore up the overall protection of the base and guard strategic points that are not watched during the day. In my combat regiment in Calvi there used to be between 40 and 50 men on guard duty at various posts throughout the night. Quite a substantial number. So, you can easily find yourself on one guard detail or another two or three times during the *semaine de service.*

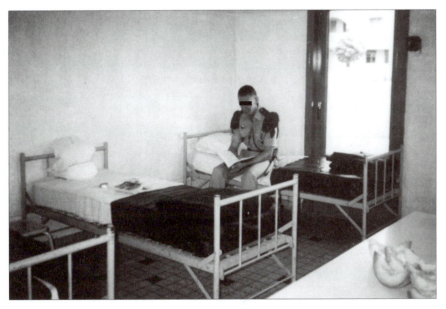

A *légionnaire* relaxes on his bunk between guard shifts. The red *épaulettes* are worn only for guard duties or parade ceremonies.

Other duties you may be required to perform during the *semaine de service* are things like working in the main mess hall, the officer's mess, the NCO's mess, doing environmental chores such as raking leaves, working in a supply warehouse, and basically anything that requires labor. When not involved in one of these assignments you might be occupied with more training or a make-work project to keep you busy. There are also chores to be done at a company level on a daily basis, such as sweeping, mopping, and cleaning common areas. These are not all day affairs, although they are usually done three times a day. These same chores are also conducted at a *section* and *groupe* level and are carried out morning, noon, and night as well. You can see that keeping things clean is a big part of life in the Legion and that being employed to complete these tasks several times a week is not unusual. As I said before, you will come to hate the word *corvée*. Even once you've progressed to one of the combat companies these chores and duties never end. You'll be all but fed up with brooms and mops and buckets by the time you've completed your stay in the Legion. Your only escape is through gaining some rank, but even then you'll be supervising it in one form or another.

Corporal Punishment

Corporal punishment is an aspect of Legion life that you may see rear its ugly head while you're at Castel. Granted, this practice had all but been eradicated by the time I finished my contract in '94. When I joined in '89, corporal punishment was still a part of the way things were done, although to a lesser degree than it probably was years ago. Unfortunately it is still present, albeit on a limited scale, since there still exists a small number of heavy-handed Neanderthals who often feel that the only way to get their point across is through physical force. There are a lot of hard men in the Legion and for many this is the language that they speak. I witnessed several incidents over the years where this accepted policy was utilized and came within a hair's breadth on three occasions of being a recipient of it myself. While most occurrences are negligible in the greater scheme of things, it is nonetheless an unpleasant and scary event to behold.

All of this may sound a little unnerving, but as I said most incidents are not that serious, even though you will always feel that any sort of attack directed at you is not something to be taken lightly. You might receive a poke or a jab from a superior with a short fuse for screwing something up, but you won't be beaten to a bloody pulp over it. By the same token, bruises, black eyes, and bloody noses are not uncommon. The really frightening part of this is that you are mainly defenseless against this type of punishment. Don't think that you can't defend yourself, but you do have to be careful as to how far you go. This is touchy subject matter. The most I would suggest you ever do in defending yourself would be raising your arms to fend off a blow. I would not advise retaliating with force even when you may be justified in doing so. You can anticipate that any kind of assault on a superior will be dealt with severely whether or not you are in the right. Remember Part 3 of the

Code of Honor where it says *"attaché a tes chefs?"* It's taken seriously and expected to be followed. This can definitely be a hard pill to swallow, but sometimes if you stand up for yourself you can deter this type of harassment in the future. Bullies are congenital cowards and any display of retaliatory action on your part is often enough to make them think again about any kind of altercation with you.

I recall an incident in Sarajevo in '93 where one of our *section* commanders, who was an NCO of the old school and well known for the use of his fists, had struck a fellow *caporal* for whatever reason. I'm not sure of the exact details but it was over something minor. Instead of taking his lumps and licking his wounds, my comrade engaged his tormentor in a petty scuffle and prevailed in the outcome without inflicting any injury of note on the NCO other than wounded pride. The NCO had him marched up in front of the captain but, to the delight of us all, he was not further punished over the matter. A few years earlier he most likely would have been harshly reprimanded. While a crack on the jaw may have been an effective method of instruction or correction in times past, the continued scourge of desertion has made it necessary for the Legion to tone down these methods as it is a contributing influence to this problem. With any luck, corporal punishment will never become a factor for you.

The preferred manner for enforcing discipline in the Legion is to have you spend time in the lockup to answer for your indiscretions. Every base has a jailhouse located at the guard hut and to be sent there is known as being *en taule* (pronounced toll as in toll booth). You will notice that it is never empty. While in most other armies, being condemned to a military prison is usually a rather grave matter and the result of a serious offense such as drug possession or theft, in the Legion you can be sent there for relatively minor infractions such as being late for roll call. The general attitude of those who spend some time there is that it's not a very big deal, since almost all forms of misconduct are punished in this fashion. In fact, I suspect few men make it through five years without having spent at least some time there, although some do. But, it's not exactly a picnic on the beach and you do spend exceedingly long days toiling at various forms of labor to work off your sentence. At night you are securely locked away in your cell and aren't let out until morning. Your pay is forfeit for the length of time you spend there. There is a record kept on you, but it may be wiped clean after two years of good conduct. Even though it's not the end of the world if you are

sent there, it's not exactly a fun way to spend your time. Do try and be-
have yourself, especially when you're in Africa. Filling sandbags in that
heat all day long is not something to be relished.

Don't get the idea that you can do whatever you want whenever you
want then just spend a few days in the lockup to atone for your misbe-
havior. The Legion will tolerate someone's screw ups for a surprisingly
long period of time, but it has a limit as to how much it is willing to put
up with. The guys who end up in jail every month or two are really push-
ing their luck, and it's only a matter of time before the walls come tum-
bling down. The Legion is not reluctant to kick someone out if they become a constant problem. There are plenty of volunteers to fill the void. I
knew several people who were given the boot after prodding the Legion
one time too many. I remember one guy who was an ex-boxer that wanted
to fight with everybody anytime alcohol touched his brain. He was finally
kicked out after punching it up with the *PMs (police militaire)*. Another
fellow I remember as a terrible drunk went AWOL for something like 56
days then showed up back at the Legion expecting to do some jail time
then be taken back in. The regiment checked with Aubagne who ordered
him released from the Legion the same day, with no jail time to be served.
They weren't about to waste another moment with him. You may be able
to get away with a lot of shenanigans in the Legion that no civilian
employer would allow for a second, but that doesn't mean you have a
license to go berserk.

Writing and Phoning Home

After being in Castel a month or two you will finally be permitted contact with the outside world and allowed to write and mail letters. You
may or may not be authorized to make phone calls at this point, but
don't be surprised if you can't. It is much easier to plan a desertion with
a phone call than it is through a letter. If they do let you phone you can
purchase phone cards from the *foyer* for fixed amounts of time that are
inserted into a pay phone and count down as you use them. Don't think
you can easily acquire a phone card from somewhere then slink off to
make a call whenever you choose. As I mentioned before, your whereabouts are strictly controlled and known at all times. For instance, I remember our *section* had 10 seconds to properly assemble in the hallway
of our barracks when any superior called *rassemblement*, following which
we were always counted.

If you're not allowed to phone from Castel, be patient as you will be at liberty to do as you please once you're in your combat regiment. If you receive any parcels or packages in Castel, be prepared to have to open them in front of a member of your *cadre*. This shouldn't be a problem in your combat regiment. Be mindful of whom you contact if you had your name changed at Aubagne for whatever reason. If your family suddenly starts receiving mail from a Foreign Legion address or phone calls from there it won't take much for authorities to piece things together. It could cause you and your family a lot of unwanted problems.

If you do anticipate problems of this nature you may want to consider looking into a confidential mail forwarding service before you enlist. There are several listed on the Internet that you can investigate.

Doing Laundry

Doing your laundry is a chore you will find bothersome while you're in Castel. There are no laundry facilities on base other than your washroom sink, a bar of soap, and a brush. In other words, all laundry is done by hand. I was never able to figure out if this was arranged deliberately or whether it was a severe lack of foresight on someone's part. For such a new base it's hard to believe there aren't appropriate provisions for washing your clothes. A wash basin large enough to lay out your clothing instead of having to wash each piece in sections would have sufficed but all that is available to you is a regular sink about one foot by a foot and a half. As far as drying your laundry goes, you have to hang it on lines on the balcony which is fine in the summer but during the winter months it can take four or five days to dry during which you hope it doesn't go missing. Because of this, you are not required to wash, dry, iron, and properly store and account for each article of clothing you were issued on a daily basis as is very much the case in other army's basic training courses. Neither is it necessary for you to be wearing a clean uniform every day and spots and stains are habitually overlooked.

I'm all for building character through the use of some well-planned hardship, especially when it can be put to practical use in future situations such as when you're overseas in Africa, but I always found this situation a bit ludicrous. Even Africa had suitable locations for doing laundry. The combat regiments do have proper laundry facilities, however, and some now make use of electric washers and dryers. As for myself, I spent the first four years of my time in the Legion doing laundry by hand before being assigned to a *section* that had its own washer and dryer.

Meals

Three times a day you will be herded en masse to the mess hall to partake in the bounty that is served up there. These are usually hurried affairs that leave little time for digestion. For breakfast you are given a loaf of bread called a *baguette* to be divided between four men, a bowl for your coffee or hot chocolate; yes, a bowl not a mug or a cup, a wee portion of jam or butter to be profusely applied to your chunk of bread and there you have it. Breakfast! What more could a man want? You can check any fantasies you may have about bacon and eggs, ham, toast, milk, orange juice, cereal, pancakes, etc. at the door, because these items simply don't exist in the Legion. Bread and coffee is how the Legion starts its day off right. The crust of the bread is usually quite robust and durable so it will probably have to be softened in your coffee which, I suppose, helps explain why bowls are used. For the noon and evening meals you assemble as a company and are marched to the mess hall, singing as you go. This formality does not take place at breakfast and you are just marched over by your *caporal du jour.*

For each meal the food is served on collective platters to be apportioned, once again, between four men after they are seated at their table. This is a quick and efficient way to get everyone through the food mill post haste and works quite well except for the occasional fight over the size of the portions. If there is any food remaining after all the companies have been served the cooks will yell out *rabiot!* (rab-ee-oh) which means leftovers. A mad dash for the serving counter usually follows this prodigious announcement which is more than understandable since you will almost always feel hungry while you're at Castel. I remember that distinctly.

The food itself is mediocre at the best of times, but your opinion of it will depend on where you're from. Having been well fed in a western army before joining the Legion, I found the cuisine to be a striking decline from what I was used to, but I know several people from eastern bloc countries who said it was a definite improvement. A simple matter of perspective. The efforts of the cooks are not so much at fault as is the lack of quality foodstuffs from which they can fabricate an appetizing meal. When supplied with proper materials at certain times of the year such as Christmas and Camerone, they usually put on an excellent spread. The food is not really that bad overall, but when a plate of malodorous tripe is staring you in the face you'll understand what I've been talking about.

A standard meal comprises some type of meat such as a pork chop (don't expect steak, as I never saw one in my five years in the Legion), a type of vegetable ranging anywhere from canned spinach, to potatoes in the form of french fries, to some weird and exotic species of plant life, an inevitable piece of cheese, and some kind of dessert. Due to the predominance of Roman Catholicism in France, fish is served each Friday. Unlike in other armies, there is only one choice of serving available. There is a variety of beverages to drink, normally in the form of soda pop. Once you get to your combat regiment there is also beer and wine on tap to freely consume at your discretion. Be careful with this, especially at noon. It's easy to quaff down a healthy portion of wine and not feel the effects until it's time to go back to work. One interesting feature they've installed in the mess hall lobby at Castel are vending machines that dispense bottles of beer. While new recruits normally can't sample the goods from this novel innovation, those who are in Castel taking courses or for other reasons regularly indulge in a brew or two before getting their meal. Helps with the digestion!

You frequently won't have much time to eat at a leisurely pace and will often have to engage in nothing less than a feeding frenzy in order to get your meal eaten. A rule of thumb to follow is that once your *caporal du jour,* who gets his meal after your whole *section* has gone through, has finished eating — you'd better be.

Since there is no civilian help in the kitchen, and in order to give the kitchen staff one partial day off out of seven, the noon and evening meals on Sunday are composed of bread and individual plastic baggies that contain tins of *pâté,* potato chips, a piece of cheese, a bit of fruit, and possibly a drink of some kind. Barely enough to sustain life. This happens weekly in the regiments as well.

You will notice that the French are quite particular about how a meal should be eaten, whether it's dining on fine cuisine in Paris or simply filling your face in a clamorous army mess hall. I had the misfortune of being seated opposite a French *caporal* one day and, quite on a whim, decided I would inhale the main course before consuming the *entrée,* or salad. He immediately launched into a lengthy harangue on what an uncouth barbarian I was, along with a few other defamatory innuendos.

Weapons

Weapons training is a considerable part of the overall program, and you will be given instruction on the principal armament utilized by all French infantry units. The main focus of this training will be on the *FAMAS,* which is the primary weapon of the French soldier. It is an assault rifle of a compact bullpup design, 5.56 mm, capable of firing single shots, three round bursts, or fully automatic. It can fire different types of rifle grenades and may be used by left or right handed shooters. It is a versatile weapon and you will have many chances to learn its capabilities and strip, assemble, fire, and clean it while you're at Castel. For all of its attributes, it is a bit of a pig to clean which you'll quickly discover. There is a modern 200 meter (219 yard) indoor rifle range on base where you will be indoctrinated in its use. The range utilizes mechanical knock-down targets that fall backwards when they are hit, then stand up again after a few moments. The *FAMAS* has a bipod built into its design and is

A *légionnaire* cleans a Browning .50 caliber heavy machine gun at the Arta camp in Djibouti. The .50 caliber is the equivalent of 12.7 mm when converted to metric and so is known as a *douze-sept* in French.

usually fired with it in use. This doesn't necessarily make you a better shot, but it can help if used correctly. There are tests of your marksmanship toward the end of your training so try and properly implement everything you are taught. You will also receive instruction on grenades, the 9 mm automatic pistol, and the 89 mm and 112 mm anti-tank rocket launchers. The rocket launchers and grenades are fired at a range off base. Anything not covered at Castel will be shown to you in your combat regiment.

All weapons are stored in armories and have at least two people working and living in them 24 hours a day. An armory is never left completely unattended for any reason and loaded pistols are kept within easy reach in case of an attempted break in. At night the armorers seal themselves in and don't emerge until morning. The entire procedure concerning the security of an armory is taken seriously due to the constant threat of attack by anyone seeking weapons. If you've served in another army you may have been allowed to sign out your weapon and clean it whenever you wanted. You will never be allowed to do this in the Legion and all weapons are signed in and out under the careful supervision of an NCO. Considering the number of desertions in the Legion this is an understandable and necessary process.

Physical Training and Tests

Training of a physical nature is a never-ending process throughout your entire time in the Legion. You will be expected to develop and maintain a minimum fitness level, which you will progressively improve during your time in Castel and continue to nurture once you've reached your combat regiment. Your personal physical condition is an extremely important part of everyday life in the Foreign Legion. You won't see many overweight, out of shape people, although there are invariably a few that fall into this category.

A number of tests are used to assess your overall physical ability, of which, due to the amount of time involved and the exertion required, the 8 kilometer (5 mile) run with a 12 kilogram (26 pound) rucksack on your back is the most demanding. There is a canal that runs beside the base at Castel and you will spend a lot of time circling it in preparation for the final test, which must be completed in less than one hour. Many people are able to attain this objective even on a first attempt without being in particularly good shape, but this does not mean that the test isn't exceedingly difficult. It does take a great deal out of you. It's no simple task straining against a swaying rucksack while you're running steadily for upwards of an hour. There are those who can complete this run in roughly 30 minutes, but an average time for this test would be around 45 minutes. The test is done while wearing your combat uniform and boots which adds a notable amount of weight to your feet and legs. Also, it is often preceded by a 1.5 kilometer (1 mile) run with combat boots and rucksack just to get you warmed up. A small word of advice I want to pass along concerns the rucksack itself. On the side that rests against your back there is a triangular piece of foam in three parts that is meant to provide some cushioning against the weight of the pack but which digs into your back more than it protects it. Don't be afraid to cut out at least the bottom piece that rests against the small of your back. I wasn't aware of the damage it could do until I had completed one of these runs for the first time. I still carry the scars that resulted when that piece of foam chewed a chunk of skin off my back the size of my hand.

Another tribulation used to appraise your running capability is the *teste Cooper*. Quite simply, it measures how far you can run in 12 minutes. It's normally conducted on a 400 meter (437 yard) oval sports track, and when the whistle blows you basically give 'er hell until it blows again. The minutes are yelled out to you each time you complete a lap to help you pace yourself. On your first attempt it will be difficult to estimate how hard to push yourself and go the maximum distance without playing out before you've finished, but you should have several test runs to feel this out. Anything over seven laps or 2,800 meters (3,062 yards) is a good run. This test is done in regular sports gear and running shoes.

One of the tougher trials tests a combination of your overall strength, speed, and agility through the use of a 16-obstacle course. You will be shown proven techniques to get through each obstacle as expeditiously as possible, then it's up to you to show what you're made of. The course looks deceptively easy, especially when you only train on one or two obstacles at a time, but it doesn't take long to realize how difficult it actually is. It only takes an average of between three and five minutes to complete, but it is likely the most exhausting few minutes you will ever spend on anything. I recall my lungs feeling as though they were burnt raw after completing the course. Those who are in very good shape and proficient with this course can complete it in less than three minutes, which is a spectacular effort. The obstacle course is located off base in

Castel itself so your *section* will usually jog the two or three kilometers to get there. This test is done in combat uniform and boots.

Climbing ropes without the use of your feet is a tried and true method of measuring the strength of your grip and upper body. This is definitely one of the harder physical endeavors you will undertake. It's hard enough getting up a rope with the use of your feet let alone without them. Most new recruits can only manage a few short feet on the rope unless they already possess exceptional upper body ability. There is a bit of technique involved whereby you kick your feet in a rhythmic manner to gain some momentum but most of it is just pure grit. It takes time and steady effort to reach the point where you can ascend a rope with relative ease. The test at the end of your training merely consists of how many times you can climb and descend a rope without stopping.

Another test you will participate in is a 100 meter (109 yard) dash carrying a sack full of sand which weighs roughly 40 kilograms (88 pounds). Anything under 20 seconds is a decent time. The sack is on the ground to begin and when the whistle blows you pick it up and haul ass down the track. One tip I'd like to pass along is to take an extra second or two and hoist the sack properly onto both shoulders before you start running. A lot of people only get the sack onto one shoulder and end up cradling it in their arms when it slips off, which ultimately slows them down.

Additional tests will incorporate the unavoidable pushups, situps, and chinups, the goals of which I mentioned at the beginning of this document. There are also a series of swimming tests to face as well. If you can't swim you will be coached along to help you evolve into something that can move in the water.

You will find that you won't receive a failing grade, as such, for any physical area in which you're not up to standard by the end of your training. Nor will you flunk basic training itself for physical or other inadequacies discovered in the course of your time in Castel unless you are somehow grossly incompetent. Even then, it would take an extreme case for you not to progress from basic training to one of the combat regiments where your shortfalls will eventually develop into assets. It nevertheless behooves you to put your best foot forward and increase your physical ability as much as you are able while at Castel. Life doesn't suddenly become sunshine and lollipops once you've gotten through basic training. Your body will undergo extreme physical demands many times throughout your sojourn in the Legion.

March or Die

At some stage of your training your *section* will embark on a journey to a small, remote village in the Pyrenees mountains known as Camurac. The Legion maintains a humble abode in this cozy hamlet similar to the farm house where you will have already spent some time. You will probably be here a week undergoing more training. The one memorable experience you may derive from your stay in Camurac is an introduction to marching in the mountains and the pain associated with it. Most of the marching you have done up until now will have been on flat terrain, and a trek in the Pyrenees will definitely expand your consciousness as to what a march is all about.

Our *section* set out on a day long hike with rucksacks and rifles starting at 800 meters (2,625 feet) above sea level, climbed to 2,000 meters (6,562 feet) then descended back to Camurac on a circular route that seemed to have no end at all. While it's not exactly climbing Mt. Everest, marches like these test your constitution to its very core. Being still in the process of turning your body into a hardened, muscled, useful entity, these types of walks can be nothing short of horrendous. I vividly recall many recruits whimpering, crying, dropping their rucksacks, refusing to move another step, and generally giving in to the overwhelming agony their bodies endured on this march. Not a pretty picture. It's something you will get used to though. The Legion thrives on this type of activity. You may have heard the ominous motto "march or die" associated with the Legion and its past. Things may not be this severe anymore, but the spirit of those words lives on without question.

The final days of your training will culminate in a prolonged expedition called a *raid marche*, which loosely translates as a "raid march" implying that you walk a lengthy distance, then simulate an attack on some predetermined target. During basic training it is actually not much more than an endurance test in which you march for what seems an eternity, but does include a few subsidiary activities such as rappelling and the use of rubber dingies called Zodiacs. The march unfolds over the course of four solid days and will take you through roughly 150 kilometers (93 miles) of foot pounding anguish. You will be on the move for 50 minutes of every hour, eight hours a day until you've completed the march, pausing only briefly for lunch. Your feet will cramp, blister, chafe, and burn, and every step will cause you torment. I've known people who have lost a few toenails on these types of walks. Marches of this kind are an inescapable element of all your days in the Legion.

The Regiments

A week or two before you are finished at Castel you will be asked for your top three preferences as to which combat regiment you would most enjoy being posted to. You will have received instruction on the regiments during your training and will have heard enough about them that you should have a fairly clear idea which one would best suit you. It may seem surprising that they are willing to consider your desires and oblige you as much as they are able, but there's really nothing to be gained by assigning someone to the parachute regiment, for example, if he strongly feels he will never be able to jump out of an airplane. That's enough to induce someone to desert. However, there are no guarantees, and you will be sent to where you are most needed regardless of your wishes.

Below are listed the regiments of the Foreign Legion:

1er RE – 1er Régiment Étranger (1st Foreign Regiment)

Located in Aubagne, it conducts the main administrative duties of the Legion. It is also home to the *Musique Principale* which is the prestigious band of the Foreign Legion.

1er REC – 1er Régiment Étranger de Cavalerie (1st Foreign Cavalry Regiment)

Located in Orange, it is the Legion's only armored regiment.

1er REG – 1er Régiment Étranger de Génie (1st Foreign Regiment of Combat Engineers)

Located at Laudun, it provides the Legion with an engineering capability. On July 1, 1999 the numerical designation for the *6e REG* was changed to the *1er REG*.

2e REG – 2e Régiment Étranger de Génie (2nd Foreign Regiment of Combat Engineers)

Located in the Marseille region, it is the Legion's newest regiment. Created in 1999 it augments the engineering capacities of the Legion.

2e REI – 2e Régiment Étranger d'Infanterie (2nd Foreign Infantry Regiment)

Located in Nimes, it employs wheeled armored personnel carriers in conducting its operations.

2ᵉ REP – 2ᵉ Régiment Étranger de Parachutistes (2nd Foreign Parachute Regiment)

Located in Calvi on the Mediterranean island of Corsica, it is the Legion's lone parachute regiment.

3ᵉ REI – 3ᵉ Régiment Étranger d'Infanterie (3rd Foreign Infantry Regiment)

Located in Kourou in French Guiana, South America, the regiment carries out jungle operations and is responsible for the security of the Ariane rocket site.

4ᵉ RE – 4ᵉ Régiment Étranger (4th Foreign Regiment)

Located in Castelnaudary, it is responsible for the basic training of new recruits, NCOs, and for providing specialist training.

5ᵉ RE – 5ᵉ Régiment Étranger (5th Foreign Regiment)

Located on the islands of French Polynesia in the South Pacific, it was involved in activities supporting French nuclear test sites. The regiment was officially dissolved on June 30, 2000.

13ᵉ DBLE – 13ᵉ Demi-Brigade de la Légion Étrangère (13th Half-Brigade of the Foreign Legion)

Located in Djibouti, it provides a security presence to this strategically positioned country on the horn of Africa.

DLEM – Détachement de le Légion Étrangère de Mayotte (Foreign Legion Detachment of Mayotte)

Located in Dzaoudzi on the island of Mayotte in the Comoros archipelago, it is responsible for ensuring the security and continued French autonomy of the island.

You will be informed before leaving Castel to which regiment you are being sent. Prior to departing Castel your *section* will assemble for a formal presentation to the *Chef de Corps* and you will learn your ranking regarding where you finished on your basic training course as opposed to your peers. All the tests you go through on everything you have been taught count toward this final standing. This really doesn't have much bearing on anything because you aren't going to fail basic training. Throughout all the training and courses you will take during your time in the Legion, there is a great deal of emphasis placed on how a person measures up as compared to those around him. So much so, in fact, that any training group is habitually assembled at the end of a course and the standings read aloud for everyone to hear, with little commiseration shown to those who may have placed near the bottom. There's nothing like boosting a person's morale with some public humiliation. Don't be too concerned if you do happen to finish last in any of your courses. You can fully expect to be thoroughly berated and viewed with disgust by your superiors but they'll get over it. We used to have a saying that went, "What do you call someone who finishes last on his *caporal*'s course? *Caporal*." Enough said. In case you're wondering I finished somewhere in the middle on my *caporal*'s course.

After saying goodbye to Castel, it's on the train again and back to Aubagne from where you will be redirected to your combat regiment. If you develop any sort of warm, fond memories of Castel, fear not as you'll be seeing her again. In five years I spent a total of ten months there.

Your stopover in Aubagne will be short and sweet, lasting only a couple of days. It was during this time that three of our fellow recruits, who had made it clear that they did not want to continue in the Legion, were released from their contract. We were also individually asked if we might be interested in a career with the *Musique Principale*. This may have an appeal for you if you found during basic training that you weren't really suited to a life in a combat regiment, but still want to remain in the Legion. The *Musique Principale* does produce quality work and I never failed to be impressed on the occasions I heard them play. They travel worldwide performing their shows.

You may find that you're at liberty to indulge in a few simple pleasures such as relaxing in the *foyer* and drinking yourself sick for the first time since you've joined the Legion. It is unlikely you will be allowed out in town for a night off during basic training so you'll have four months of accumulated steam to blow off. You certainly have every right to celebrate your passage through Castel but don't get too carried away or you could quickly be wearing a reflective vest sweeping streets around the base. In other words — *en taule!*

Once these minor amenities have concluded you will assemble on the day of your departure in groups bound for your respective regiments. There will be a representative of each regiment to accompany your group on the journey. From this point on I will cover regimental life but, unfortunately, will only be able to accurately present the perspective of the *2ᵉ REP (2ᵉ Régiment Étranger de Parachutistes)* as it is the only regiment I served in. Other than the fact that the *REP* is the sole regiment involved in parachuting activities, life throughout all the regiments is quite similar.

Chapter 5

REGIMENTAL LIFE
IN THE *2ᴱ REP*

⎯

Since Calvi is located on an island you will be taking a ferry from either Marseille, Toulon, or Nice to reach it. Only in summer do ferries run from the mainland directly to Calvi, so in the off season Bastia is the regular port of call, with Ajaccio and Île Rousse sometimes being used. When taking a ferry either to or from the island you normally embark in the evening and spend the night making the crossing that takes roughly twelve hours, depending on the ports being used.

Your tickets will have already been arranged for you. For a modest sum, usually less than 150 francs, you can pay for a bunk in one of the sleeping cabins. Your ticket won't include this extravagance so you will have to sleep in the regular seats on the upper decks if you don't purchase a berth. It's worth the minor expense to pay for a bunk if you can afford it. You may not possess enough money, having just left Castel and a couple of drunken nights in Aubagne behind, so you might end up roughing it on your maiden voyage. You should have adequate funds on subsequent sailings so this won't be an issue. Most sleeping cabins have four bunks in them so, if possible, try and get a room with a few of your mates. When the ship is crowded the pursers will assign anyone to a room in order to fill the bunks so it's entirely possible that you could be sharing your sleeping arrangements with a group of civilian strangers. This doesn't make for a particularly comfortable night's sleep. Don't

2ᵉ REP regimental insignia. The dragon is indicative of Legion parachute units having served in Indochina.

ever think that because you're a rough and tumble Legionnaire you would never be robbed, or worse. I'll relate a few stories to you later on illustrating this. If you're not certain how you'll be berthed, make sure you get the details from the purser.

If your passage to Calvi happens to co-incide with a unit from the *REP* returning to the island, you will most likely be used for guard duties keeping watch over vehicles and equipment on the lower decks. This is the penalty for being one of the new kids on the block, but should only take an hour or two of your time.

Normally on these ferry crossings you are free to do as you like until the ship docks in the morning. Most Legion members tend to gravitate directly to the alcohol establishments and maintain a constant vigil there until they close. There will be a buffet and restaurant on board if you get hungry or tired of drinking. The vessels used in making this transit are as modern as you will find anywhere and have sufficient facilities to keep you occupied until you decide to turn in.

Parachute Training

Upon arriving at Camp Raffalli in Calvi you will likely be met by the *caporal* of your *promotion* or *promo* for short. This is a term that describes your parachute course and the activities associated with it. He will escort you to barracks reserved exclusively for this purpose and you will be billeted there for the duration of the course which lasts anywhere from three to six weeks, depending on the availability of aircraft.

The number of men in each *promo* varies greatly, but they are run irrespective of size. They don't wait around to fill any quotas. The size of our *promo* was only seven men, of which six successfully completed the course, one having been hampered by real or imagined medical problems. Only three of us honored our contract and remained in the Legion five full years. The other four all deserted within the first two years.

The *promo* is run by a senior NCO with a *caporal* as second in command. The first two weeks will be devoted to instructing you on everything you need to know about the equipment and procedures necessary to get into a parachute and out of an airplane. By the third week you'll be ready to do it for real.

French parachute wings.

A lot of time is spent improving your physical condition, especially your upper body strength. You'll be hanging from a chinup bar several times a day. Strive to be doing at least 10 chinups before completing your *promo.* After I had been in my combat company awhile, a newcomer from a *promo* was posted to our company who could not execute even a single chinup. He had somehow slipped through the whole system, completed his parachute jumps and received his wings, without being able to perform the one act vital to a parachutist; having the upper body strength to pull a slip on the risers of a parachute to steer yourself away from potential harm. This caused quite a sensation in our company and throughout the regiment, as he should never have been allowed to don a parachute and make a jump. He was threatened with having his wings revoked unless he got himself up to standard, but ended up deserting within a few months. The moral of the story being that you must take some personal initiative in getting yourself in shape. Your physical training has to be more than just those times someone is standing over you making you do something.

There is no physical qualifying test before you're allowed to commence the course, so once you're told at Castel that they're posting you to the *REP,* you're on the course whether you're properly in shape for it or not. One morning after assembling in running attire we were told that we'd be doing a *petit footing,* or brief jog, for that morning's physical recreation. This quickly turned into a 10 kilometer (6 mile) trot through the Corsican countryside which is nothing less than can be expected in the *REP.* If you are not yet in prime form, now is the time your weaknesses will surge to the forefront. In general, it is safe to say that the men in the *REP* are in very good condition overall and surpass the physical standards of all other Legion regiments. The *REP* sees and conducts itself as the elite unit it is considered to be.

The *REP,* and I believe the French army as a whole, does not make use of a mock tower in its parachute training. If you've never heard of one, it is a structure used to simulate jumping out the doors of an airplane. The platform is 32 feet off the ground and has a cable and pulley system to which a jumper attaches himself before leaping out the door. I had found it much harder to spur myself out the doors of a mock tower than the actual doors of a plane when I took a parachute course before joining the Legion. The mock tower is just at that height where it is psychologically difficult to follow through on the drills whereas a plane is high enough at jump altitude that it's not as much of a factor. Repeated jumps from the tower also beat the tar out of you when you are jerked to a halt as opposed to the comparatively cushy feel when your parachute opens in the air. So, for those of you who may have wondered, you can breath a sigh of relief. You won't be using this torture mechanism. The *REP* does use a rickety looking apparatus to practice landings, but it's a walk in the park compared to a mock tower.

The drop zone, or *zone de saut,* at Calvi is located right beside the camp with the airport only a few kilometers away. This is an efficient arrangement and allows for a lot of jumps to be conducted when an aircraft is present. The drop zone is rather small though. It only allows for a limited number of men to jump on each pass of the plane and, since it is in such close proximity to the camp, cannot safely be used when the wind picks up. There have been several instances of jumpers landing on the roofs of buildings in the camp or smacking against objects when the strength of the wind was miscalculated. Because of these problems an alternative drop zone called Borgo is often used. It is situated south of Bastia, so it is possible for you to spend a couple of days on the other side of the island getting some jumps in.

You will have to carry out six jumps to complete the course and be awarded your wings. Previously, one jump had to be at night, but I believe this is no longer required. The main aircraft you will jump from is a C160 Transall with a C130 Hercules being used on occasion. You may eventually get to jump out the rear of a Puma helicopter but this will come much later. For some reason the French do not make static line ramp jumps, or exits off the cargo ramp when it is lowered, and all jumps are done out the aft side doors of the aircraft. Having done ramp jumps prior to the Legion, I can say that it is a preferable method of exiting the plane. You aren't blown, twisted and turned by the prop-wash as you plunge out the side door, but rather have a smooth, straight drop until your parachute opens.

There is a definite adrenaline rush when you strap that parachute on for the first time and climb aboard an aircraft knowing you won't be landing in it. There have been times when the excitement of a jump has gotten the better of people and they have frozen moments before going out the door and refused to jump, but try not to think about this sort of thing too much. The safety records of parachute units around the world speak for themselves. They are almost flawless. Leave your mental junk in the barracks when it's time for a jump. When the green light comes on and the buzzer starts sounding get your ass out the door and don't think twice about it. You'll be glad you did.

A C160 Transall drops a stick of parachutists over the drop zone at Borgo. Training jumps are made from an altitude of 400 meters.

Having said that, I'm going to regress for a moment in order to make you aware of an unnecessary mishap I observed on at least three occasions. When your static line is hooked to the cable, make sure it does not pass in front of your neck under any circumstances. For example, if you will be exiting the right-hand door of the aircraft you will be facing the rear of the plane while your right hand holds the fastener with it hooked to the cable. The static line should run unimpeded from your parachute to the cable. It should not be passing over your left shoulder, in front of your neck, and then to the cable. If you're jumping from the other side of the plane the opposite is true. The static line is colored a nice bright yellow so it's easy to see. When the three victims of this serious neglect exited the plane they fell with the line continually tightening around their necks until the parachute was ripped from its pack whereupon it probably came close to strangling them. While they all survived, they each had a permanent reminder of their inattention by the layer of skin swathed off their necks. This is known as being clotheslined or getting a *cravate* (tie). In each case they were not exclusively at fault, as the jump master is supposed to check this, pick up on the error, and correct it but this procedure depends on both parties doing their job. The worst episode

Legionnaires prepare to board a C160 Transall to make a jump on the drop zone at Calvi. The men are members of the *REP*'s 1st Company as indicated by the green *foulard* on the left shoulder of the jumper facing forward and by the green triangles painted on the backs of the helmets. The number 4 in the triangle means the jumpers are from 1st Company's 4th *section*. The helmet covers are gray cloth held in place by a piece of tire inner-tube stretched over the helmet rim.

I ever witnessed was a jump master who almost jumped an entire stick of men, myself included, with everyone's static line crossing in front of their necks. Luckily most of us noticed the mistake immediately and straightened him out in time. All of this really goes without saying if you've completed the course, but it's easy to become complacent at anything when you do it over and over without incident. Don't let it happen when you're about to jump out of an airplane.

Other than going through the drills several times, there are no tests that you have to pass in order to make a jump. Unlike many parachute courses in other countries around the world, the Legion does not weed people out by having them pass a series of checks, so pay close attention to what you're being taught. Everyone who is posted to the *REP* goes through the parachute training and jumps out of planes for a living.

While you're on your *promo,* you'll be asked which of the six companies of the *REP* you would like to be sent to once the course is over. They'll listen to your preferences then put you where you're most needed. They probably won't be as considerate about your choices as they were at Castel. I'm not even sure why they bother asking, but I guess there's no harm in it. Most of the people in the *promos* tend to be sent to a company

A Transall buzzes a group of parachutists on the *Petit Bara* in Djibouti as they pack up their gear. The jump was cancelled due to winds exceeding 10 meters per second which is the safety limit the *REP* adheres to. The vast, empty stretches of Djibouti's *Grand* and *Petit Baras* make ideal drop zones for parachute training operations as there are no obstacles for jumpers to hit or have their parachutes tangle on. The ground can become as hard as iron though. One of our Legionnaires snapped the bone on his upper arm like a twig when he made a bad landing on one of these jumps.

This photo was combined with the *REP*'s 1st Company color standard (flag) and made into Christmas cards in 1992.

as a group rather than individually to different companies. The six companies in the *REP* are as follows:

CCS – Compagnie de Commandement et de Services (Commandment and Services [Headquarters] Company). Company color is yellow.

Provides all command, administration, maintenance, support and service requirements for the regiment.

CEA – Compagnie d'Éclairage et d'Appui (Heavy Weapons Support Company). Company color is blue.

Utilizes heavy weaponry in support of the regiment such as MILAN anti-tank missiles, 20 mm anti-aircraft cannons, and 120 mm mortars. It is also home to the *REP*'s own elite Deep Reconnaissance Commandos.

La 1ᵉʳ Compagnie (1st Company). Company color is green. Specializes in night combat and fighting in built-up areas.

La 2ᵉ Compagnie (2nd Company). Company color is red. Concentrates on all aspects of mountaineering.

La 3ᵉ Compagnie (3rd Company). Company color is black. Concerns itself with amphibious techniques. Conducts much of its training from the amphibious center, *centre amphibie,* located on the beach a few hundred meters from camp.

La 4ᵉ Compagnie (4th Company). Company color is gray. Conducts rear-action operations requiring sabotage and sniper capabilities.

While each company may focus on a specific area of expertise they all cross-train on the specialties of the other companies.

So, after three weeks or more of training and wondering whether or not you will actually be able to fling your carcass out of a skyborne airplane, the great day will arrive when, having done just that, you will be presented with your jump wings. The wings you are given have a serial number engraved on the back and you will be required to memorize it. Do not wear these wings other than for parades, guard duty, or other special occasions and even then think twice about it. You are not normally obliged to wear them for any reason; at least no one checks to see if you are, so do your utmost to safeguard them. It's not an exaggeration to say that you could spend some time in the lockup or at least be doing extra work details if you lost them. On one occasion we were required to produce them for our *section* commander on short notice and demonstrate that we had the serial number memorized. Don't wear them on drunken forays into Calvi whatever you do. You can purchase duplicate sets at the *foyer* that work just as well.

During our *promo* we were visited by an insurance salesman who signed us up for a comprehensive policy that would cover us in the event of any injury incurred on the job. You aren't required to buy insurance, since the Legion will fix you up if you get hurt, but you may want to consider it anyway. If you are injured to where you are permanently disabled or even crippled, monetary reparations can go a long way toward easing your suffering. Jumping out of airplanes has its risk and people do get hurt.

Parachutist Certificate.

With Castel behind you and the *promo* under your belt you will now be assigned to the company and *section* with whom you will conceivably be spending the next several years. Many people spend the bulk of their careers in the Legion with one company. Other than being posted to one of the overseas regiments or possibly to the *CCS* (Headquarters Company) in the future, it is unusual to be sent elsewhere. Changing companies within a regiment does not happen much, nor does changing regiments within metropolitan France. To do this you would normally do two years in an overseas regiment then request a different posting upon your return. Once you've settled into your new home you're there for a while, like it or not.

Commando Training

Our *promo* was posted to 1st Company, and the introduction to it was a whirlwind affair, leaving little time to get oriented. The company was in the process of leaving for the Mont Louis Commando Training Center, located in the Pyrenees mountains 20 kilometers (12.5 miles) from Spain, and we arrived one morning in the midst of the preparations for departure. We were quickly issued lockers, bunks, rifles, and other material and equipment. By that afternoon we were on a plane wearing parachute gear and made a tactical jump into a drop zone not far from Mont Louis a short time later.

Commando badge. The number in the red shield refers to the designation of the training center. In this case the 1 indicates the Mont Louis commando training facility.

France has several commando facilities throughout the country and overseas and puts them to good use rotating units through the training and often hosting contingents from other countries. The course is normally three weeks long and concentrates on advanced soldiering techniques. One week is completed in Mont Louis and focuses on mountaineering and a diversity of other training, while the next week is carried out on the coast at Collioure, located south of Perpignan, and conducts mainly amphibious related activities. The final week is used for a *raid marche* to consolidate the lessons of the previous two weeks.

The course is quite involved and will keep you hopping from start to finish. You can expect to cover the following:

- Rappelling and scaling techniques using several different systems allow you to ascend and descend various structures. You'll scramble up and down the walls of the forts learning these procedures.

- Confidence and obstacle courses that emphasize heights as the medium in building your physical self-assurance. They often incorporate heavy wire cables strung high in the air which you must cross using the methods you are shown. You are connected to most obstacles with a safety line that will prevent serious injury should you slip or fall off. These courses require exceptional upper body strength to pull you up, around, over, or under the obstacles and are exhausting if you don't possess arms of steel. The rappelling and scaling techniques you learn are often applied in these courses.

- Instruction on boobytraps and explosives. You will be shown how to prepare and employ different types of explosive devices including plastic explosives, dynamite, shaped and cutting charges, anti-personnel and anti-tank mines, and how boobytraps can be fashioned from these materials. There is normally a live demonstration on most explosives then personal hands-on training. The French maintain an ample arsenal of this type of weaponry, and you'll have plenty of chances to put it to use.

- Hand to hand combat. This is one of the more physically demanding parts of the course. You are made to run around to the point of exhaustion for the sake of staying warm and loose so that when you apply the techniques on each other no serious injury results. You are shown how to administer and escape from holds, how to kick and punch and fend off the same, methods of tackling and incapacitating an opponent, and of a more serious nature, how to garrote and break the neck of an adversary.

- Touching the tracks of a tank or armored vehicle as it rolls towards you then letting it roll over you as you lay between its tracks. A great confidence builder.

- Building rope bridges to cross rivers or ravines. Done as a team effort.

- Fighting methods for built-up areas such as towns and cities. The French have constructed miniature villages expressly for this purpose. You are shown how to enter and clear buildings while utilizing blank ammunition and dummy grenades. It quickly becomes apparent how dangerous a task this is, and how Germany could have lost an entire army fighting for Stalingrad in World War II.

Commando trainee leaps from a platform onto a metal free-swinging pole hanging 50 feet above the ground.

A commando trainee descends a cable slide over 100 meters long from the top of a cliff before terminating with a drop in the sea.

A commando prepares to descend a cable wearing a rucksack. For this technique you don't climb on top of the cable but rather grab onto a rope attached to it via a metal ring and hang from it as you descend. Once the obstacles and techniques for surmounting them are learned there are usually individual and *groupe* competitions to determine who can complete the courses the fastest.

A commando slides down a cable having a downward slant of roughly 30 degrees. The right foot rests on top of the cable and is used to help push you along. The left foot dangles freely with the arms outstretched for balance. The carabiner that connects your safety line to the cable is placed between your waist and the cable and serves to reduce the friction so you can descend as fast as possible.

- Instruction on the use of kayaks and Zodiac inflatable dingies. You'll practice things like flipping a Zodiac over then hiding in the air pocket underneath, or bailing out of a parent vessel with a Zodiac and boarding it in open water. Basic stuff but quite a chore if you don't move well in the water. Life vests are always used.

- A swim in the sea without life vests sporting rucksacks and rifles. In Djibouti you complete an obstacle course in the water in this configuration. Great fun if you can't swim.

- No amphibious commando instruction would be complete without the forced feeding of raw sardines. You are made to choke down a raw sardine — scales, fins, bones, tripe, arsehole — everything, while your instructor stands over you and ensures that you do. Some raw mussels are also provided for dessert and are a little easier to get down your throat. The reasoning behind this is that if you've run out of food on a mission, managed to catch a fish but have no means of cooking it, you wouldn't have any qualms about eating it to stay alive. I suppose this must be true after watching an instructor gulp them down like they were chocolate bars.

After you have rotated between Mont Louis and Collioure you will terminate your commando training with a *raid marche*. Things such as building a rope bridge, rappelling, rafting in Zodiacs, and simulating an attack on a target are all part of the march. It is more of a tactical exercise than simply a route march, and is quite grueling at times. One evening

Zodiac training.

Kayaking.

Commandos practice an emergency evacuation of a vessel that has brought them close to shore. Zodiacs are heaved into the water followed by everyone bailing out with oars in hand. Upon swimming after them the Zodiacs are then boarded.

after eating and waiting for the sun to set, we commenced a leg of the march that lasted 13 hours before we reached our objective, pausing only about ten minutes every hour along the way. This is probably the longest I ever had to march at any one time in the Legion but overnight excursions of eight to ten hours aren't out of the ordinary.

Once this is finished, you will receive your *brevet commando,* or commando insignia, for completing the course. It is worn on your parade uniform but unlike your jump wings, has no serial number. Duplicates can be acquired from the *foyer.*

Daily Life

After having gone through nearly six months of uninterrupted training we finally had a chance to settle in and adjust to our new home at Calvi. This lull in the action lasted maybe two weeks before our company packed up and shipped out to Djibouti for a four-month tour there. A typical day in your regiment will be scheduled something like this:

5:00	Wake up call
5:30	Roll call
5:30–7:00	Breakfast, ablutions, *corvée* duties
7:00–7:30	*Corvée quartier*
7:30	*Rassemblement compagnie*
7:30–9:00	Sporting activities such as running or playing soccer

9:00–9:30	Showers, *casse croûte*
9:30–12:00	Morning training, work details
12:00–13:30	*Soupe, corvée* duties
13:30–14:00	*Corvée quartier*
14:00	*Rassemblement compagnie*
14:00–17:30	Afternoon training, work details
17:30	*Soupe,* end of work day
17:30–21:30	Free time for yourself
17:30–5:30	Allowed to be absent from camp if you've applied for and been granted a *permission* slip
21:30	*Corvée* duties
22:00	Roll call
22:30	Lights out

This is the standard routine you can expect to follow every day in the Legion. There will be little deviation no matter if you're comfortably in your regiment, in Africa, or on operation somewhere. You can see by the schedule that the Legion still intrudes in your life and has its hook in you even at the end of the work day. It takes getting used to the fact that you don't have the freedom to do everything you please and that all phases of your life are regulated by the Legion.

The work or training you conduct during the day is nothing out of the ordinary. It is just the normal business that can be expected from any combat unit in keeping its armor well polished. I knew people who'd been in other armies before coming to the Legion, including myself, who said things were generally not much different than what they had seen before. Same shit, different pile, as the saying goes.

Your living quarters are rooms that you share with six or seven other men. You have a bed and locker for yourself. You are allowed to have televisions and VCRs in your room and many rooms do have them. You can also have items such as a fridge. In most cases the inhabitants of a room will pool their money to purchase expensive merchandise that everyone uses.

All camps have modern facilities or are in the process of improving them. There is nothing lacking in basic necessities. Each regiment has a *foyer* and gymnasium in which to spend your free time. There is not a lot to do in camp when the work day is done other than frequent these places. You can go into Calvi after work but there is not a lot to see or do there either. Members of the mainland regiments at least have the luxury of being close to larger cities where they can keep themselves amused.

A regular distraction for many is drinking beer in the *foyer.* Since there isn't much to do at the end of the day, it's not unusual for people to fill hours of boredom by having a few beers to relax. France and the Legion have an open-minded approach to alcohol consumption as evidenced by the availability of beer and wine at the mess hall, the use of which is tolerated at almost any time during the day. No one will say anything if you have a beer at 9:00 A.M. with your *casse croûte,* or snack, after you've finished your sporting activities. As long as you can do your job no one will get too excited about it. I've spent days painting and wallpapering rooms where everyone was constantly dipping into a case of beer. This isn't to say that the Legion is full of alcoholics, but it is more permissive of this type of behavior than you would probably find anywhere else. At the same time, this sort of activity is becoming less and less prevalent. When I first got to the *REP* the *foyer* was full of people drinking beer every night, yet five years later near the end of my contract, practically no one was spending their time drinking in the *foyer.* It is hard on the body to be hung over every morning and trying to run 10 kilometers (6 miles).

A better way to occupy yourself is by participating in one of the clubs that are organized by the regiment. Skydiving, scuba diving, skeet shooting, orienteering, and cycling are a few of the diversions one can seek out. Unfortunately, these clubs are run only on weekends and then only at irregular intervals. Another drawback is that, in clubs like skydiving, there are a lot of officers and NCOs who take part and shamelessly throw their rank around to force their way past subordinate ranks for seats on the plane.

I'll talk more about daily life in the section on desertion, since much of what does go on every day largely contributes to a person's decision to desert.

Africa

Preparations for your departure to anywhere in Africa will entail a cursory medical and dental examination, a few inoculations, and the issuance of personal clothing, material, and equipment exclusively for use in Africa. There is seldom a reason anyone is prevented medically or dentally from a *tournante,* or tour, in Africa, and the procedure is just a formality. The gear you are given is not part of your regular gear and has to be drawn and returned for each tour. You will also be required to empty your locker and store all personal items not accompanying you on the trip in barrack boxes that are placed in a storage room for your *section*. The entire company does this and nothing remains in company living quarters when that unit is away for any length of time.

The standard size of a company embarking on a *tournante* is 150 men, and your company will be reinforced from other units in the *REP* to make up for any shortfalls. A company will have five *sections* of 30 men each, of which four make up combat *sections* and one a headquarters *section*. Each *section* is further comprised of three *groupes* of usually eight men with a smaller *groupe* acting as a headquarters team for the *section*.

You will need to get yourself a civilian shirt for the flight to Africa. You can do this any time you go into Calvi for the evening. For reasons unknown to myself, we weren't permitted to wear military apparel on any flight to Africa but instead wore civilian shirts with our parade uniform dress pants so that we always resembled a traveling choir or band. This may be done because of the unpredictable nature of some airspaces, such as over Libya and Sudan. This way, in the event of an unscheduled landing in one of these places, any disembarkation would not be cause for alarm. So, even though the cargo holds are crammed with weapons and military gear, and carry-on luggage consists of sensitive night vision equipment and small green backpacks clearly indicating militaristic use, you wear civilian shirts. This never entirely made sense to me, but neither did I inquire as to why it is done.

I had the good fortune of being among the last members of the *REP* to go on a tour to Djibouti. For years the *REP* continually had one of its companies stationed at Arta, which would rotate with another company every four months. This operation was discontinued before the end of my contract and the camp at Arta vacated and returned to the locals. The *13ᵉ DBLE* and a small detachment from the *REC* located at Oueah remain as the sole Legion units in Djibouti. The French do maintain a sizeable military force in Djibouti due to its strategic location at the mouth of the Red Sea, but regular French units bolster this garrison. Formally known as the French Territory of the Afars and the Issas, Djibouti gained its independence from France in 1977 but still welcomes the security of French military occupancy.

Chad was the only other African nation I was favored to visit, but I was lucky enough to do two tours each of both Chad and Djibouti. If you average one *tournante* per year during your time in the Legion the Gods are smiling on you. Chad is also independent from France but, like Djibouti, is content to have French military forces positioned there. The French presence in Chad is formidable and is known as *Opération Éper-vier,* or Sparrowhawk, of which the main force is stationed in the capital of N'Djamena with a smaller unit in Abéché. A Legion regiment will normally send two combat companies and a part of headquarters company to assume the duties in Chad. The headquarters detachment and one combat company will be stationed in N'Djamena, with the second combat company being sent to Abéché. The two combat companies will rotate with each other after two months. Regular French units also reinforce the military might in Chad. There aren't many other countries you would likely be sent to in the normal course of events, but French interests in Africa are still widespread and the potential is always present for the necessity of troops being deployed there. Africa is truly a volatile continent because of the constant tribal disputes that simmer unabated. Through the duration of my contract, the Legion either responded to, or was on alert for, crises in both Chad and Djibouti, Central African Republic, Gabon, Mali, Somalia, Togo, Rwanda, and Zaire.

When you set foot in Africa for the first time you will likely experience a stunning measure of culture shock. The sights and sounds are sure to be an enormous contrast to what you're used to. The initial things you will notice are the ever-pervasive heat, the unique smell of Africa which is equally prevalent, and the camels which seem to be absolutely everywhere. No matter how you slice it, Africa is one hot mother of a place. Djibouti and southern Chad are both within 12 degrees of the equator and temperatures over 40 Celsius (104 Fahrenheit) at midday are commonplace. It feels like you're carrying an extra weight on your shoulders, it can be that oppressive. There is a distinguishable odor that permeates Africa no matter where you go, but it is not necessarily unpleasant or offensive. It simply reiterates the fact that you are now in a very different world. You'll know for sure you're in Africa when you see camels being lead through the streets of Djibouti City or N'Djamena. Analogous to horses in the frontier days of the American West, camels are major forms of transportation for the nomadic peoples of the African Sahel region, and these guttural beasts are as plentiful as motor vehicles. Donkeys are also abundantly employed as a means of conveyance.

Something else you can't fail to notice is the exigent level of poverty and squalor, particularly in the cities. Chances are you've never seen anything like it. Everywhere you look are dirty, run down buildings, people in filthy, disheveled clothing, crippled beggars crawling through the streets on their hands and knees, other people with obvious medical problems, and an extensive seediness in many urban areas. It's not all bad, but there is a great deal of human misery and suffering that is endured throughout. There is a shantytown on the outskirts of Djibouti City that epitomizes what I'm talking about. It resembles nothing less than a refugee camp with shacks constructed of corrugated strips of metal, cardboard, mud, and any scrap of material that could be used to construct a wall or roof. Thousands of rusted tin cans are scattered for hundreds of meters across the ground along with other accumulations of litter, so that it appears the inhabitants live in the middle of a garbage dump. Really a terrible looking place.

That the general populations of these areas are poor is beyond question. In fact, there were many times I had to marvel at how some of these people could subsist at all. Rural denizens seem to fare better by living off agricultural produce and livestock but this self sufficiency doesn't predominate built-up areas. Many city dwellers are not engaged in productive labor and do whatever is necessary to survive. For many, depending on their level of desperation, this means theft.

On my first trip to Chad in 1991, we shared our camp with a Chadian military unit who had recently been involved in the government takeover there. Local civilians were also largely present in the camp. Within minutes of unloading our gear into our barrack block and assembling outside, several locals broke through a window in the rear of the building and made off with a number of duffel bags full of gear. Most of it was recovered as they didn't get too far, but it was an eye opening introduction to the problem that is a constant anxiety in Africa. You have to be incessantly vigilant. If you are on a vehicle patrol and you stop anywhere, whether it be in the country or city, you are immediately beset upon by throngs of curious locals who aren't the least bit shy about asking for handouts. In Djibouti they yell *bakshish, bakshish* which is Arabic for a material or monetary gratuity. In Chad it's *cadeau, cadeau* which is French for a gift or present. We often weren't averse to giving them candy or biscuits from our ration packs or other non-essential articles. It really didn't seem to matter what we gave them. They were always thrilled to receive a gift of any kind. Even something as mundane as a plastic throw-away mineral water bottle is seen as a prize, and a mad skirmish will result if you throw one into a crowd. Unfortunately, this kind of benevolence leads to a ceaseless bombardment of requests for charity and can become rather annoying. It's nice to be in a position to help others but you can't save the world. Among those asking for hand-outs are opportunity seekers who wait for the moment your attention is diverted then swipe whatever they can grab and run for dear life. Keep your guard up at all times.

We were involved in protecting an anti-aircraft missile site beside the airport in N'Djamena after the military coup. The site was encircled with barbed wire and had several observation towers around it. At night it was a never-ending battle to keep the locals from entering the compound and stealing us blind. With the help of night vision equipment we usually deterred their efforts, but not always. One night after a guard had radioed in that some locals had entered our enclosure, we scrambled to intercept them and barely managed to catch one of them before they fled back through the barbed wire with a heavy rimmed truck tire. The only reason we did catch the one was because our guard had fired an unauthorized warning shot at them. Here is a prime example of how the language barrier can be a detriment. We had been specifically told we were not to use our weapons and he had not understood the order. Luckily no harm befell anyone. A search of the compound turned up another infiltrator and they were handed over to the local *gendarmes* and an unenviable fate.

Once, while guarding this place, we found that we did not have enough manpower to fill all the guard towers during the day and had to quit using one tower. Within 24 hours a group of locals had discovered this weakness in our defense, slipped through the wire in broad daylight, and attempted to remove a metal Transall cargo pallet being used as roofing in one of the bunkers. They didn't quite get away with it as they couldn't get it back through the wire before we caught up with them. The chances they were willing to take was amazing. It certainly kept us on our toes.

We had a good chuckle about one minor incident when a *caporal-chef* was on his way to the swimming pool just off base and was approached by a local who snatched the sunglasses he was wearing off his face then ran like a scared rabbit. The *caporal-chef* was too astounded to do anything, and by the time he realized what had happened the perpetrator was long gone. I wasn't laughing a week later while on a brief jeep patrol into N'Djamena. We stopped for a few moments and were surrounded by locals within seconds. I mistakenly turned my head away from this one fellow for a split second and he relieved me of my wristwatch. He stuck his fingers behind the watch face, twisted it so that the pin broke, and was gone. With the help of my counterparts and a Chadian soldier who happened to be blocking his escape, we managed to catch him and persuade him to give it back.

A frightening occurrence of attempted theft happened within a week of our departure from Chad. I was driving a jeep on an orientation ride into N'Djamena for the NCO who was taking over our duties. My commander inexplicably decided to turn down a decrepit side street that we never used to show to the new NCO. As usual, we were overwhelmed by a mob of locals, one of whom made no bones about trying to snatch the glasses off the face of the new NCO while we were moving in the jeep. He was unsuccessful but his attempt encouraged others to grab at the jeep and its contents, including us. The crowd was thick enough and their actions so dangerous that I briefly considered driving over those in front me and possibly using my rifle to disperse them. Fortunately for everyone, the crowd abated and we got out of there in one piece.

I'll never forget the time we were assembling for lunch in camp one day and a Chadian soldier came screaming past us in a panic. He was being pursued by two others cracking bullwhips at him. We didn't know what had happened but it was probably theft related. Third World justice at its harshest. After seeing the debilitating poverty all around you, it is more than understandable that someone would risk bodily harm for personal gain, but theft can't be condoned under any circumstances. Without the right to property anarchy ensues.

The worst example of destitution I ever observed was during an armed garbage detail in Abéché. We had towed a trailer full of garbage to the dump and were met there by a horde of desperate locals. They swarmed the trailer and proceeded to empty its contents, fighting each other for whatever scraps they could get their hands on. Many were there not only for the material debris we were unloading but for anything edible they could find. Several of them wasted no time in eating remnants of food waste they discovered. The plight of some of these people is heartbreaking.

The soldiers in the camp we shared with the Chadian military at N'Djamena were barely better off than the local populace and were no more bashful about asking us for handouts than the civilians. The pay they received was a pittance when they were paid at all but at least they got regular meals every day. Many of these soldiers had been POWs in Libya for years before being released, and even though they were better off than before, their existence was still squalid. It was hard having so much and working opposite those who had so little. An older fellow I remember named Service — his father had named him Service because he himself had done a lot of service in the army — had visited his brother in Paris and couldn't believe that toilets were on the same floor in his apartment and that you didn't have to descend to the ground floor to relieve yourself. It was especially disconcerting to drink and eat in front of them during Ramadan, where they aren't allowed to eat or drink between sunrise and sunset. You feel a little bit awkward taking a big slug of water in front of a fellow guard who can only watch you thirstily. The really moving part of working with the Chadian military was seeing ten and twelve year old kids riding around like desperados in Toyota pickups armed to the teeth with AK47s, rocket launchers, and heavy machine guns when they should have been in school. Things aren't right when kids have to take up arms to get a meal in their belly.

Within a week of arriving in Africa you will develop an appreciable case of the backdoor trots or *la chiasse* as it's known in French. You can almost set your watch by it. Your system won't have a ready defense for the new and unusual forms of bacteria, so it responds by disintegrating your solid waste matter into a fluid evacuation. You'll be clenching your butt cheeks together and making a hasty dash for the crapper many a time before your system achieves a balance. There are a few self-proclaimed medical consultants who will tell you that healthy doses of beer, whiskey and other spirits of choice will stave off the effects of gastrointestinal challenges, but this is more an excuse to indulge in their favorite pastime than anything. Everyone is afflicted with the runs sooner or later. If you acquire any form of illness while in Africa don't delay in telling your *section infirmière,* or medical representative. Health issues can quickly compound themselves in the Dark Continent. Avoid drinking water from a tap while in Africa and instead drink only bottled mineral water. In Chad, *Opération Épervier* provides this to you free of charge, but you will have to purchase it yourself from the *foyer* while in Djibouti. This extra expense may not seem too appealing but your health is always worth it.

A Chadian soldier sits in the back of a civilian Toyota Land Cruiser mounted with an anti-aircraft cannon. A Russian-made RPG-7 (Rocket Propelled Grenade) is hanging beside the passenger door. The passenger door also appears to have several bullet holes in it.

Now is as good a time as any to pass along an interesting peculiarity you will eventually discover for yourself concerning French commodes. In certain regions of France itself and other areas to which it has strong ties, there is a propensity towards squat toilets. These are bothersome devices whereby you poise yourself over a hole in the ground on a porcelain covering, complete with little raised steps for your feet on either side of the hole, in order to go about your business. Ordinarily you adopt a skier's stance over the hole and try to maintain it until you've done your duty. It's actually good exercise for your legs and you can sometimes break a sweat during prolonged bouts on the roost, but it's hardly the occasion for excessive exertion. The first time I saw one of these I thought it was a shower of some kind. The most irritating problem with these contraptions is when you have a case of Aztec revenge and relieving yourself results in it spraying all over your boots, legs, and the back wall. Why the French still use this archaic means in such modern times I don't know, but I believe it may be due to the influx of Arabic culture into their society. When we were with the UN in Sarajevo we shared responsibilities there with the Egyptians and Ukrainians. One of my colleagues who worked alongside the Egyptians in a central Headquarters building said that they left footprints on the seats of the toilets since they were used to squatting over, instead of sitting on, the throne.

There are two basic precautions you will have to adopt in order to thwart any possibility of your becoming infected with malaria or *paludisme*. Both Chad and Djibouti are affected by it to some degree and, while it may not be of epidemic proportions, you don't want to take any chances with it. First of all, make sure you take your daily dose of quinine in the form of Paludrine tablets. It is distributed with your noon meal while in camp, but you may be given a small container of pills to use on your own while in the field. Taking it on a regular basis keeps it in your body at a steady, constant level so that your system is better prepared to ward off the effects of malaria. Secondly, ensure that you sleep under the *moustiquaire,* or mosquito net, that is issued to you. During the day the extreme heat keeps mosquito activity restrained but they are out and about once it cools down and you can't fend them off when you're sleeping. You won't be able to completely avoid being bitten, but these measures go a long way to ensure that you depart Africa in a healthy state.

While you're in Africa the daily routine does not diverge much from the habitual goings on in Calvi. Unless you're on duty, you still take part in the daily *rassemblements,* a period of physical training before the sun gets up, then a day of work or training according to your *section* commander's agenda. One major variance, of an agreeable nature, is the *sieste* or nap period between noon and 4:00 P.M. Because the mid-afternoon heat is so strong, the French have adopted an intelligent method of dealing with it which is to do as little as possible while the sun is at its apex. During this interval you are free to do as you like such as sleep, read, or relax at the swimming pool, if your locale has one. Something that may be frowned on is any attempt to get a sun tan during this time. Not only can a serious sunburn be disabling, but basking in that furious heat can really sap your strength. Whether or not you're allowed to sunbathe will depend on where you are and who's in charge. Most rooms on any important base are equipped with air conditioners and ceiling fans to keep you nice and comfy so staying indoors and out of the sun is not stifling. To make up for the time lost during *sieste,* the regular work day is usually extended to 6:30 P.M. but this is a small price to pay for a few hours of respite from the heat.

A Legion combat *section* conducts a morning *rassemblement* in the Chadian desert. The truck on the right is a *VLRA* and is used for patrols in the African wilderness.

One nice thing about being in Chad is that *Opération Épervier* hires locals to do laundry for you, work in the mess hall, and handle most of the routine *corvée* that would normally fall on you to perform. Each room of seven or eight men is assigned a local, known as a *boy*, who's job is to keep the room clean and do the daily laundry of each person in that room. This is all fine and dandy until you consider that for his efforts your *boy* receives the whopping sum of approximately 50 U.S. dollars per month which, even in Africa, does not translate into very much money. Talk about your exploitation of labor. Considering that each article of clothing he washes is done individually by hand then dried and ironed by him, and this abuse is all the more apparent. The local who looked after our room told me that he could barely buy enough food for his family each month based on what he earned. While this might sound unfair, the French don't pay more than that because they really don't have to. For one thing they could find hundreds of people on short notice willing to do the job, and for another it would be nothing for us to revert to doing these chores for ourselves. Without this opportunity to work most of them would have no source of income at all. Labor laws are non-existent and the French don't take it upon themselves to initiate any changes.

This leads back to what I mentioned earlier about theft. While most *boys* are trustworthy enough this is not always the case. Make sure you keep careful track of all your belongings and lock away anything you can. There are times during the day when they have a free run of your room and there's no sense in leading them into temptation. In the last week or two of your *tournante* do not give your *boy* any more of your laundry to do or it could go missing. It's much better if you do it yourself. He will be fully aware of your departure date and knows there is little, if anything, you can do to retrieve lost articles of clothing in the final days of your time there.

One of the most flagrant examples of theft by a *boy* happened on my second tour of Chad. A fellow *caporal* in my room wanted to purchase several pieces of memorabilia as souvenirs a few weeks before our departure and unthinkingly gave our *boy* the equivalent of three or four month's wages in cash so he could purchase these items in N'Djamena and bring them back. Needless to say, we never saw him again and weren't too thrilled with suddenly having to do our own laundry.

If you're wondering whether or not racism is much of a factor in the Legion, unfortunately I have to tell you that it does exist in all of its ugliness. It would be nice to think that a neutral sphere like the Legion, where so many different races and cultures come together under one roof to work in conjunction towards common objectives, would serve as a catalyst to eliminate any feelings of malice people might have towards each other. Regrettably, the Legion is completely unable to filter any moods of antipathy that recruits bring with them when they join. People don't suddenly shelve years of rancor at the injunction of a third party.

Racism is not an overwhelming problem and, in actuality, has very little impact in the daily affairs of the Legion. In most cases people do put their differences aside and attempt to get along, but undercurrents of malevolence are there and often make their presence known in the form of spiteful words or actions.

During basic training our *section* had one recruit from Syria and another from Lebanon who, by the ill-starred caprices of fate, ended up as *binômes* because their last names were side by side alphabetically and the fellow from Lebanon was fluent in French. The political and religious divisions between their countries, which they carried with them into the Legion, were only aggravated by their involuntary proximity. Their mutual hatred often erupted into tirades of Arabic vitriol terminating in a fist fight. In spite of all this, they somehow managed to suspend most of their reciprocal loathings in order to complete basic training.

Incidents like this are common enough in a situation where people from countries with opposing foreign policies or questions of faith resolve matters of opinion with a racial slur or physical confrontation. The most overt and untenable incidents of racism I saw in the Legion though, were towards the populations of black Africa. For whatever reason, many of our troops treated the locals there like they were dirt and undeserving of even the smallest fragment of respect. It's easy to feel superior to someone who is impoverished, uneducated, dressed in rags, and desperate to the point of despair, but this mean-spirited behavior has no reason for occurring other than because of narrow-minded bigotry. Even the handful of Africans who joined the Legion were not always given their proper due and often endured barely concealed disinclination from others.

The one event which really opened my eyes to this problem was when we were departing from a four month tour in Africa the first time I was there. As we were cleaning up and discarding unwanted material, many of our men went to great lengths to ensure they thoroughly destroyed anything of value that could later be retrieved and used by the locals. Instead of showing a bit of compassion toward someone who barely had enough to eat every day and relinquish a few belongings they no longer had need for, they chose to render these possessions useless.

Not everyone is guilty of racial prejudice. Most aren't, in fact, but you'll see enough of it to be conscious of how noxious it can be. If you do join the Legion, you can expect problems of this nature to be relatively minimal. Everyone is in the same boat, after all, and most strive to keep things on an even keel. Don't be surprised, however, if someone does take a disliking to you because of the color of your skin, your country of origin, or political and religious beliefs.

At given times during the *tournante* your *section* will go on field excursions known as *sorties terrains* for the purposes of patrolling, training, acclimatization, and just seeing the sights. This is a grand opportunity for experiencing the bucolic aspects of Africa and becoming better acquainted with its hinterlands. Normally these outings involve the use of vehicles and each *groupe* in your *section* is assigned its own to use and maintain. The French utilize excellent vehicles for preclusive employment in Africa that are known as *VLRAs* or *Véhicule Léger de Reconnaissance et d'Appui* (Light Reconnaissance and Support Vehicle). They look like over-sized half-tons, can carry ten men and their gear comfortably, have virtually a go-anywhere capability, and have the invaluable feature of a 200 liter (53 gallon) water tank built into their underbellies, although drinking from them results in a metallic taste in your mouth.

A top-heavy tractor trailer passes a small roadside market selling mangos in Chad. Dangerously loaded vehicles such as this are common and many come to rest on their sides after unskilled or inexperienced operators drive them too fast on roads in no condition for high speeds.

These jaunts into the African wilderness usually cover several days and quite a distance. Djibouti is a comparably small nation, so it doesn't take an inordinate amount of time to cover the accessible territory. Chad and most other African countries are substantially larger than Djibouti, so you spend more time getting from place to place. This means more time in the heat and longer intervals bouncing around in the vehicles. The roads are terrible once you leave the cities, and riding in the back of the trucks is akin to riding a roller coaster with a blindfold on. There isn't much of a highway department in these lands to maintain the roads. The plethora of tractor trailers that have flipped over on these ill-maintained routes and been left to rot where they lie attests to this fact.

A nice characteristic about Djibouti is that it does abut the Red Sea, so it's not unheard of for your *section* to spend a few hours relaxing on one of its beaches and going for a swim. The water is beautifully warm, and if you like snorkeling, there's an abundance of marine life to observe. On one of these trips our *section* commander decided he would like a feed of fish that night. He dropped a bangalore torpedo, along with a couple of hand grenades, into the water a few feet offshore and, without further ado, we collected enough seafood off the top of the water to last a week. For those of you not familiar with a bangalore torpedo it is a metal tube filled with explosives used for breaching barbed wire, and it packs quite a wallop. Fishing with one is an illegal practice in most places, but Djibouti has nothing in the form of conservation laws or any way of enforcing them.

It is common practice for a unit in the field to supplement their rations in whichever manner is deemed appropriate. There is often a modest budget in place for this purpose that is used to acquire things like fresh fruit and vegetables or fresh meat in the form of a live goat or sheep from the local populace. During one of these back country junkets our *section* did, in fact, purchase a sheep from a vendor, then set about slaughtering, skinning, dressing, stuffing, roasting, and finally eating the damned thing. After a considerable amount of time was expended on this culinary catastrophe we dined on what amounted to boot leather. The rueful part of this whole affair is that it was completely unnecessary. We had plenty of food with us and had no need whatsoever to butcher a sheep. It was done more to fulfill the requirements of tradition than anything. Most of the men I served with preferred to stick to the rations they were issued and not go through this type of *sketch,* or charade, with elaborate food preparations. But because the forefathers of the Legion used to do this sort of thing, it is still practiced regularly today.

The evening meal on these field expeditions is often a three hour affair and tends to exasperate and whittle away the patience of pretty much everybody. While a nice hot meal can certainly be a boon, devoting three full hours to it is disproportionate to its benefits, especially when your serving is so modest. We ended up giving the remains of the sheep to the locals who invariably hover on the edge of our encampments wherever we happen to be. In fact, no sooner had we gutted the sheep and buried its entrails, than the locals who were on standby, so to speak, dug them up and claimed them as their own. Nothing goes to waste in their meager world.

Water is perpetually at a premium while you're in the field. A sufficient quantity is regularly carried by all units but it is not always easy to estimate the rate of consumption. We once spent four days transiting the 800 kilometers (500 miles) from N'Djamena to Abéché and almost ran out of water before arriving. It can usually be obtained from any village,

Chadian locals gather on the edge of a Legion encampment in anticipation of hand-outs once the Legionnaires are done with their breakfast.

A Legionnaire tries his hand at extracting water from a well using a bucket.

but there are often lengthy stretches between watering holes. Many villages don't have running water and the inhabitants extract it from wells using a bucket and rope so you wouldn't ordinarily stop at such a place for this purpose unless absolutely essential. Water is rationed to the degree it is necessary. It is normally freely used although it is not squandered needlessly. If you're thirsty you drink. You shave and sponge bath daily. The nightly cooking ritual also consumes a lot of water in the preparation and cleanup activities, but none of these routine matters are interrupted in order to stretch the supply.

Your water will reach temperatures equivalent to the daily heat which is to say well in excess of 40 Celsius (104 Fahrenheit) and drinking it when it's that hot is not pleasant. It definitely doesn't cool you down or quench your thirst. Each *section* usually carries a large cooler or two filled with ice to keep foods chilled, and water and the evening beer ration at consumable temperature levels. But they aren't always used for drinking water. You may or may not be given a bottle of chilled mineral water in the morning for your personal use, depending on the circumstances. A clever technique to keep your drinking water cool is to wrap your canteen or water container in a wet cloth then expose it to moving air, such as when your vehicle is in motion. You'll have to do this continuously during the day but the result is more than worth the effort.

Throughout the day your *section* will traverse hill and dale, field and stream, near and far in executing its duties. There won't be much relief from the sun beating down on you. Many of the roads you use are nothing more than dirt tracks and, when riding in a vehicle convoy, you will inescapably be covered in dust from head to toe by day's end, but there's little you can do about it. You are issued goggles and a cloth head and face covering called a *cheche,* that you see Arabs wearing. The French use a handy piece of equipment called a *housse,* which is a covering with a Velcro seam, to keep most of the dust off your weapon. Weapons can still be slung with this covering in place and quickly extracted if need be. Everyone carries at least one magazine of live ammunition in the field. A lot of the time you won't do much in a day other than sit in the back of your vehicle and be driven all over the country, enjoying the sites. This might not sound like a bad day's work, but it can be tiresome if the roads are rough.

Often a road that is clearly marked on a map is not as distinctly visible in the open country. When roads are not located where they're supposed

A Legion convoy halts for a break while on the move in Chad. The local populace is never long in arriving anytime a convoy stops for more than a few minutes.

to be, there is a tendency to make your own. This happened to our unit on one unforgettable day. We were wending our way south from Abéché when our commander decided that taking a shortcut would speed things up. When the road gradually petered out then disappeared altogether, he remained steadfastly convinced that forging ahead would carry us through to our objective more quickly than turning around. The modern Legion takes full advantage of prevailing technological advances and our commander was confidently endowed with a GPS (Global Positioning System). This is a hand held device that receives signals from satellites to give you your position and can plot a course for you to follow. It is accurate to within 10 meters (11 yards) and our commander felt that following its guidance would see us through. This may well have happened without a hitch had it not been for the 17 flat tires our convoy sustained trying to plow through the Chadian scrub brush. These trees were dry and brittle and had thorns an inch or two long that thoroughly wreaked havoc on our tires as we drove amongst them. When all of our spare tires had been used we had to patch new flats on the spot. I think we averaged two or three kilometers (about 1.5 miles) an hour for about nine hours before we finally got back on a road. Few days are this bad but an average day in the field is still long, hot, thirsty, and dirty.

When the sun finally sets and its searing rays take their nocturnal hiatus, you can begin thinking about bedding down for the evening. Unless your *section* is involved in some manner of tactical training, a bivouac

A convoy lines up to board a ferry at a river crossing near Lai in southern Chad.

for the night is decidedly non-tactical. Other than the customary positioning of sentinels, your encampment won't be much different than if you were camping in a National Park somewhere. You unload tables and chairs to eat on, cooking supplies and utensils, string up lighting, dig fire and garbage pits, break out the beer, eat, drink, and be merry, and generally cause a resounding clamor in the African twilight. You may even have to sing around the campfire, whether you want to or not. For all of its toughness, the Legion is not about to renounce any luxuries in the field. This is undeniably preferable to digging trenches in the dark, eating from a ration pack, sleeping with your boots and clothes on, and abiding a 50 percent sentry watch from a hole in the ground.

Once the evening meal is complete and guard schedules arranged, your *section* will settle into a state of blissful repose until morning. Even though the sun takes a leave of absence until dawn, the heat tends to linger well into the morning hours. In fact, you will find that you will have to lay on top of your sleeping bag wearing only your underwear until around 4:30 A.M. when the heat, at last, disappears for a couple of hours. This does depend on the time of year. The drawback is that you are now exposed to the many and varied desert creepy crawlies that insistently make their presence known at night. Varieties of big, scary, long legged, hairy spiders skitter across the sand and give you a case of the willies. One night we camped next to a wooded area of dried out timber that was absolutely infested with ants. They weren't the kind that bite but they were big and moved quickly, destroying any plans I had for sleep that night. Changing spots didn't help since they were all over the place. Most of the time these pesky insects are not much of a problem, but they can be if you find yourself in the wrong place. The Legion doesn't use tents of any kind whether in Africa or France or elsewhere. The only time I saw them at all was during basic training. The most you ever use is an overhead covering such as a plastic tarp, or *bâche,* so animal and insect life can easily become your bedfellows. Just ask anyone who spends some time on a *mission profonde* in French Guiana. I've heard some wild stories about that place.

At times, your field sorties will involve marching with rucksacks and rifles and include segments of tactical drills and exercises to keep you honed to a razor's edge. These types of activities are difficult enough on their own, let alone throwing some African heat into the stew pot. The exertion required to perform this training can rapidly deplete your reserves of strength and energy, and because of the ever-present danger of heat exhaustion, you are never far away from vehicular and medical support. On more than one occasion we'd be running during a mock assault with our lungs feeling utterly scorched by the hot, dry air. You can barely generate saliva afterwards.

Our company once set out for a two or three day exercise in Djibouti and commenced things with a parachute jump into a devil's cauldron called Gaggadé. It was one of the more remote regions of Djibouti and temperatures were well over 50 Celsius (122 Fahrenheit) when we hit the drop zone that evening. We marched for a few hours then cozied down for some sleep which proved almost impossible. The heat never did dissipate and when combined with a wind that picked up, produced the effect of being inside a blow dryer. On these types of marches you carry almost nothing but food and water and we had consumed a substantial portion of our water before even twelve hours had passed. You are given salt tablets in an effort to assist your body in retaining water and reducing the amount you perspire, but you still consume water at an accelerated rate. At sunup we began marching again, then holed up in defensive positions under our tarps around noon to get out of the fierce midday sun. Most of the water was gone by then, and because we were on exercise and had units strewn all over the landscape, we had no ready means of resupply. By this time several people had become sick from the heat and before the afternoon was finished we had 11 or 12 men

A Transall makes a desert landing as a group of locals look on.

A team of Legionnaires takes up position on a bridge with a .50 caliber heavy machine gun while the rest of their *section* advances through a dry river bed on the right.

A convoy stops while en route from N'Djamena to Abéché to await the arrival of a sandstorm that is bearing down on it.

incapacitated by heatstroke. Since events had deteriorated into a considerable dilemma, helicopters were radioed in to medevac those who were ill, and the exercise was cancelled.

The African climate can be described in two words. Hot and hotter. Days of roasting heat are incessant but from time to time it will rain. When it does, it comes down violently and drenches everything in its wake in a few short minutes, leaving you thoroughly soaked if you're caught in it. Because of the fury and suddenness of these storms, flash flooding is not unheard of. Since a bivouac for the night is sometimes made in a small ravine, this is a situation you need to be aware of, especially on sentry duty, even though the likelihood of your unit being swept away by floodwaters is remote. Another weather phenomenon you may experience is a sandstorm. Our unit got caught in one on the leg between N'Djamena and Abéché, and it turned day into night for about 15 minutes. You couldn't see your hand in front of your face. There's nothing particularly dangerous about a sandstorm but the wind does increase and the dirt it blows around may obstruct your vision momentarily. Apart from these elements, weather conditions do not vary much from the constant, steady heat.

In Africa you can be seemingly lost in the middle of bloody nowhere and, from out of the blue, you'll see one of the locals ambling along without a care in the world with a herd of goats, or camels, or by themselves headed who knows where. We could establish a remote bivouac somewhere, believing nobody was around, and within a very short time be approached by inquisitive members of the surrounding areas. Having to walk protracted distances in order to find food, water, firewood, or other essentials has no deterrent effect at all for them. Once we stopped briefly in a village and, while waiting to leave, a friend of mine asked one of the children to fetch him a couple of nice cold Cokes and said he would pay him once he returned. While the boy was gone our *section* commander finished his inquiries with the villagers and we all departed for a bivouac site a number of kilometers from the village. An hour or more later, after we had made camp for the night, who shows up but this young lad with the Cokes wrapped in wet cloth to keep them cool, determined to deliver them to my friend. Amazed at his persistence, my friend paid him and gave him a hefty reward for his service. The boy wasn't about to let five or six kilometers stand between him and his profit.

The people of Africa are most assuredly a hardy lot. They survive the harshest of environments in conditions of scarcity and take it all cheerfully in their stride. In the countless times that we came across the inhabitants of the places we visited, rarely did I hear a baby cry. Their mothers normally have them slung across their backs in a large piece of cloth and there they hang for hours on end with the sun baking their bare heads while the mother goes about gathering food, water, and firewood, cooking, and making a home. They say that a working mother toils the hardest of any member in a society, and nowhere is this more evident than in Africa. While the women may not hold paying jobs, they labor tirelessly at the duties their culture imposes on them. It's not difficult to commend their efforts when you see them with one or more infants tied to them while they strain under heavy loads of water or firewood balanced on their heads. What are the men doing when there is work to be done? Nothing. We sometimes pulled into a village that was completely devoid of women. They would be off performing their never-ending chores while the men remained behind lounging around on ground mats in a state of complacent apathy. To be sure, they were only following the dictates of their civilization, and they doubtlessly did something worthwhile in the course of a day, but what that may have been was not discernible.

Unfortunately, the ruggedness of these people does not make them immune to disease and malnutrition, and scores of them suffer the crippling effects of easily remedied afflictions. We stopped in a village one day and were soon besieged by the citizenry, among whom was a young boy shyly

A Legionnaire stands beside a grass hut characteristic of the people of southern Chad while a group of toddlers watch shyly from the shadows.

cradling one of his arms beneath his robe. When one of our people asked him to reveal his arm, he uncovered a dirty, swollen, mangled claw for a hand that had stiffened into a hook at the wrist and appeared to be in a state of decay. He couldn't move his hand, and it didn't look like he would ever be able to use it again. It had probably been infected somehow and, because of the lack of simple medication, it had progressed to where amputation was a conceivable possibility. Sadly, there was nothing we could do for him at that time and place and had to leave him to his fate.

There were occasions where assistance could be rendered. *Opération Épervier* in both N'Djamena and Abéché provided daily medical services to the local population free of charge. In Abéché, the locals would congregate in multitudes outside the main gate of the camp before the daily quota was allowed to trickle through for treatment. A friend of mine who worked in the infirmary told me more than a few unpleasant tales of what happens when pestilent medical problems fester unhindered. The number of people with genitalia ravaged by venereal disease was staggering. Children with a profusion of ailments were pandemic, and their mothers struggled at the gate each morning to have them admitted to the camp. Countless others were affected by any variety of maladies, many of which could have been prevented or alleviated with reasonable access to medication. It's tragic to think of the infinite magnitude of humanity the world over who have no help available to them.

A monkey has no scruples about climbing into the cab of a *VLRA* in the camp at Abéché.

Field outings will also bring you in contact with an assortment of indigenous wildlife, the camels and donkeys which I've already mentioned being the most abundant. You might also see antelope, monkeys, baboons, vultures, ostriches, hippos in Lake Chad, and a wide variety of marine life in the Red Sea. We used to have large groups of baboons pass through the camp at Arta regularly, stopping to rummage in the garbage bins before scampering off.

Because you will encounter such a rich panorama of persons, places, things, and events, you should consider making every effort to procure a camera, preferably before arriving in Africa. Use it without discretion every chance you get. If you're the least bit interested in photography you'll be in seventh heaven. One regret I have is that I didn't take nearly as many pictures as I should have. Cheap cameras are easily obtained from your regimental *foyer* as are higher end models. Your time in the Legion is filled with golden moments to take innumerable photos as a history of your passage through there. Don't bring a camera when you join the Legion, but do invest in one as soon as you are able.

Legionnaires approach a camel in Djibouti as it rises to its feet. Further back, herds of goats gather in the shade of some trees to keep out of the sun.

The Legion prints its own monthly magazine in Aubagne called the *Képi blanc* that has color photos from all the regiments in each issue. It is an excellent publication — one of the best I've ever seen that is produced by a military unit — and may offer you the opportunity to submit photos. You won't receive any form of payment if you do, but you may have the satisfaction of immortalizing some of your snapshots.

If you'd like to gain some insight into what the modern Legion is like, you can inquire about subscribing to it at the following address:

Képi blanc
BP 78 - 13 673
Aubagne, France

The magazine is wholly in French, but its emphasis on numerous color photos and simple captions makes it easy to read with the help of a dictionary. Single issues are only 22 francs plus shipping and handling. It cost me a total of 66 francs, 22 francs for the magazine and 44 francs for postage, to have the January 2000 copy sent from France to North America. Forms of payment are made out to:

Foyer D'Entraide de la Légion Étrangère

If you want to get information about the magazine before sending payment, write them a short letter saying the following:

Je cherche des renseignements pour souscrire a la revue Képi blanc. Je voudrais que vous m'envoyer une liste des prix et une manière pour la commander.

They will probably just send you an order form. If you just want to order the February, 2001 copy, for example, by sending payment outright you can say:

Je voudrais commander la revue Képi blanc du Fevrier, 2001.

I suggest you include a French money order for at least 100 francs to cover all the costs. It might cost you more this way, and I cannot guarantee fulfillment of your order, but you won't go bankrupt if you do lose 100 francs.

Another toy you may want to consider purchasing is a small world band receiver so you can tune in to your homeland and listen to the news each day. It's nice to hear what's going on back home when you're on the other side of the world somewhere. Most countries have an international radio service you can listen to throughout the day, but even if you can't tune in to it you can almost always get the BBC which, I believe, has the most extensive radio broadcasting service in the world. In every place I've ever been, I could always pick up the BBC. We even used to be able to dial it up on our Morse sets while on patrol in the middle of Africa. A radio I picked up in Gibraltar and have used for years that I would recommend to anyone is the Sony ICF-SW7600. It's about the size of a pocketbook and doesn't weigh too much. There is a smaller model of the same design that is even better but it will cost you more.

After flexing your muscles in the field, it'll be time for some well deserved R&R. All work and no play will make Johnny a dull Legionnaire, so you'll surely want to take full advantage of any occasion for blowing off steam. The weekend in Djibouti and Chad falls on Wednesday and Thursday rather than Saturday and Sunday in accordance with Islamic decree, but this isn't a difficult adjustment to make. Even though Chad and Djibouti are visibly indigent nations, they boast an abundance of bars, night clubs, and restaurants in the capitals that cater to your hedonistic cravings. Many of these establishments are remarkably first class.

It is not unusual for the bulk of several *sections* to descend full force on the nightlife together in groups. A very good idea is to pair up with at least one other person and keep an eye out for each other during the night. There are certain areas in Djibouti City and N'Djamena that are perilous after dark to say the least. You never want to accidentally turn down a wrong street by yourself in a drunken stupor. This happened to one fellow I served with in N'Djamena and he returned to camp clad only in his underwear. One night a bunch of us piled, destination unknown, into a cab in N'Djamena which drove us deep into the city. When we finally stopped we had no idea where

A *légionnaire* wearing his *tenue de sortie,* or dress uniform, is ready for a night out in Djibouti.

we were. We had to arrange for the driver to pick us up a few hours hence or we may not have found our way back. You would be crazy to try something like this on your own, sober or drunk, and even being in a small group it was not extremely intelligent. Some people in these areas are desperate to the point that they would have little remorse about assailing you. All it takes is a few of them to marshal a plan of attack and you've had it. When you go out for the night you are dressed in your parade attire, complete with white *képi* and all the bells and whistles that clearly identify you as a Legionnaire with money in his pockets, which acts as a magnet for nefarious beings and their evil deeds. Your vulnerability is also increased the more you drink, even though your brain will tell you otherwise, so be careful out there.

In Djibouti you can paint the town until sun-up, as long as you're back for roll call in the morning. In Chad, because of the operational status of all activity there, you are only allowed out until 1:00 A.M. in N'Djamena. Needless to say, this seriously cuts into your carousing and

Legionnaires from the *2ᵉ REP* relax in a bar in N'Djamena. Each regiment has a number of indicators that are worn on the dress uniform to identify the affiliation of their members. Someone belonging to the *2ᵉ REP* is quickly distinguished by the parachute wings worn over the right breast pocket, the triangular regimental insignia that hangs from the button on the same pocket, and the red *fouragère* worn around the left shoulder. The parachute wings are worn by any member of the French armed forces who has completed parachute training but the regimental insignia and red *fouragère* are unique to the *REP*.

rabble-rousing, but sacrifices do sometimes have to be made and your hangover won't be as severe. In Abéché you aren't allowed out at all and your festive pastimes are confined to the camp *foyer*. When you do *sortie en ville* you will have to take a few party hats with you. Your *section* commander will often pass inspection to satisfy himself that you are carrying at least three condoms or *capotes* and you may not be allowed out if you haven't any. They are easily obtained from your *section infirmière*. Don't ever think you would never have use for them. Some of the women you will meet in the bars and clubs of Africa, especially Djibouti, are exceptionally beautiful, with outgoing, uninhibited dispositions and resisting their alluring siren calls takes more will than most mere mortals possess. Having your senses blunted by alcohol won't help either. The moment you walk into any entertainment establishment you are greeted by a variety of women who want nothing more than to spend a little time with a Legionnaire and his money. They receive a small commission if you buy them an overpriced drink, so zealous competition for your attention is very much the norm. It's nothing for a young lass to latch onto your arm and pull you away to a corner for the evening. You can pretty well pick and choose any maiden that may tickle your fancy, and they'll be more than happy to extend you their courtesies.

Other than getting out on the town for a bit of recreation there isn't much else to keep you amused. All camps have a *foyer* of some kind that serves beer and has a television to watch, but beyond that, entertainment is what you make of it. Djibouti at least has the luxury of having beaches where you can relax. You'll have to seek out a distraction to assuage your after-hours tension and boredom or you'll find yourself in the *foyer* with beer in hand most nights or in town spending your money faster than you earn it. In Abéché, where you can't leave the camp at night for the two months you're there, it's the *foyer* or nothing. These weeks of privation definitely make you appreciate the moments you are free to do as you please.

The months you spend in Africa are a considerable personal sacrifice where duty clearly comes before self satisfaction. It's not out of the ordinary to spend several days in a row cooped up in camp, especially if you're on duty, and this can wear on you after awhile. As a radio operator on my second tour of Djibouti, I once spent six straight 24 hour periods (roughly 144 hours) in the radio station due to all other operators in the company being deployed elsewhere at the time. The only time I left was to eat, go to the washroom, and take an evening shower. It was like being released from a jail cell when I was finally replaced.

It is often a huge relief to escape the confinement of the camp perimeter for any reason, be it recreation, a work detail, field excursion, fitness training, or what have you. Most mornings your *section* will take a prolonged jog encompassing many kilometers. In Djibouti there is a span of desert known as the Grand Bara which is a flat expanse of hardpan that extends for 15 kilometers (9.3 miles) in an unbroken stretch from start to finish. There are no trees, rocks, or other obstacles for its entire length, and you can't see one end from the other. The Legion, being gung-ho as it is, enjoys running its full extent just because its there, and the *13ᵉ DBLE* habitually organizes an annual run in which the whole regiment participates. Once, someone had been well into the run when he could no longer prevent his bowels from purging themselves, and he was forced to perform his intestinal eliminations in full view of the entire regiment as they ran by, since there was nothing to hide behind.

Before you know it, your four months will be at an end and you'll be winging your way back to home base. You might have had the occasion to obtain amounts of contraband during your stay in Africa. You may come in contact with prohibited material such as when one of our *sections* found a warehouse full of weapons, ammunition, night vision equipment, uniforms, radios, explosives, and all manner of military paraphernalia after the coup in Chad. Unfortunately, availing yourself of such victor's spoils won't benefit you much. Regulations controlling goods of this nature may be quite lax and unorganized in Africa, but this is not the case in France.

Immediately upon your return to the regiment, your unit assembles on the parade square with all personal baggage and you are made to display your belongings to the military police who methodically rifle through it. If you are found in possession of illicit merchandise, you will be put in the lockup forthwith and may eventually be court-martialled or face prosecution in a civilian court. Don't even think about trying to smuggle back a pistol, grenade, or similar item in your luggage. You will be told before leaving Africa what types of souvenirs you are allowed to take back. If you have any doubts make sure you ask someone.

Legionnaires from the *2e REP* enjoy a few beers at the airport in Djibouti as they wait for their flight back to Calvi after completing a four month tour. The tan uniforms they are wearing have since been replaced by a light gray model.

Vacation Leave

Anytime a unit returns from a lengthy duty outside the regiment, they are given a leave period of anywhere from two to four weeks. It can also be given to a unit at specified times during the year. Before joining the Legion I had been fully prepared for a stark life of deprivation and sacrifice, spending all my spare time in a desolate camp somewhere, earning only enough money to keep me in beer, cheap wine, boot polish, and toothpaste. Never did I think that you would actually be permitted to take a vacation beyond the outer limits of the camp and its environs, which goes to show how much I knew about the Legion before I joined. This may have been how it was years ago but the overall severity of existence in the Legion has diminished as it continues to advance and improve itself with time.

You are, in fact, granted a significant amount of freedom during your leave period. You are allowed to go where you like with the understanding that you remain within the borders of France. If you are still fairly new to your regiment (less than one year of service), you may not be authorized to take leave outside your regiment but will still receive the same amount of time off as the rest of your unit. This will depend on the regiment and the attitude of the hierarchy. Each regiment maintains a *centre de repos,* or rest center, for this purpose and for those not desirous of leaving the area due to lack of funds or personal preference.

Leave, known as *permission,* or *permission longe durée (PLD)* for extended periods, is usually given to a company as a whole, except in headquarters company where you can apply for it individually whenever you feel like taking it. You are entitled to 15 working days of paid leave in your first year which increases each year to a total of 45 days in your fifth year. Yes, that equals nine weeks or over two months of paid leave in a year. Not too shabby. It was a far cry from the despondency I expected. The trick is saving enough money to enjoy all those days off, which is not especially difficult with a bit of discipline. You are paid better in the *REP* than the other regiments because of your airborne status, which helps you stash some cash for a rainy day.

While still on your *tournante* your company may ask you where you plan to spend your leave, and may go as far as to arrange a plane ticket for you, the usual destinations being Paris, Marseille, or Nice. This is a congenial thing to do as it prevents a hundred or more men from trying to secure a flight from Calvi to Paris at the last moment, for example, and not getting tickets. If you ever take leave on your own, you can easily reserve a seat by phoning the airport. Don't bother with trying to cross to the mainland on a ferry. They may be cheaper than a flight, but they're slow, and if you can't get one out of Calvi you'll have to travel to another port on the island by taxi which will end up costing you more. When you get leave you'll want the quickest, most efficient route off the island.

You are required to wear your dress uniform when you depart for leave, keep it on all the time you're at the airport and for the duration of the flight until you arrive at your destination, after which you can change into civilian clothing. The *PM*s monitor comings and goings from the airport, so there's not much chance of avoiding this detail. Other regiments are more lenient with this procedure but the *REP* is not as gracious. The problem that arises by having to wear your dress uniform is just exactly what to do with it. Are you going to cart it around for a month while you gallivant all over France? A *képi blanc,* along with your shoes and uniform, takes up a lot of space in your luggage and is easily warped or crushed if mishandled. If you only plan to visit one location, keeping it with you is not a major headache but most *permissionnaires* move around considerably while on leave and don't want to bother with it.

You may want to leave it in a bag in long term storage at the train station in the city you fly into and will depart from after your leave. Make sure the bag you put it in can be locked and won't reveal its contents. Whatever you do, don't tell the baggage handler that you're a Legionnaire wanting to store your uniform for awhile or it could fall prey to souvenir hunters. You can usually store it indefinitely, but you'll have to pay handsomely to get it back. I once paid over 700 francs to retrieve mine after leaving it in storage for a month in Paris. You will also need to purchase a travel iron. Don't dare return from leave wearing a uniform that looks like its been slept in.

The question that begs asking is why force this imposition on someone if they're only going to wear their uniform once on departure and once on arrival? If you serve in the *REP* you will find that the phrase "anal retentive" is an appropriate description of much of the activity that goes on there. Common sense is habitually discarded to preserve a grandiloquent air of elitism. No one would dare affront this image, and certainly not to appease any murmur of discontent from the rank and file. Tradition is the expression that is bandied about with resplendent fervor when any method of doing things is challenged. Don't complain though. Any leave at all is infinitely preferable to moping around in camp.

The first time I got leave was after the tour in Djibouti that followed six months of basic and commando training. Since we'd hardly stopped to catch our breath for all that time, we arrived in Paris wearing only what we had on our backs, which is to say our dress uniforms. Strolling the streets of Paris in Legion garb is a great way of drawing attention to yourself. It is fun to imbibe copious quantities of liquor with *les anciens* or ex-Legionnaires who seem to ferret you out and regale you with tales of Algeria and Indochina. And, as much of a magnet as it can be to members of the fairer sex, you'll probably want to shed it as soon as possible and purchase some new clothes. Technically speaking, you aren't allowed to possess civilian clothing while in the Legion, at least before your first five years are complete, but this is entirely impractical and is not enforced. However, the clothing you do buy and bring back to Calvi will have to be stored away in a foot locker until your next leave period. A Legion track suit is the only clothing you are permitted to wear after hours other than your uniform.

Before departing for leave, your regiment should issue you a card which provides you a 75 percent discount on all train travel within France and will be valid for the length of time you serve in the Legion. When you grow weary of Paris just hop on a train for the French Riviera. And you thought life in the Legion was difficult? Just present your card when you buy your ticket and ask for a *tarif militaire.*

I mentioned that you may do as you wish on leave provided you stay in France, but don't take this as rote. The vast majority of non-French Legionnaires depart France on leave whether they are authorized to or not. The outlook on this situation is one of grudging compliance by the Legion as there isn't much it can do to prevent anyone from leaving the country nor to prove that they did. As long as you aren't blatant about your absence and don't rub anyone's nose in it, your truancy is tolerated. My own reasoning on the matter was that if French-speaking Legionnaires could go home and visit their families while on leave, why shouldn't the rest of us be able to? This may be why no one will say anything if you do leave the country. You are supposed to provide your company with the name and phone number of where you're staying in the event the regiment has to recall you from leave for a crisis of some kind, but this is just protocol and is not at all practical. It's unrealistic to

expect someone to stay put for a month in the same hotel. You are expected to keep your regiment informed if you do move around but, as
you can guess, no one is going to phone and say they're back home in
Walla Walla when they're supposed to be in France.

After returning from a tour in Chad I once got three week's leave
ahead of my company because I was scheduled to take a course in Castel during the time the company was to take its leave. Upon his adamant
insistence, I gave my *section* commander the name and phone number
of the hotel I would be staying at in Paris. After five days of reveling in
the benign splendor of that beautiful city, I decided I would head for
Nice and the Riviera. Being a non-European I resolved, after four more
days in Nice, that I would attempt to cross into Italy sans passport and
take better advantage of my time in Europe. I'd already spent a previous
leave period in France and wanted to broaden my horizons a bit. I took
a train as far east as you can go in France to Menton, got out and walked
the road to the border, not sure if they'd let me into Italy or not. I handed
the border guard my Legion I.D. card, which he glanced at with surprising disinterest, and let me pass. I then walked another eight kilometers
(five miles) to Ventimiglia and got a train to Rome. I went on to Florence
and Venice before I had to return to France. When I got back to the regiment my *section* commander asked me how the weather was at home,
knowing full well I had not dallied long in Paris. I believe he actually
contacted the hotel concerning my whereabouts and, even though he
could have made my life hell after I returned, he relented to my wayward
whimsies, content that he didn't have another desertion on his hands.

There is an administrative procedure known as *rectification* where
you can apply to have your passport returned to you long before your
initial contract has expired. It can be done with a year's service, or possibly even less, and only requires that you take the initiative to start the
ball rolling. I'm not sure of the exact criteria for being *rectified,* and I
don't think that everyone who applies is successful in this venture, but as
long as you're aware of its existence you can give it a whirl. Its main
purpose is to reestablish the correct identity of those who had their
names changed when they joined the Legion, Frenchmen included. You
will notice that people you have known for a few years will suddenly be
wearing new name tags as a result of this system. Those who aren't able
to be *rectified* usually have ongoing personal problems that began prior
to their joining the Legion. Even if you didn't have your name changed

when you joined, you will still have to go through the process to get your passport back. To do so, you will need to obtain a copy of your birth certificate from your homeland and have it sent to you after you've joined. Bringing one with you when you join will speed up the whole operation, though it may be better to send for it later to reduce the chances of it going missing. When your unit gets the copy it is sent to Aubagne where it is translated into French. Your passport is returned to you once the paperwork is complete. When you get leave afterwards, you can request to depart France and do so legally in the Legion's eyes.

If you aren't able to reclaim your passport via *rectification* when you want it, you can try your consulate or embassy if your country has one in France. Whether or not they'll be willing to assist someone who voluntarily relinquished their passport to the Legion will only be known when you present them your lamentable tale of woe, but they are usually quite helpful. They may not be too impressed with your laxity but, as far as I know, joining the Foreign Legion is not a criminal act, even if you did give up your passport. Whatever the circumstance may be that confronts you, I would strongly urge that you do whatever it takes to get your passport back or have a new one issued to you. Europe is a treasure trove of things to see and places to visit and you'll surely want to explore some new vistas.

Having had the good fortune of crossing unobstructed into Italy and back with only a Legion I.D. card, a friend and I determined during a two week leave that we would make a similar attempt to enter Spain. Our main goal was to see a bullfight. We hopped a train from Marseille to Barcelona but after arriving at the French-Spanish border I was removed from the train because I did not have a passport. My friend had a second passport due to his having dual citizenship, and was allowed to remain but got off with me anyway. We were then summarily put in a train car and sent back into France. Having ascertained that Spain was not as sympathetic as Italy in letting just anyone stroll into their country, we hatched a stratagem that we hoped would get us where we wanted to go. Not anxious to spend another leave in France, and because we only had two weeks to play with, and because we were almost in Spain already, and because we really, really wanted to see a bullfight, we decided that we would mosey on up the road on foot to the border crossing and see if we could walk across the border as I'd done in Italy. It was almost midnight as we approached the end of the hairpin turn where the border crossing was situated. We realized that there was probably little chance of us crossing on foot if we hadn't been able to on the train. We then reasoned that we wouldn't be doing anything wrong if we only climbed the hill a bit and just had a little peek on the other side into Spain. Once at the top we again reasoned that since our intentions were honest enough, why let the lack of a pesky passport prevent us from doing what we wanted. With this delusion firmly in our minds, we crossed into Spain.

We still felt a patent amount of trepidation in spite of our flawed logic. We had no desire in being picked up and held accountable for our actions. When we got back onto a road on the Spanish side, we were only a few hundred meters from the border crossing and our immediate concern was that a border guard driving home might spot two men walking down the road away from the crossing knowing he hadn't allowed anyone through his post on foot. Because of this we bailed into the ditch at the sound of every approaching vehicle. It was also for this reason that we did not try and get a train from the border town of Portbou — in case we ran into the guards that had originally taken me off the train. Instead, we continued on past the town, spent the night sleeping in a ditch, then walked 20 kilometers (12.5 miles) to Figueras the next morning where we finally got a train to Barcelona.

After arriving in Barcelona, I rationalized that it would probably be to my benefit to see the consulate about obtaining a passport since the prospect of crossing back into France via our method of entry had no appeal. They directed us to Madrid, where I explained how I had entered the country with only an I.D. card from the French military, omitting the ignominious details of how we actually got in, and was wondering if there was any way of having another passport issued since we'd gone through a lot of hassle when trying to enter. If they had questioned me with any scrutiny, I would have divulged what had taken place, but they weren't overly interested. A major stroke of luck was that my old passport had expired and since it was no longer valid, a new one could be issued without a lot of wrangling. I'd also memorized the serial number long before, and they were able to promptly verify that it was expired. Upon completion of the paperwork explaining where my passport was and why I was not in possession of it, I was issued a brand spanking new passport. I can't tell you what a relief that was. With the freedom of movement this document brought me, we finished our visit in Spain, stopped for a few days in Gibraltar, and made a quick visit to Andorra before returning to France. If you ever get a chance to see a bullfight, by the way, be sure and take one in. It's the most compelling spectacle I've ever witnessed.

The planets and stars must have been in proper alignment for us during this whole affair because we sure had a favorable run of luck. Looking back on it now, and even while we were in the midst of it, I realized that it was probably the single most reckless thing I'd ever done in my life, other than joining the Legion perhaps. If we'd have been caught we could have languished in a Spanish prison for who knows how long, then presumably have spent time in a Legion lockup after returning there. Any manner of unpleasantness could have befallen us, but as it was we came through it safe and sound.

Because I now had a valid passport and, essentially, a ticket to anywhere, I was able to visit Greece, Vienna, Berlin, Potsdam, Belfast, Dublin and Southern Ireland, Scotland, England, the Canary Islands, Singapore, Hong Kong, Macau, Malaysia, and Oktoberfest in Munich during the remainder of my leave periods in the Legion, all unauthorized. Like I suggested, do what you have to in order to get a passport. To allow five years to go by and not take advantage of your location in Europe would be a sorry waste.

A real concern while you're on leave is the money you carry with you. You are paid in cash and can't have a bank account in France outside the Legion so you are saddled with an enormous amount of liquid capital that you have to protect during your furlough. This places you in a rather precarious position. Staying in hotels every night and traveling around for a month is expensive. You will need a significant stake to sustain your activities. Cutting your vacation short because you've run out of cash is not something you even want to think about. On most leave periods I had around 25,000 francs in currency on my person, which is not exactly a safe thing to do. If you're ever robbed or lose it you could end up stranded somewhere without any means of extricating yourself from that situation. Basic precautions are necessary to prevent such a calamity.

One of your first priorities should be converting enough of that cash into travelers checks so that you're not completely wiped out in the event of an unforeseen misadventure. Another cautionary step is to use a money belt of some kind to keep that huge wad of cash securely attached to you. Never keep a sum of money that large in a wallet that you pull out and expose every time you buy a beer. I used to keep my excess cash in a pouch that was originally meant to be worn as a shoulder holster, but which I modified so I could carry it tucked in the front of my pants just above my groin. It was impossible to detect, and there was no chance it could ever be pilfered.

An important additional consideration is if you cross any borders to another country carrying your tremendous stash of loot. If, for example, you enter the United States with more than $10,000 cash and it is discovered, you could be detained and held indefinitely. Those assets could be seized and possibly never returned to you, under the suspicion of you being a filthy drug dealer. Who else carries that kind of money around with them? In many places in the world you are guilty until proven innocent. To avoid this type of interruption in your sabbatical, take the time to find out what the regulations are particular to your destination. Don't think you won't ever find yourself with this much cash. One guy I knew spent the equivalent of $15,000 U.S. during a four week leave after our tour in Sarajevo.

Pay

At this point you're probably thinking: Bloody hell! Just how much do they pay you in the Legion anyway? I was as ignorant to the amount of money you earn as I was about taking leave before I joined. I figured that a few hundred francs would be somberly doled out to you each month which would quickly evaporate in beer fumes and a few other basic necessities. The sum I had fixed in my mind was the equivalent of roughly $200 U.S. per month or somewhere in the neighborhood of 1,000 francs. How wrong I was! Of course when you're still a tenderfoot *légionnaire* you don't earn much but things do improve in your favor. The published pay table below gives some approximations as to what you can expect to earn.

Grade	Base Pay
Legionnaire	5,500 francs per month
Caporal	6,000 francs per month
Caporal-chef	6,300 francs per month

You make more in the *REP* than the other metropolitan regiments, although I can't speak for the overseas regiments. This became glaringly obvious while I was taking a radio course at Castel as a first class *légionnaire* with two year's service under my belt. We were paid a little over 6,000 francs a month, but a fellow course member from the *2ᵉ REI* was given four measly 500 franc notes for the month. What really demonstrated the disparity in wages was the fact that we received slightly more as first class *légionnaires* with the *REP* than a *sergent* did with the *4e RE*. A *caporal* in the *REP* will make around 8,800 francs each month, which can almost double for a four month tour in Africa. A *sergent* on tour in Africa can make well in excess of 20,000 francs per month.

The partial pay stub below shows what I received as a *caporal* in the *REP* for June 1994 while on a tour of Chad. My total pay for the month in cash was 16,426.83 francs.

On the following page is the pay stub I received in July 1994 after returning to Calvi from the tour in Chad. You can see that my pay was almost half of what it was for an overseas tour, being paid only 8,781.44 francs in cash for the month.

MINISTERE DE LA DEFENSE

ARMÉE DE TERRE

	N. O.P.	Décompteur	Identification Affectation	Livret de solde
	131	D702	00200255	6025432

O.P. 131
C.T.A.C. 131
CASERNE DU MUY
13998 MARSEILLE ARMEES

Bulletin de solde

du mois de **JUILLET   1994**

ADRESSE FISCALE :

2 REP
CAMP RAFFALI

020260
CALVI

CAPORAL

2 REP CALVI   20CALVI

3037/3

ELEMENTS DE BASE UTILISES POUR LE CALCUL DES INDEMNITES ET RETENUES														Nombre d'enfants				MUTATIONS EFFECTUEES SUR LE MOIS EN COURS	
Echell.	Echon	N.Maj	Indic. pens.	Indic. res.	Zone Fam.	Sit.	SFS	RSFS	ICM	AF	+ 10	+ 15	APJE	CFFN	MICM	ISSP		ECHELON	
3	02	0289		2	0	00	00	00	00	00	00	00	00	00	00	00		ENFANT	
																		INDEMNITE	X

Libellé des indemnités et retenues	Date début	Date fin	Type	Taux base	Montant + ou -	Montant imposable
SOLDE BRUTE	01 07 94	30 10 94	A	6 015,90	6 015,90	6 015,90
IND DE RESIDENCE	01 07 94	30 07 94	A	60,30	60,30	60,30
IND SERV AER TX 1	01 07 94	30 07 94	S	2 746,50	2 746,50	2 746,50
IND CHARG MILIT TL	01 07 94	30 07 94	A	497,58	497,58	
RETENUE MUTUELLE	01 07 94	30 07 94	M	135,00	-135,00	
				SOUS TOTAL	9 185,28	8 822,70
COTISATIONS SOCIALES						
RETENUE SS TERME B	01 07 94	30 10 94	A	373,50	-373,50	-373,50
RET FONDS PRE.AERO.	01 07 94	30 07 94	A	41,19	-41,19	-41,19
				SOUS TOTAL	-414,69	-414,69

Contribution Sociale Généralisée				Total Solde	8 770,59	8 408,01
Assiette	Déduction 5%	Taux 2,40	Baisse pension	Total Rappel (*)	10,85	
				Net à Payer	8 781,44	8 408,01

Ventilation et cumuls des sommes imposables en fonction des régimes d'imposition			MODALITES DE PAIEMENT	
	METRO/FFA	ETRANGER	Fraction principale	8 781,44
Territoire			NUMERAIRE	
Montant	23668,83	22724,91	Cpte: Frac.sec. ou cvf/dm	
Avant.Natures	480,00	640,00	Cpte: Troisieme frac.(FFSA)	
			Cpte:	

DANS VOTRE INTERET, POUR FAIRE VALOIR VOS DROITS, CONSERVER CE BULLETIN SANS LIMITATION DE DURÉE

* : (A)utomatique,(S)emi-auto,(M)anuel,(D)ette (*)Les situations intermediaires ou les rappels sont détaillés au verso

We used to talk about what an unrivaled situation we were in as far as saving money went. Because your overhead living expenses are almost non-existent you can literally save thousands of dollars each year. To show you the potential of the money you can amass, I estimate that I was able to preserve an average of over $10,000 U.S. for each of my five years in the Legion, and walked away with a very comfortable nest egg. After completing a six month UN tour in Sarajevo as a *caporal,* I was able to bank about $20,000 U.S. because there is almost nothing to spend money on in a war zone.

One fellow I knew who had lived in severe poverty in Buenos Aires, Argentina confided in me that he had saved over 200,000 francs, and this was long before the end of his first contract. What I found interesting about his situation was that he was often chided as being cheap, but he was only taking every precaution that he would never again live in dire need of anything. Many others renew their contracts for exactly this reason. They are unlikely to find a similar cornucopia anywhere else. Those that come from nations suffering from high unemployment or a host of other social ills are not quick to surrender this type of abundance and return home to an uncertain future. There is a price to be paid for continuing a career in the Legion, but it is not so high as to warrant the departure of those who've found their horn of plenty.

The actual process of being paid is still resolutely based on the mores of tradition. On the monthly pay day, your company is assembled wearing their *képis blancs,* and is marched to the pay office in formation singing the company song on the way. When you arrive at the pay window you salute the officer, remove your *képi,* present yourself to him, and give your I.D. card. Once he gives you your pay, or *la solde,* you tuck it away, come to attention, slap your thigh, and be on your way. If you aren't comfortable carrying your entire month's wage around in your wallet you can deposit some of it back into the account the Legion maintains for you. It won't earn any interest but at least it's safe. You can also look into having it forwarded to an account in your home country. They will need the account number and address of whichever bank you want it sent to so you'll have to organize these matters before joining.

Personally, I never did use any method of transferring money from the Legion to an outside bank account but you shouldn't experience any problems if you choose to. Start with small denominations until you get comfortable with the procedure and you're sure your money is arriving safely at its destination. I used to mail considerable sums of cash to my parents in 500 franc notes that they would then deposit into my bank account. I never had a single one go astray. Whatever method you decide on, have a plan in place to adequately safeguard the fruits of your labor.

A friend of mine who renewed his contract and stayed in the Legion a few more years informed me that the Legion may be moving toward providing its members with accounts through the national post office. These accounts would allow the Legion to directly deposit wages rather than paying everyone in cash. You could then withdraw your money as needed. My friend said one of the reasons this may be happening was because a Legion payroll bound for the *REP* was hijacked directly off the plane by the Corsican Mafia when it landed in Bastia.

Theft

Theft is rampant within the ranks of the Legion and I could recount dozens of tales where people had their entire pay or large portions of it stolen by the two-faced bastards that infest every single Legion formation. Allow me to vent for a moment. There can be no lower form of human life than a thief. This contemptible personality trait is reprehensible at the best of times, but in a close military environment it is unforgivable. It can collapse the spirit of trust and confidence that is critical to the members of a combat unit where lives may hinge upon knowing whether or not you can depend on someone. It is a mannerism that has to be annihilated without mercy. The Legion does act with a vengeance when someone is caught with their hand in the cookie jar, but most larcenists are not apprehended. It is difficult to prove that someone stole your money unless you actually see them do it, which is one of the big problems with being paid in cash. The vermin that engage in their quest for easy money are usually quite careful in their pursuits.

If you are caught in an act of thievery, you may as well kiss your career in the Legion goodbye and desert the first chance you get because your life will be a litany of torment. Two people indicted for stealing were hounded out of the Legion and deserted in short order even though they could have continued their careers if they had chosen. One of the most satisfying closures concerning robbery happened when a *caporal* in my company was finally jailed for his sticky fingers. It could never be proven but he had long been suspected of the mysterious disappearance of money from other people's wallets. Incredibly enough, he had once threatened a new *légionnaire* with bodily harm if he told anyone he had seen him pinch some cash from his locker as he returned from the shower. The new *légionnaire* had felt powerless to do anything about it, but word of the incident did filter through the grapevine and only confirmed what everyone already knew. When he was eventually charged for an unrelated event and put in the lockup, he cut himself and wrote on a wall in blood, "I didn't do it." In due time he left the Legion in disgrace.

Don't lend money to anyone or be careful who you trust with small loans. When living in close proximity with others it doesn't take long to know who has money and who doesn't. It can be difficult to budget your pay over a full month when you get it all at once, and many don't have the foresight to do this successfully. When you consider that no one really has any overhead, those that can't mete out their income in moderation and spend it all within a week or two are not people you would want to lend money to. They are serious credit risks and have likely already borrowed from others before coming to you. You'll probably be proven wrong if you think they'll be dependable in paying you back. An incident that took place on a number of occasions was that someone short of money, or possibly not, would ask for modest loans from many people at the same time with the full intention of deserting once he had accumulated enough to take flight. With this in mind, never lend money to someone just before they go on leave as this is when most desertions occur.

A factor that contributes to a lot of material theft is an administrative policy. It has a dual purpose of punishment and accountability, but inadvertently backs people into a corner and prompts them into a course of action they may otherwise not have considered. If you lose any article of your issued gear or any bit of material you are entrusted with, you are made to write a *compte rendu,* or report, by hand in triplicate explaining the circumstances surrounding the matter. There is a strict format to be followed in composing this document and any errors you make could result in having to rewrite it until it's perfect. Getting it right is a painstaking chore. I had to do one for a piece of equipment I lost on a march and would have considered almost any alternative to avoid doing another. No one is going to endure this bureaucratic nonsense and the castigation of their superiors because they lost one of their shirts or had a pair of pants stolen off the clothesline. The most pathetic example I ever saw of someone trying to escape the aggravation of a *compte rendu* was when one of our *sergents* lost his *cheche.* He openly took one from a *légionnaire,* forcing him to do the report. One way to dodge this nuisance is to try and obtain surplus items from anyone who deserts and quietly stock-pile it in anticipation of future need. When the gear from a deserter is returned to the quartermaster it is never fully accounted for. Another way to acquire something you need is to talk to others around the regiment. A few beers in payment is usually all it takes.

The largest case of theft I experienced in the Legion occurred when our company was on a tour in Chad. While there, word got back to us that one or more thieves had broken into the storage rooms in our company's vacant barracks. They had ransacked all the foot lockers that were stored there, strewn the contents of each up and down the hallway and caused a terrible mess. When we returned we had to sift through piles of personal possessions to try and reclaim our own property. The miserable human garbage that did this was never caught and got away with whatever valuables they managed to steal. This may have been an instance where the theft was not an internal issue. If I had to guess, and it's only strong speculation, I would suspect that a few civilian contractors who had been erecting a new building beside ours had gotten into the barracks knowing it was vacant. They would have had all the time in the world for treasure hunting and could have rapidly quit the premises at the first sign of danger. Unfortunately no one could prove anything and did not have much interest in further investigating the matter.

It may be to your advantage not to accumulate anything of value while in the Legion. Nothing is safe. There are those who feel that you're the one at fault if you leave them an opportunity to steal from you, and they have little compunction about doing just that.

A theft of sorts occurred when I was still a recent addition to the *REP*. A new *Chef de Corps* had just assumed command of the regiment and one of his first duties from his totalitarian vantage point was to freeze all bank accounts in the *REP* in an effort to stem the tide of desertions, as if doing that would really have any effect on anyone determined to get the hell out of there. Needless to say morale plummeted, the desertions persisted, and things continued pretty much as they always had.

Because we weren't allowed withdrawals from our Legion accounts and were forced into accepting our pay in full in cash, everyone commonly had reams of money on them, just prime for the plucking from any thieving S.O.B. that found it. There were people with thousands of francs sitting in their accounts that they could not get at without a proclamation from on high, and you couldn't you have it sent outside the Legion because you might desert.

I, along with most others, could not fathom the reasoning behind this oppression and seethed with injustice during the two years this restraint was in place. I was never able to generate a shred of respect for this *Chef de Corps* during his tenure and always considered him as much a bandit as the kleptomaniacs in our ranks. It can only be guessed what happened to the appropriated funds from the accounts of those who deserted. Regardless of whether someone deserted or not, the money in their account had been earned for services rendered, and they should have had the unrestricted right to do whatever they liked with it. Punishing the many for the actions of the few is a superficial method of addressing any problem. No one could have gotten away with a comparable persecution had it occurred in any place except the Legion, but this *Chef de Corps* did, to his eternal damnation.

Desertion

Desertion is the Achilles heel of the Foreign Legion. It is a curse of epic proportions, a bane so comprehensive and unending that it debases and undermines the entire foundation the Legion is built on. It is an enigma that can never be eliminated and will dog the Legion until it ceases to exist. Despite the best of efforts and good intentions to retain its members, there is little it can do to prevent someone in renouncing their obligations if they no longer want to be there.

The desertions from the Legion each year number in the hundreds. Within the first two years of my being in the *REP*'s 1st Company, there were over 100 desertions from this single company. One time, after returning from a morale-deflating tour in Chad, we lost approximately 20 men from our company who did not return from leave. I don't know if other regiments are as bad for desertions as the *REP*, since it tends to be much more rigorous on its members, but they have their fair share. No unit can claim immunity from this pestilence.

There is no single prominent reason why someone decides to escape the indentured servitude of their contract. They yield to the culmination of a variety of factors that reach a boiling point and result in their quitting the Legion's ranks. Have I mentioned that life in the Legion was tough? You are subjecting yourself to one of the harshest tests of your manhood that you could expect to find anywhere in the world. When I talk about deprivation and sacrifice they aren't just prosaic locutions to quaintly describe the ambience you may encounter, but are the reality of the situation. It's not an exaggeration to say that you live a monk-like existence in the Legion, especially in the *REP*. We used to joke about this or equate it to being in prison, but it is very true. You simply do not enjoy the same liberties that you would as a civilian, or even in other military units, and have consented to their abdication by signing your contract. Many only become aware of this after treading into waters deeper than they can negotiate.

I don't know how many times I saw the look of dejection on people's faces when they finally realized what they had gotten themselves into. For the majority, this disenchantment will take hold during basic training or within the first few months of being in their combat regiment. It is probably safe to say that most desertions occur within the first two years of a Legionnaire's contract. When the facts concerning the circumstances of living in the Legion at last become clear, they conclude that they are not willing to waste another three or four years of their life mired in misery in an effort to prove something to themselves. They then begin casting about for a means of escaping. For many, joining the Legion is taking a definite step backwards from the status or the comforts of life they are used to. In an age of instant gratification, they aren't willing to sit still and remain in a situation that is not satisfying to them. Some people really have no business being in the Legion in the first place but only discover this after seeing it for themselves.

You may now be wondering just what is causing the enormity of disappointment which impels so many to rescind their agreements with the Legion and flee its bondage. This is not an easy question to answer. A young man who first prophesies a stint in the Legion customarily harbors grandiose illusions of adventure, fame, romance, and prestige with a reasonable amount of hardship thrown in to test his mettle a bit, but nothing so difficult that he can't withstand it. He's probably read a few sketchy magazine articles on the subject, maybe seen an obscure documentary on television or a movie à la "Beau Geste" or "March Or Die." He may also have heard some second-hand accounts of what it's all about. Even though none of it provides much detail or only presents things in a glamorous light, he doesn't let this bother him. Then, deciding this is for him, he makes a fateful determination based on shockingly incomplete information, little suspecting the seriousness of his fallacious reasonings. With stern words of discipline, honor, fidelity, images of grueling marches, exhaustive training, a grim life of austerity, and other visions of sugar plums all dancing in his head, he departs into a great unknown, ill-prepared to meet the substance of these flights of fancy face to face. Sure, he could be killed or worse, but he's young and invincible and that sort of thing always happens to someone else. Signing away five long years of his life? Nothing to it. A mere drop in the bucket on his life's time clock. He'll still be a young man when he gets out.

As you can well imagine it isn't long before the bubble bursts and he lands with a painful thud back into the real world. As he soon discovers, life in the Legion is not an orgy of guns and glory. You spend more time behind a broom than you ever will behind a rifle. When the lifestyle of thankless drudgery is laid bare before him, these fantasies fall by the wayside and a pervading sense of claustrophobia can set in. He either gets tough and braves its chokehold, or he deserts. Men that have a bit of living under their belts and have undergone their share of rigors already in life tend to better manage the adversities of the Legion. Those less experienced in the ways of the world are more apt to struggle and lose heart when their machinations don't pan out as they had anticipated.

One of the first things you encounter that will begin putting you off about the Legion is the endless *corvée,* which I've already touched on. It is a perpetual daily grind that slowly gnaws at your enthusiasm for being in the Legion. I have nothing against keeping things clean. It is quite necessary and it wouldn't be so bad if you only overhauled everything once a day. But, the Legion insists it is done three times daily. Can you imagine cleaning your own home three times daily, day after day? I don't think so. When your name appears on the *corvée* duty roster you are responsible for completing that chore at the prescribed times throughout the day. The different duties you can look forward to on any given day are *corvée chambre* which is keeping your *groupe*'s room clean, *corvée couloir* which is cleaning the hallways of your *section, corvée chiote* which is cleaning the toilet areas, *corvée compagnie* which is cleaning the common areas of the company, and any number of ancillary *corvées* depending on how your barracks are structured. You would normally sweep and mop each of these areas. Because there are so many duties to be carried out each day you can expect to be doing something every second or third day or more if your *section* is short of people. I remember a time when there was only myself and one other person in our *section* to perform these chores for over two weeks. One of the worst things about *corvée* is that it can prevent you from going out into town for the evening. I don't think the other regiments are quite as exacting as the *REP* as far as *corvée* goes, or most other things for that matter. You may find that it's not the same headache if you end up in another regiment. Much of the nonsense you find in the *REP* serves an important function during basic training but to continue these stringent inanities in the regiment is senseless. You will quickly become aware that being in the *REP* is like never having left basic training.

Another mind-numbing daily duty is *corvée quartier* which is a garbage sweep of the exterior company areas that takes place before the morning and afternoon *rassemblements*. All *légionnaires* assemble in a line, with the *caporals* behind them as overseers, and walk around the company areas picking up all manner of trash including cigarette butts or *mégots*. If you are a non-smoker you will have little appreciation for picking up after filthy tobacco puffers who discard their butts with indifferent neglect for those who have to clean up. This is a catch-22 like you've never seen it. People throw their butts on the ground because they know they'll be picked up yet they wouldn't have to be picked up if people didn't throw them on the ground. Even *légionnaires* who will have to pick those butts up assert their rights as idiots and toss them around haphazardly. The mind-boggling stupidity of this is completely overwhelming. I can't begin to tell you how frustrating it is to have to do this every day.

The ones that really need a good, old-fashioned boot to the hindquarters are the fearless leaders of the Legion who proclaim that because they had to pick up butts as *légionnaires,* they will be sure to leave an abundance of the same for those that follow in their footsteps. This is like someone saying that "because I was wronged, I will therefore commit wrong." Where does it end? If there could be found any one reason, although there were many, why I could never have signed an extension of my contract, it would be because of *corvée quartier* and cigarette butts. It might sound like a small matter but it reflects a distinct mentality that courses through the Legion's veins. Most people endure *corvée* with the expectation that it will eventually abate, which it does as you gradually gain your standing in the company, but it's one of the straws that pile up on the camel's back and go a long way toward breaking it.

Another bothersome item on the daily agenda is roll call or *appel.* Once again, it's not a major event in most other regiments but the *REP* just has to milk it for all it's worth. At 5:00 A.M. the *caporal de semaine* whistles *"Appel!"* and at 5:30 A.M. your company assembles on the parade square to be counted by the *sergent de semaine.* Not all companies in the *REP* go through this rigamarole, but instead employ common sense and leave it to the *caporal du jour* to account for everyone rather than hauling the entire company out of their bunks. As in basic training you are constantly accounted for during the day to thwart any ideas you may have about absconding. At night there is yet another *appel* at 10:00 P.M. with lights out for the whole regiment at 10:30 P.M. The evening *appel* is substantially more irritating than in the morning. *Corvée* is done in all areas of the barracks for the third time that day just before *appel,* and the *sergent* will inspect things when he makes his rounds. For the *appel* itself you either have to be in bed sleeping, or pretending to sleep, or be standing at the foot of your bunk waiting to be counted. The aggravating thing about evening *appel* is that between the time you finish work at day's end and the time you start gearing up for *appel,* you have maybe three and a half hours of time for yourself — in any 24 hour period — and even then you are subject to the whims of chance and could be commanded at any moment to perform any necessary chore or duty. It's very difficult to relax and unwind after working all day when you have to plan your evening activities around this type of foolishness, and it does begin to wear on you before long.

This is an example of how a lack of perception and remaining rigidly inflexible creates unnecessary problems. To rob someone of their spare time in an already difficult environment so they can sweep and mop even more floors, and then, in effect, have a lack of trust displayed towards them is asinine. There wouldn't need to be an *appel* if people didn't desert and yet, people would conceivably be less inclined to desert if there wasn't an excess of stupidity over issues like *appel.* The problem with a unit like the *REP* is that since it is regarded worldwide as an elite unit, it has to constantly search for ways of reinforcing that image, whether its procedures are practical and make sense or not. Because of this, few in positions of authority have the necessary daring to break with firmly embedded customs.

The Legion is steeped in tradition which provides an extremely important basis from which it operates, but some healthy changes could be effected without its core values being rent asunder. Much of the desertion could be allayed and a lot gained if the Legion would lighten up a bit and take note of the grumblings of its soldiers, though there is hardly any chance of this happening.

Most officers are completely out of touch with their men as is common in all military organizations. They seem to have little or no knowledge of disaffection in the ranks, and aren't overly concerned when they do find something amiss. Rather, they clamp down even harder, thinking that will squelch the problem. Officers are normally at the helm of their post for two short years, even though they may spend many years in the Legion, and an appointment to any position in the Legion is a decided boost to their careers. As long as they keep their ship pointed along the straight and narrow and don't rock the boat too much, problems they encounter eventually become someone else's. There's no need for them to initiate any changes to placate dissension. They can't be faulted for following a doctrine that's been in place for decades. Tradition is a great and noble word, but it can have a repressive influence on personal initiative.

You will share your living quarters with a *caporal* or two, one of which will be the *chef de chambre* who ensures the room is kept in constant order. Having to live in the immediate vicinity of this type of authority figure can really grate on your nerves, especially if you have a mutual animosity towards each other. When this happens, you are constantly on edge from a palpable sense of unease and are never able to fully relax. If a *caporal* has taken a disliking to you, there isn't much you can do except endure as best you can. He can abuse his power and make your life miserable without thinking twice about it. I know of several instances where *légionnaires* were thoroughly bullied into deserting because of the indignities suffered at the hands of despotic *caporals*. There's only so much a person can take, and you don't have many options available to you in resolving ill-treatment. You can't go whining to anybody that *caporal* so and so is picking on you and you want him to stop. No one will grant you an audience or care enough to investigate the matter. Nor can you send a *caporal* the message that you won't be trifled with by giving him a bloody thump on the nose and expect to get away with it. He's got right on his side even if he is wrong, so you either sink or swim against any type of unfair treatment.

The single most pitiful example I ever saw of the impertinent misuse of authority conferred on a *caporal* was during basic training. Two of these contemptible cowards took it upon themselves to harass the weakest member of our *section* until his eyes blackened, his lips and nose bled, and he was wetting the bed at night, knowing full well there was little he could or would do about it. To his detriment this recruit was painfully out of his element by being in the Legion, but he should not have had to prevail against this sort of craven tyranny. He requested to be released from his contract at the end of basic training and his wish was granted. These *caporals* overstepped the bounds of decency and made a mockery of the power entrusted to them, without the slightest repercussion. If this sounds scary, that's only because it is. New recruits aren't exactly welcomed with open arms into their regiments and are likely to be initially viewed as fresh meat to be played with until they've proven their worth a bit. You're going to feel like you're walking on eggshells for the first few weeks or months, but if you can get through this period reasonably unscathed you should be okay. Even though it may seem like you're in for a hellish ordeal, most *caporals* are easy enough to get along with if you keep your mouth shut and do as you're told.

One thing I will say in the Legion's favor is that they don't engage in initiation-type rituals. In many armies around the world or in organizations of people associated by common interest, induction ceremonies of a contentious or controvertible nature are conducted as a mandatory rite of passage. These practices can be as straightforward as excessive bouts of drinking or as extreme as hazing and physical violence. To its credit the Legion neither compels its men to act in this manner, nor does it tolerate immoderate levels of intemperate behavior. Completing a phase of training is not seen as cause to run amuck and intimidate fellow Legionnaires through ridiculous customs.

An element concerning your living arrangements that slowly rattles your cage is the fact that you have no privacy at all. For your entire five years in the Legion you will share your living quarters with several of your fellow comrades and are thus constantly exposed to the racket created as a result. Most rooms have at least seven *caporals* and *légionnaires* residing within, and getting any peace and quiet is almost impossible. There is always someone talking, making noise, or causing some sort of disturbance which, when combined with things like snoring, body odor, drunkenness or other irritating behaviors, is enough to drive you off the deep end. Televisions and VCRs are allowed in the rooms as well, and are nearly always turned on after work. The only place to get anything resembling a moment of privacy is when you go to the toilet and lock the door, but this is hardly a propitious locale in which to relax and read a book or contemplate worldly affairs. You can't very well read from a squatting position either. Even outside your room there isn't any place on base where you can find some quiet time for yourself. It is a factor you will definitely have to adjust to, even if you are the type of person who likes the constant company of others. Everybody needs an occasional bit of serenity. A couple of things you can do to contend with this lack of solitude are to purchase a Walkman and lots of music to drown out the din, or just buy some earplugs if you want to concentrate on reading or writing a letter. Communal living of this nature takes some getting used to.

An additional irritant is the way in which the barracks are constructed. Some of the living quarters for the company *sections* are situated on the second floor of the same building where the administrative offices of the company are located. To reach your room, you are required to pass in front of areas that your superiors frequent. The closeness of these two domains creates an awkward situation and only contributes to an already ostensible level of tension. Add to this the fact that a great deal of your daily work involves being in your room. For example, there generally isn't any classroom space in the companies for instructional training, so a lot of it is done in the rooms with everyone sitting on stools or on their beds. Any time weapons are cleaned everything is spread out on a rain poncho covering your bed. Never being able to completely separate your work environment from normal living conditions really exacts a price after awhile.

As for your evening leisure time, there is not exactly an overabundance of things you can do with it. There isn't much to do on base other than go to the *foyer* to drink and watch television, rent a movie, spend some time in the gymnasium and weight room, or swim in the pool. The *foyer* and company clubs close at 9:00 P.M. which permits little opportunity to let your hair down and have a few beers. One of the big problems in all regiments is that there is no where to go in camp where you and your buddies can get together and raise a bit of hell after hours without disturbing anyone else. In theory, you aren't allowed to bring alcohol into your rooms, but this is seldom complied with and rarely enforced by the *caporals*. Drinking in the rooms is common. Difficulties arise when several people decide to continue their binge after lights out and

Legionnaires whoop it up after hours in one of the barrack rooms in camp Raffalli. Two brands of beer act as staples for the Legion. The more popular is Kronenbourg which is contained in diminutive .25 liter bottles. Heineken is the only other beer normally seen on Legion bases and is contained in regular .33 liter bottles — just in case you were wondering.

do it in the midst of others who are trying to sleep. It's not unusual to find a few guys sitting around a case of beer in the shower or toilet area in an effort to keep their uproar to a minimum.

The only way to really get away from things for a few hours is to go out on the town. During the day, if you plan to go into town that evening, you would fill out a *titre de permission,* or overnight leave pass, then give it to your *caporal du jour* who forwards it to your *section* commander for final approval. This pass allows you to be absent for the evening *appel.* Without one, you can still go into town provided you return by 10:00 P.M., or sooner if you have a *corvée* detail. To leave the camp you have to be wearing your good dress uniform complete with *képi blanc.* You pass by the *chef de poste,* who passes a casual inspection on you and can prevent you from exiting the camp if your uniform is not up to standard. This requirement is a genuine pain in the backside. The uniform you wear is typically the same you use for guard duty, and keeping it clean while you're eating and drinking in town borders on the impossible.

Not to mention the amount of time you can spend getting it up to standard merely to march through the front gates. Because of this, there are those who seldom leave camp at night. I was lucky if I got out once a month.

Calvi is a tiny community about 5 kilometers (3 miles) from camp, and taxis are always waiting outside the gates to shuttle you back and forth. A trip will cost you about 50 francs each way. It's really in your best interest if you buddy up with someone when you go into town. It may not be the danger zones of Africa you're heading into, but you are always vulnerable when drunk and alone and wearing a Legion uniform. There have been cases where Legionnaires have been shot and wounded while in town. Other times they've been cornered and beaten senseless by a cowardly gang of locals. These are rare occurrences but they can happen. Corsica is home to a quasi-terrorist organization known as the *FNLC (Front National pour la Libération de Corse),* and while it doesn't normally target the Legion or cause extreme chaos throughout the island, its minions are everywhere and don't need many reasons to pick a fight. They have no reservations about gunning down *gendarmes,* so shooting a Legionnaire would not be cause for lost sleep.

Tourists fill Calvi to capacity each summer. There's not much danger in being physically menaced by them but there are those who will try and filch a Legion souvenir such as your *képi.* Most Legionnaires who enter a bar put their *képis* on a shelf somewhere out of the way. Doing this can expose *képi* to theft. It's not much fun trying to sneak back into camp because you've lost your *képi* and don't want to explain it to the *chef de poste.* Any tourist that steals from a Legionnaire is gambling with their life because there are Legionnaires who wouldn't hesitate for a second to cause crippling bodily harm to them. Stealing a *képi* is not only theft, it's sacrilege.

Even though Calvi becomes a regular boom town in the summer with lots of pretty girls flocking to its beaches from all over Europe, it dries up into a veritable ghost town in the winter months and women are not at all plentiful. This dearth of feminine presence can have a serious effect on fellows in their late teens and early twenties who want nothing more than to sow their wild oats as far and as wide as possible — something that isn't readily viable when obligations to the Legion come first. The other regiments don't really share this problem but Calvi is isolated enough to where it is a distinct concern for young men. Some guys might have a steady girlfriend year round, but this is the exception rather than the rule. Having a girlfriend is actually not so important as having opportunities to pursue this enterprise to your heart's desire. Weeks and even months can go by in which you are completely devoid of close female contact. What's especially demoralizing is missing the summer months at Calvi due to being on course or overseas somewhere, in which case we're now possibly talking about a year or more without the company of a lady. To say this is tough on a young guy laden with testosterone is an understatement. I wasn't kidding when I compared your life in the Legion to that of a monk. Most people don't find a life of chastity too appealing.

Calvi sports what has to be one of the finest beaches in the world, with beautiful sandy shores that slope gently into the clear Mediterranean waters. You are more than welcome to enjoy this small corner of paradise after work or on the weekends, but there are a couple of small rules you'll have to follow in order to do this.

First of all, you will need to purchase proper beach apparel from the *foyer* which consists of a white shirt, white shorts, white socks, and white shoes, that you'll have to wear while on the beach. You'll then have to pass by the *chef de poste* again who will inspect your attire to make certain it's clean and neat, after which you can spend a pleasant day at the beach or in the taverns that line the waterfront.

A second rule you'll have to comply with is that you can't enter Calvi itself in your beach clothing but must remain on the beach. To go into Calvi you have to be wearing your dress uniform so if you planned to extend a day at the beach into a night on the town you first have to return to camp and change your clothing. I don't think there would be a problem if you wanted to stroll along the beach in your dress uniform though. Go figure. The beach and town are both patrolled by the *PM*s who keep their eyes open for wanton violations like this, so there's no point in wasting your time trying to outfox the system.

The sheer monotony and boredom of life in the *REP* can't help but weigh on a person. You aren't able to hop in a car and go for a drive, attend a movie or sporting event, play a round of golf, go cycling, or seek other distractions to stave off the tedium of garrison living. Nor do you have any privacy to speak of to quietly indulge in a hobby or other pastime you have an interest in. This inability to release the steam on the pressure cooker creates a restlessness that can manifest itself in many forms of damaging behavior. Some people drink beer every single night for lack of something better to do. Others are habitually late for *appel,* display a lethargic approach to their work, develop attitudes that they "just don't give a shit" about anything, and spend a lot of time *en taule* as a result. Still others take their feelings of desperation to the extreme and attempt desertion. If you are going to survive in the *REP* you have to find a way of dealing with the mundane or you won't make it. I had considered taking a correspondence course to put my spare time to constructive use, but found the cramped living ill suited to study.

The only real diversion I was able to find in the Legion that had any form of practicality was reading. I easily read over 100 books of various length, tackling compositions like *Moby Dick, East of Eden, The Complete Works of Edgar Allan Poe, The Rise and Fall of the Third Reich,* and *War and Peace* to name a few. You can obtain some publications from the regimental *foyer* in English such as *Time* magazine or *Newsweek,* but books or other forms of reading material will have to be sought elsewhere. A larger variety can be found in Calvi but to acquire anything of substance you will have to find the English bookstores in Paris or Nice. On our first leave, a friend and I bought about 20 books each and mailed them back to ourselves in the regiment. We then swapped back and forth once we were finished with them. Toward the end of my contract, myself and a few other fellows purchased a couple of bookshelves which we mounted in our room. We gathered all the books we had laying around and put them on the shelves for anyone in the regiment who wanted to read them. The Legion espouses an exemplary attitude of trying to leave things better than it finds them. In our own small way we had tried to do the same. I've no idea if this legacy is still in place, but if you make it to the *REP,* go visit the guys in the *CCS Section Transmissions* (Headquarters Company Radio Section) and they might be able to fix you up. If you're in Paris looking for a bookstore you can try Brentano's, 37 Avenue de l'Opera, 75002, Paris. Tel. 42 61 52 50. There is also a W. H. Smith store at 248 Rue de Rivoli beside the Louvre.

A major form of discomfiture for many is having to adapt to a different culture and modus operandi. One of the reasons there has always been, and will continue to be, so much war, strife, and conflict in the world is because of humankind's innate intolerance towards those whose ideologies differ from their own. Arriving in the Legion and having to suddenly conform to a new way of thinking and acting, not only on a military level but at a civil equivalent, all while in the throes of learning a new language, is no easy task. It so happens that the Legion is mainly influenced by French culture, which only makes sense since France created the Legion. This results in a set of standards that everyone uses as a common point of reference on how to conduct themselves. If any of these standards challenge your own convictions, you could experience a weighty aversion towards your surrogate society. You might find living under the French rules of life a disagreeable undertaking, but it really wouldn't matter if the French Foreign Legion was British, German, Mexican, or Japanese. Each would have their idiosyncrasies and anyone convening at its doorstep would need to make certain modifications to adjust to their new surroundings.

It is easy to criticize and find fault with anything, so even though it is not my desire to denounce French custom, I am nevertheless going to point out a couple of things about their ways that you may find difficult.

Probably the biggest issue I had in opposition to their methods was a deficiency in leading by example. The French tend to rest heavily on their laurels, feeling that once the rank of *sergent* or above is attained, there is no longer a need to hyperextend themselves in demonstrating the heightened level of proficiency that should accompany this position. The old adage of "do as I say, not as I do" is very much in evidence, which might work with children but not with adults who see right through feigned airs of expertise and superiority. Rank does have its privileges but reaching a rung on the ladder does not mean you've transcended from mortal to demigod and are suddenly justified in a dereliction of duty. As an example, *sergents* and above never clean their own weapons, whether it be after a session on the rifle range or a routine march in the field. Their weapons are pawned off to *légionnaires* who must also clean their personal arm. If you've had any military experience at all your mouth is probably hanging open in disbelief, as mine was the first time I became aware of this conduct. If there could be cited a cardinal sin as it applies to military etiquette anywhere in the world, not cleaning and caring for your own weapon would surely top the list.

You may have heard it said that the French can be somewhat rude and arrogant. You will likely find this is not an inaccurate summation. I'm not going to bother with a list of petty grievances on their hereditary characteristics, but will instead leave it to you to form your own opinion. For the most part they aren't that bad, but there are occasions when their impudent demeanor can give you a sore neck from shaking your head so much. Many of the officers especially, seem to think they're direct descendants from God and therefore enjoy some sort of divine right.

One event that really exemplified this haughty attitude took place during a leave period in Paris while completely independent of the Legion's influence. I had walked into a bookstore beside the Sorbonne to have a look around. No sooner had I entered the establishment than the female clerk began to chatter like an angry squirrel. I had offended her decencies by not saying "Hello, how are you, isn't it a nice day?" and whatever else she was expecting me to say and I was therefore deserving of a royal scolding. She then proceeded to set me straight with a quick course in social graces. Being of a "live and let live" mentality, I was quite taken aback by her attitude and left promptly without buying anything.

Another telling display of this temperament was during the Gulf War when France exhibited a stubborn reluctance to cooperate with the coalition forces. France is replete with a hearty anti-American sentiment and was not about to relegate its troops to American command regardless of how much easier this would have made coordinating offensive actions. France did participate in the war and was an important ally, but did so on its own terms and consequently was involved in more skirmishing on the sidelines than in bearing the brunt of any major engagement. This detail did not diminish the consummate glory France was able to achieve in its own eyes for some minor successes on the battlefield.

One attribute I feel compelled to tell you about is the French habit of shaking hands. They feel absolutely required to shake hands with everyone they come in contact with daily, even though they may live amongst and see those same people every day. Some unwritten rule binds them to this behavior to where it is an obligation, and while this is a friendly enough gesture, to apply it in everyday circumstances reduces its impact, which probably accounts for most of the dead fish handshakes that are offered up. Instead of simply grunting "hello" in the morning, it's not unusual to see a large group of men spending several minutes shaking hands with each other before morning *rassemblement*. To give you an idea of how strongly this urge is rooted in their psyche, I once saw two Frenchmen approach each other from opposite sides of a chain-link fence whereupon one of them extended his pinky finger through the links which the other clasped with his own pinky finger to complete the transaction.

It may be considered somewhat forward of you to extend your hand towards a superior in greeting. It's best if you only salute, then allow your superior to make the first move if he wishes to shake hands with you. Once again it's really not that bad of a practice and its general purpose is companionable in nature. I only mention it as an illustration of how a cultural difference can have an adverse effect on you. Personally, and I know many other non-French Legionnaires shared my point of view, I found the penchant the French have for excessive handshaking overdone to the point of absurdity.

Overall, the French aren't really that bad to get along with and even though I could carry on at length on the infinite trivialities about them that may rub you the wrong way, there's little justification in doing this. Every country in the world has its oddities of custom and you would have to adjust to them no matter where you went. Most Frenchmen you will meet are pretty good fellows and with a bit of mutual give and take you should coexist with them admirably. Besides which, they just won the Euro 2000 soccer championship and the 1998 FIFA World Cup so, what the hell, they can't be all bad! Still, it's those niggling little peculiarities that can feed fuel to the fire of any inclination you may have in deserting. Keep in the back of your mind the fact that you are going to have to make concessions from your old way of life in order to succeed in your new one. There's no way around it.

On a more serious note, a dominant influence that can force people to desert is nothing less than the threat of war. This might sound strange if you have the impression of the Legion being a spirited fighting force that attracts young men eager to test themselves on a distant battlefield somewhere, but this is not the case at all for the great many who join. A large number who enlist seek only the path to a better way of life and are prepared to brave the five long, hard years so that they may qualify for French citizenship, but are not so motivated that they would jeopardize their lives in order to reach that goal. There is a running joke in the Legion about those who only join for the food and have little interest in soldierly pursuits. They are known as *engagés gamelles,* or mess tin recruits. Others, having joined in the spirit of youthful adventure quickly realize, when the specter of war suddenly looms large in front of them, that the potential of being killed is not exactly what was on their agenda. It goes without saying that no one joins to die, and anything you may have heard about Legionnaires gladly laying down their lives for the glory of France and the Legion is an unmitigated load of claptrap, although instances like the battle of Camerone don't exactly help to dispel this image. When it became known that the Legion would be sending troops to the Gulf War, the regiments involved suffered a spate of desertions from those completely unwilling to risk injury or death regardless of the personal reasons that brought them to the Legion.

There are countless other factors that may seem insignificant on the surface but which sow the seeds of dissatisfaction. Doing all your laundry by hand, for instance, becomes a tiring task when compounded over several weeks, months, and years. Not being able to live off base, own a car, or come and go as you please, and requiring authorization to do anything from owning a bicycle to getting married, all take their toll.

The Legion works Saturday morning until noon which reduces your free time on the weekend and, in effect, leaves Saturday evening as the only reasonable night to go out on the town. You might only get one or two Saturdays a month when you're not on duty or busy at something else.

Every day at noon your company is marched to the mess hall while singing your company song en route, which is fine during basic training but is an aggravating display of Legion pomp and ceremony in the regiments. Yes, you sing for your pay and you sing for your supper.

A note about meals in the regiments: eating at the mess hall is compulsory for the noon meal but optional for the evening feed. At noon your company assembles on its parade square to account for all the *mangeants,* or eaters, and you are handed a meal card with your name on it which you then turn in as you pass through the food line. Those who don't want to choke down the victuals have someone else sneak their meal card in then go eat at the *foyer.* If you wish to dine on the evening offerings, you must indicate such to your *caporal du jour* in the morning, who submits your name with the *appel* slip. Once your name has been turned in you must be present for the evening meal or face reprimand for your absence, which can lead to you doing the fandango with a broom and mop in your spare time. This doesn't allow you to change your mind during the day, or if you do, no one will make the effort to remove your name from the list. You may also be commandeered during the day to perform duties somewhere and not be able to make it back in time for dinner, through no fault of your own, and are then left to explain to the *sergent de semaine* why he was holding an extra meal card. One time a *caporal* had mistakenly put my name in to eat that evening when I had no desire to do so. The *sergent de semaine* tracked me down wanting to know where I'd been. It was only through some fast talking and vehement denial that I avoided cleaning inconspicuous corners of the barracks that night. For some reason the Legion wants to account for every blessed potato and piece of cheese at each meal, which must certainly reduce the amount of waste that is generated, but seriously restricts your freedom of choice. I don't see where throwing a bit of excess food in the garbage is such a crisis. Many decide it isn't worth the hassle and find another source of evening nourishment.

Many who join, especially disgruntled ex-soldiers from other armies, expect the Legion to be an elite corps of men that will somehow fulfill their visions of impeccable training and professionalism. The Legion does satisfy to some degree, but tends to fall short of these expectations. When people see tables and chairs in the field for the first time along with the same kind of nonsense they thought they were leaving behind, their illusions start to falter and their convictions begin to waver, often ending in desertion.

Personal or family matters back home are often enough to make someone fly the coup. The Legion will usually grant bereavement leave but circumstances don't always permit the smooth implementation of this sort of request. While on tour in Djibouti, a fellow *légionnaire*'s mother had died but he was made to finish the tour before he could go home for the funeral. He didn't desert but would have been justified in attempting it. Another guy learned that his girlfriend was pregnant and raced back to England the first chance he got, never to return. It doesn't take much of an emergency at home for someone to abandon their ties with the Legion.

What can also happen is that someone is suddenly told without warning that they are going to be sent to an overseas regiment whether they like it or not. I knew a few people who had settled into a comfortable routine with their regiment and completely balked at the idea of a two year tour away. Faced with such an ultimatum, they chose desertion.

When someone finally arrives at the realization that they'll be enduring these types of things for five long, drawn-out years, they aren't exactly clicking their heels with delight. The physical side of life, while tough in its own right, is not nearly as difficult as the mental wars you will wage in your odyssey in the Foreign Legion. Time ticks by at pace that will seem agonizingly slow. Persisting through 1,825 days, give or take a leap year or two, will test your resolution like nothing else ever could.

Unfortunately for too many, seeing their contract through to the end is a feat beyond their endurance. Desertion becomes the only solution to their grievous mistake. I could sit here and wax eloquent on how a person should honor their commitments but there is no sense in doing this. I could never blame someone for wanting to desert. I knew a lot of pretty good fellows who had reached the end of their rope in the Legion and concluded that desertion was the only way to salvage themselves from it. On more than one occasion I shook hands with someone who said they were leaving and assisted them where I could.

Tips on Deserting

If, after having seen the Legion for what it really is, you feel that desertion is your only recourse, there are a few things you can do to help ensure your departure goes as smoothly as possible and you are not caught. The easiest method of deserting is to wait until your unit is granted a leave period, which should give you at least two weeks to find an unobstructed way out of France. Even if your passport is still being held by the Legion you will have enough time to visit your consulate or embassy in France to ask if they can assist you. I believe most consulates and embassies will be willing to cooperate, but you'll have to do as much as you can to help them help you. Having a list of people they can contact and being in possession of as much identification as you can muster will aid them in verifying who you are and speed the process toward a new or temporary passport. If the unthinkable occurs and they can't or won't help you, I've already explained how you can enter Italy or Spain where you can fabricate a story about how you lost your passport and hope for the best. Be wary, keep your wits about you, and have a story ready if you arrive at a border crossing without a passport. One fellow I knew had tried to enter Switzerland without a passport and was quickly detained by Swiss officials then handed over to French authorities who returned him to the Legion and a jail cell.

If you don't think you can stand waiting until your unit goes on leave, which could be several months down the road, your only other option is to desert in the night after having been granted an overnight or weekend pass at a time you consider to be the most favorable. To get off of Corsica you will have to catch a plane or a ferry from anywhere but Calvi, as this is the first place the *police militaire* will look for you. You should try to have plane and ferry schedules in advance to assist you in your planning. Ideally, you will want to catch the earliest available flight off the island from whichever city it is leaving to its destination in France.

The locations aren't as important as is getting off the island as rapidly as you can. You don't want to give the *PM*s any time to mount a search for you. If you can get a flight off the island around 7:00 A.M. the morning following your desertion, there should be little chance of you being caught. The only places other than Calvi that have regular flights and ferries off the island are Ajaccio and Bastia. To reach them your best bet is a two or three hour ride in a taxi which is going to cost. Make sure you have plenty of cash with you. Also ensure you have civilian clothing and don't be so undiscerning as to wear a Legion gym suit or other military attire. Keep your eyes peeled not only for the *PM*s at your point of departure, but also for regular French police who may have been requested by the Legion to assist in searching for you. Your haircut will identify you as being in the military so remain discreet for as long as possible. You may want to consider holing up in a hotel for a few days until the heat dies down a bit, especially if your way off the island is delayed. Once you're on the mainland you should have all the breathing room you will need to leave France for good.

Should you be snared by the *PM*s, you can try bluffing your way out of it by pretending you're a tourist who doesn't speak French and hope they don't know you or have your picture with them. They aren't the police and don't have the right to demand identification from a civilian or to physically detain you. Your ruse might not work, but if you're frantic it's worth a shot. If you're stopped and questioned by the regular police, you can claim you're a Legionnaire going *en stage,* or on course, to Castel. If they're looking expressly for a deserter and have your name, your subterfuge probably won't get you very far.

I should mention that the *PM*s are only *caporals, caporal-chefs,* and *sergents* that rotate into this job from the regiments for a few months and do not receive formal training in being a police officer. *PM*s are not the police and do not have authority outside the Legion. They are only concerned with enforcing the rules and regulations that pertain to the Legion and its members. The Legion polices its own and most infractions are easily handled within by the *PM*s. Any major offense would be dealt with in conjunction with civilian law enforcement agencies.

Belonging to a regiment in mainland France gives you a substantial head start over those stationed in the *REP* who must first get off the island before they can effectively take flight, and also over those stationed in overseas regiments where a valid passport is a definite necessity. I read an account years ago of a Legionnaire who had attempted to desert from Djibouti by stumbling through its arid wastelands on foot, without a passport, carrying barely any food and water. Good fortune was with him and the Legion got a hold of him before the buzzards did. To set forth on such a foolhardy scheme borders on the suicidal. Take the time to plan your actions, regardless of how desperately you want to leave.

Consider telling no one of your plot to desert, or only your most trusted confidants if you feel you want to let someone know. Nobody can stop you from deserting before you have made an attempt just because they may have heard you uttering words to this effect, but why push your luck? Your aim should be to make a quick, clean break using the element of surprise to your maximum advantage. You don't want to find the *PMs* waiting in ambush when you think you've gotten away scot free.

French Legionnaires are pretty much obligated to complete their five years in the Legion no matter how distasteful they may find it. They really have nowhere to run, nowhere to hide. I knew of a handful of Legionnaires from France who had deserted but soon found they could not remain fugitives in their own country for the rest of their lives. They were eventually caught or returned of their own volition with their tails between their legs. Unfortunately for them, this breach of deportment was a blot on their records that could not be erased and would severely forestall any chance of promotion or other benefits. It also had the potential side effect of carrying over into civilian life where they wouldn't be able to present a possible employer an unsullied account of their exploits in the Legion. During leave in Nice, I was walking down the sidewalk and came face to face with a French *légionnaire* who had deserted from my *section* a few months earlier. When he saw me he just turned away without saying a word and continued in another direction. I have to wonder if they ever caught him or if he remains truant. From what I remember of him, it would be in everyone's best interest if he did not return to the Legion.

As for those originating from outside of France, once you have made it back to your green, green grass of home, your worries are at an end. I doubt any country in the world would extradite you from your homeland to honor a commitment to the French Foreign Legion, nor does France have the authority or inclination to reach beyond her borders in search of a recalcitrant Legionnaire. As long as you stay off of French soil for the rest of your days, you won't have anything to worry about.

While still in the Legion I remember seeing articles in a British tabloid where the headlines screamed something similar to these: "I Was Hunted By Death Squads After Deserting The French Foreign Legion" or "French Foreign Legion Deserter Just Barely Escapes With His Life After Evading Death Hunt." Hysterical drivel is to be expected every now and again, when perpetrated by emotional runaway Legionnaires who feed a media that has an insatiable lust for narrative that shocks and excites. The fact that this sort of fable is difficult to substantiate by anyone other than its architect is irrelevant.

Whatever that person's reasons were for concocting such a fish tale, be they based on revenge, monetary gain, or whatever, I am here to tell you that the Legion does not employ death squads to hound your sorry ass to the ends of the earth should you choose to desert. Think about it for a moment. Does anyone honestly believe that France would risk international censure in engaging assassins to hunt down and kill a worthless deserter, especially in peacetime, whose net value to the Legion is a sum total of zero once he decides to break his ties with it? I can assure you that this does not happen. Yes, they do mount a token search for deserters and yes, if you are caught you can expect punitive measures to be brought against you which may include a certain amount of physical abuse, but you don't have to worry about being executed in some remote locale with your corpse being dumped in a shallow grave for all eternity. The Legion is not some lunatic fringe cult whose cryptic affairs of intrigue are to be kept secret at all costs. You don't swear an allegiance to a code of blood or any other such nonsense.

A stubborn pursuit of deserters may have been the rule when someone fled a remote outpost in Morocco in the early 1900s, but not in an age where modern communications and transportation allow someone to desert almost at will. Few ultimately care if you do desert and, other than a perfunctory investigation and follow-up, the general attitude toward someone who leaves is very much one of "good riddance to you." The regiments are so beleaguered with desertions that they aren't much cause for alarm and are taken in stride. There is also a feeling of smug satisfaction by those who don't desert and are able to defy all that the Legion can throw at them. Watching others abandon the Legion only reinforces this self-satisfied sentiment. Those who desert and are caught do eventually make good on their escape attempts. It's not a matter of if, but only a matter of when someone finally succeeds in leaving forever.

While desertions in peacetime may be regarded as inconsequential, deserting in time of war might be seen in a whole different light. In most countries in the world, desertion in wartime is punishable by death. The question that arises is could a French Foreign Legionnaire be sentenced to death if he deserted during a war even though he may not be a citizen of France? I honestly don't know. If I had to guess I would say that yes, he could be executed due to the fact that he signed a contract subjecting himself to the regulations of a military body governed by France. I really don't know the answer, but it's best to err on the side of caution and assume that you could be put to death for deserting in the middle of a war. I doubt anyone caught deserting before being sent to the Gulf War or while it was underway would have been executed, but any conflict that directly threatened the existence of France could be sufficient grounds for the firing squad.

The Good Life

For all of its imperfections the Legion is not as bleak or as terrible as one may believe. The impressions I have of the way it was years ago compared to how it actually is in the present are at completely opposite ends of the spectrum. Years ago a Legionnaire could expect to eke out a scanty, miserable existence in the atmosphere of iron discipline and brutality necessary to control a mercenary force. He could count himself lucky that he had a place to go that would take him in. It isn't nearly as bad these days.

The Legion may once have been considered to be the most disciplined army in the world, but this has gradually diminished as the Legion continues to climb out of the Dark Ages. Today the discipline is tempered with a measure of lenience, the brutality offset by a mellowed concept of forbearance, and the bleakness displaced by as many modern comforts as the Legion can accommodate. Don't let this fool you though. You aren't coddled to any large degree, nor has the Legion's own sense of propriety been greatly impaired. Things are better now, but its cutting edge has not been dulled to where it has been rendered ineffectual. It is still a force to be reckoned with.

Those who find that the Legion really isn't so bad discover that its benefits outshine any possible detriment. Anyone originating from a background with little to offer doesn't have a great deal to lose. They still have to play by the Legion's rules and always face the potential of becoming involved in a war and possibly being killed, but these issues pale in comparison to a life of indigence.

One of the payoffs of being a Legionnaire is that you do enjoy an unmistakable amount of celebrity status. There is an almost magical quality about the Foreign Legion and the men who serve there. Not everyone sees the Legion this way, but it still has admirers who are awed when in the presence of its members. On many occasions I observed regular French soldiers defer to the Legion and regard it with reverence. The Legion might be considered an elite fighting force in some circles but it is not infallible. It screws up as much as you could expect any military unit. In my opinion they are several units around the world that surpass the Legion in terms of being an elite unit. It does lift your ego though to see an *adjudant-chef* from a regular unit enter your drinking mess and be enraptured by having a few beers with the Legion.

There were other moments that defined how captivating the image of the Legion can be for some. When I was checking into a hotel in Rome while on vacation the clerk asked to see my passport. I explained that I didn't have one and gave him my Legion I.D. card instead. As soon as he realized I was in the Foreign Legion he began shaking my hand as did two other locals who were standing there. They all seemed fascinated that I was a Legionnaire and we talked about it for several minutes. In Paris, myself and a couple of friends were in a bar and began talking with some French women who were accompanied by a couple of slightly effeminate male friends. After learning that we were Legionnaires, one of the women leaned towards her friend and said quietly, "At last, some real men." I had to laugh when I overheard that, but it sure makes you suck in your gut and stick out your chest. The women that flock to Calvi's beaches every summer also attest to the allure of the Legion. Calvi might have some beautiful stretches of beach and a wonderful Mediterranean climate but I doubt this is the only reason they congregate here.

A major example of how the Legion is held in esteem is the awareness of photographers or film crews towards a Legionnaire's right to anonymity. Any time someone wants to photograph a Legionnaire, his permission is supposed to be obtained. Most photographers are cognizant of this requirement and most of them do ask, but I have heard of occurrences where permission had not been sought and cameras were seized and smashed by Legionnaires who were not amused with trespasses against their privacy. The Legion always has a following that wants to photograph and record its activities, but this can only happen upon the stipulation of its men.

Our *section* was on a rifle range near Calvi and was accompanied by a film crew working on a documentary to be aired in the United States. There were six of us who spoke English in our *section,* and we were asked if one of us would like to be filmed while discussing some of the weapons we were training with that day. None of us volunteered and I don't think they made much headway with their production. Even though I wasn't running or hiding from anything, I wasn't comfortable having my likeness broadcast presumably around the world. The other guys felt the same way. However, while we were in Sarajevo a news crew visited our company and asked to film me while I was working in the radio station. I said, "Go ahead," and they filmed a clip which was shown on French television that same night. But you are never obligated and always have the option of saying no. Part of why people join the Legion is because of the unwritten agreement concerning this privilege. You may not find anything on the contract you sign that guarantees you this type of immunity, but it does exist, and the Legion will stand behind you 100 percent if it is ever challenged. You will never be reprimanded if you have to enforce this rule on a photographer who won't listen.

The Legion will always have an appeal for the many who never enlist and see for themselves how it actually is. From the outside looking in it is still a place of intrigue and captures the imaginations of enthusiasts the world over. A Legionnaire walking around in his white *képi* and uniform draws attention like metal filings to a magnet. I was completely enamored with the Legion before I joined. My heart used to skip a beat and I'd feel the rush of adrenaline anytime I heard mention of it or saw a magazine article or news item about it.

Ongoing Training

Calvi is situated in a location that provides an opportune environment for the *REP* to carry on with the continued grooming of its troops. Being nestled a stone's throw away from the ocean and mountains allows easy access to these areas for the requisite instruction the *REP* engages in. Training in one form or another is a process that never ends. When your company is not usurped for the *semaine de service* or otherwise engaged you can anticipate classroom instruction, a day on the rifle range, a march in the hills, weapons training, *section* tactics, learning new songs, doing a few parachute jumps, or training on any matter considered essential. Not all days are devoted to training and there are times when your unit won't do much of anything except pass the time of day at frivolous tasks, but there's usually something to keep you occupied. If nothing else, you'll be given make-work projects to keep you busy. On three separate occasions I was involved in repainting and rewallpapering our quarters for no other reason than to be working at something. On days when things are really slow you might do monotonous drills like strip and assemble your *FAMAS* blindfolded until you can do it in your sleep.

One of the more salient features about Corsica that is put to good use is a trail that runs diagonally across the island from the northwest to southeast corners. It is known as the *GR* 20 or *Grande Route* 20. It is one of the world's distinguished hiking trails, used by both civilians and military units alike. After walking lengths of it myself, I can safely say it is a memorable experience. There are some breathtaking panoramas, but getting to them exacts a hefty price on your body.

The trail traverses the mountainous core of the island. Every effort was made by its creators to ensure it passes over the highest and most inaccessible terrain possible. Sections of it are so steep that your knees almost touch the slope in front of you as you climb. This, combined with the weight of your rucksack, can quickly turn your legs to rubber and exhaust your capacity to move forward. Unfortunately, the trail is extremely remote in most places and once you've gotten started there's no turning back. There isn't any way to get a vehicle onto most parts of the trail, and removing accident victims or those who are otherwise disabled can only be done via helicopter.

On one of these marches after our company had stopped for a break, a *légionnaire* who had reached his physical limit laid down on the ground and refused to move another step. For over an hour he lay there not saying a word and hoping, I'm sure, that his obstinate noncompliance with those who were yelling at him to get up would somehow earn him a ride in a helicopter or a makeshift stretcher. As it would have been well nigh impossible to carry someone through those mountains on a stretcher, and as our company commander was not about to bend to the will of a pigheaded *légionnaire* and call in a helicopter, he ordered his *section* to get this guy moving. Finally, after tolerating more pain from having his lips and nose pummeled than he was enduring from the march, he got back onto his feet and continued the trek. He later spent time in the lockup, then was removed from the company and given a menial job somewhere in headquarters.

Hiking the *GR* 20 with rifle and rucksack imposes an acute exertion on your body. There were times on these marches where I was in so much pain that I just wanted to sit down and cry and spent many moments whimpering like a whipped puppy. After returning from one march, I awoke the next night in our barracks with severe cramps in my abdomen. It was a delayed reaction from straining against a heavy rucksack while climbing up and down precipitous slopes for hours on end. During another march, I never got the chance to eat breakfast in the morning before setting out. It wasn't long before my body started feeling the effects of not having any fuel, and it got to where my legs could hardly propel me up even leisurely inclines. By the time we stopped for lunch the muscles in my legs were trembling with fatigue and I was on the verge of being sick. But, after getting some food in my stomach I was miraculously rejuvenated and finished that day's leg without too much additional struggle.

The *GR* 20 is usually done in legs of roughly three days. To walk its entire length would take upwards of a week or more and most units don't have the time to expend in completing the whole stretch. The march doesn't involve much in the way of tactical training and is used more for exercise than anything.

For training in the field you are given ration packs to see you through the day. French field rations are pretty good overall. Each pack consists of a full day's worth of food and includes coffee, hot chocolate, sugar, whitener, biscuits, *pâté,* or some other type of meat spread such as mackerel in white wine or sardines in mustard sauce, two large tins of stew that make up the noon and evening meals, a chocolate bar, energy bars, candies, and a few other odds and ends such as matches and a small stove and heating tablets. The older ration packs used to have unfiltered cigarettes in them, but this is no longer done. For most activities ration packs are sufficient to keep you adequately nourished, but for high performance operations like the *GR* 20 they fall a bit short. Most people supplement them with sustenance bought from the *foyer.* Almost everyone also buys small gas stoves with interchangeable cartridges for use in the field. They can heat up your food and coffee many times faster than the primitive fuel cubes in the ration packs. When it's time for chow you don't want any delays. Invest in one.

In contrast to the acceptable field rations utilized by the French, their field equipment leaves a lot to be desired. The rucksack has only one main pocket with one other smaller pouch that sits on top. Because there are only two storage areas you are constantly having to empty out or root through a lot of material to find what you are looking for. The available space is limited and by the time you get your sleeping bag, poncho, tarp, jacket, and rations stuffed inside, there isn't much room for anything else. This can be a blessing in disguise since the more room you have the more you will find things to fill it, which adds unwanted weight to your load. The rucksack does get the job done in most applications, but for prolonged field use there never seems to be enough room, nor is it particularly well organized.

The web gear is poorly designed compared to the styles now in use by other armies and it probably dates back to the Indochina and World War II eras. In most cases all it is used for is to carry a water bottle, ammunition pouches, and a cleaning kit for your personal arm. In operational modes a bayonet, gas mask, and medical pouch are added. The water bottles are large metallic containers that make a lot of noise when they are being used, and always seem to have some sort of mineral deposit growing on their insides.

The issue sleeping bags are terribly deficient. They are big and bulky and provide little in the way of insulation for keeping you warm. They really aren't much more than thick blankets. Whichever bureaucratic entity is responsible for outfitting an entire army with unsound gear like this is guilty of gross negligence. They might be fine in a Mediterranean climate in summer months, but all it takes is a bit of frost on the ground or for you to climb into the mountains a bit to feel how inappropriate they are. The last thing you want when trying to sleep is to be shivering uncontrollably. The only real solution to this matter is to purchase a quality down-filled sleeping bag on your own which almost everybody does. This shouldn't have to happen. You should be issued proper gear that will do the job it's designed for but, unfortunately, until the powers that be get their heads out of the sand and remedy these problems, you won't have any other choice. Staying warm and dry in the field is vital, and having a good sleeping bag is of paramount importance.

Another piece of equipment you may want to consider purchasing is a Gortex sleeping bag cover. Your sleeping bag fits inside this outer shell which keeps out all forms of moisture and prevents any wind from reducing the insulating effects of your sleeping bag. You can actually sleep out in the rain in one and not have any water penetrate through to your sleeping bag. One morning I awoke and found that I had been sleeping in a puddle of condensation. Not a drop got through to dampen my bedding. It is a priceless piece of gear and worth every *centime* you'll have to shell out for it.

A sleeping bag is one of the few items you will be allowed to purchase and use openly in the field. Even your commanders recognize the issue sleeping bags as being garbage. As for other military paraphernalia, you can acquire materials that you think might make your life in the field easier or more comfortable, but there is a limit as to what you're allowed to use. For example, you can't go out and buy a better rucksack and expect to tote it around in the midst of your comrades who are using standard issue. Conformity is still the code of conduct to be followed. A lot of people will buy themselves a good knife and keep it tucked away in their rucksack but never would they be allowed to hang it from their web belt or otherwise display it openly. The rule of thumb to follow is that you have to look the same as everyone else on the outside. If you want to get a few items for yourself and keep them squirreled away for your own covert usage, that's your business.

The one instance that clearly demonstrated a lack of faith in French military gear was when our unit was preparing to depart for a UN tour in Sarajevo. We were heading there in January and knew we would be facing snow and cold unlike what we were used to in Calvi. We'd heard that we would be issued special winter gear before leaving, but knowing full well what we were likely to get, we went ahead and began buying our own winter gear. I know people who spent several thousand francs in preparing for this trip. It turned out that most of the issued gear would have done the job nicely, but no one was taking any chances.

During your first year in your regiment, much of the training you receive will correspond with your company's particular area of expertise.

If you're in 1st Company you can expect to receive training on techniques for night combat and fighting in built-up areas. There is a facility in Calvi itself called Fort Charlie that has a variety of obstacles in place used for commando-type training. Near Bonifacio on the southern tip of the island there is a mock village utilized for house clearing exercises.

2nd Company will concentrate on mountaineering and scaling procedures. They often make use of the walls of the Citadel in Calvi for practicing methods of rappelling. The *REP* maintains a chalet known as Vergio year-round in the mountains south of Calvi which is used as a base for mountaineering excursions. When the snow falls units rush up there to get in some skiing.

3rd Company trains on amphibious matters and operates from the *centre amphibie* just off camp. They conduct drills using Zodiac inflatable rafts and receive training on scuba diving and underwater techniques.

4th Company concerns itself with sabotage and demolitions instruction as well as with sustaining a trained body of snipers.

The Heavy Weapons Company will train its men on MILAN anti-tank missiles, 120 mm mortars, and anti-aircraft cannons. They deploy to firing ranges in mainland France for live-fire exercises.

The fact that each company focuses on a specific area of expertise does not mean that they acquiesce solely to this one discipline. Each company is thoroughly conversant with the techniques used in the other units and cross-training is extensive. This isn't to say that everyone in 1st Company will know how to fire a 20 mm anti-aircraft cannon or will ever even see one, but everybody in 1st Company should undergo instruction on rappelling, Zodiacs, and explosives at some time or another. It often happens that one company will be tasked with running a course such as a *tireur d'élite,* or marksman course, for example, and will have several representatives from each company take the training instead of just that company's men.

Once you've been in your unit awhile you can start thinking about volunteering to take a specialist course. There isn't an extensive list of options or different career paths you can follow in the Legion, but you may want to consider what is available. You aren't browbeaten into taking these courses, but if you're getting tired of the routine in your *section* and no longer derive any satisfaction from stripping and assembling your *FAMAS* in record time, you may want to look into it. A specialist course can extract you from unfulfilling circumstances to some degree. For those who don't pursue a specialist course, their

Insignia worn by those who complete the *tireur d'élite* or marksman's course. There is another badge displaying crossed rifles that is awarded for sniper training even though the two courses are almost identical.

future lies in a narrow combat role in one of their company's *sections*. There's nothing wrong with this, but it doesn't exactly stimulate the gray matter either. I would strongly suggest aspiring to dizzying heights at your earliest convenience. It does tend to improve your standing in your unit and put you a little higher on the pedestal. Also, it reduces the possibility of ever having to work in the *SEPP – Section d'Entretiens et Pliage de Parachutes* (Parachute Maintenance and Packing Section). This place is a virtual sweatshop and the last place you ever want to find yourself employed. The people who toil here put in long hard hours, and have to obtain a quota of at least 25 packed parachutes per team each day before they can leave. I know they worked well into the evening many times trying to get done.

There are five main specialties available to you. They are *transmetteur* (radio operator), *infirmier* (medic), *mécanicien* (mechanic), *secrétaire* (administration worker), and *cuisinier* (cook). For each of these specialties it will be necessary to return to Castel for several weeks or months for the training. All except radio operator have the additional bonus of a parallel civilian applicability which may prove useful once you and the Legion have parted ways.

Old model of the seven-flamed grenade cap badge worn on the beret by all Legion infantry regiments except the *REP*. The *REC* used the same design but theirs was a silver color instead of gold. The new model still incorporates the same design but has the top extremities of the flames extending beyond the ring with the number of the regiment inside the circle of the grenade. The *REP* continues to use the winged dagger insignia as its cap badge.

Since the Legion is largely a self-contained combat force, it does not need to have men trained in roles that extend beyond the realm of its immediate internal support needs. It has the primary function of being a ground-based mobile infantry and armored corps, and so does not have a large assortment of vocational opportunities. You've taken a wrong turn somewhere if you dream of lofty scholastic possibilities. Any support requirements outside the scope of the Legion's own capabilities are supplied by regular French army units.

These courses take place several times a year and you will be among a handful of men that are sent from each regiment to be trained in their chosen field. At Castel, all course members are attached to the company that handles the training for all specialties. While on course you are still subject to things like guard duties, working in the mess hall, and the daily *corvées*. You can run but you can't hide. You will have more freedom than you did as a raw recruit and be able to put in for leave on the weekends if you're not on duty. During the week you can also go into Castel after work if you don't have too much studying to do.

When you are sent on these courses you are fully expected to return to your regiment having passed the training. There's no excuse for failure and you can actually spend time in your regiment's jail for not having successfully completed the course, depending on the circumstances surrounding your educational miscarriage. Your superiors don't take kindly to having sent you on a course only to have you fall short of expectations and return empty-handed. It wastes everyone's time. The difficulty in learning is compounded by the language barrier, but this will never be accepted as an alibi for failing the mission entrusted to you. Refer back to Part 6 of the Legionnaire's Code Of Honor. The language hurdle should be all the more reason to keep your nose to the grindstone. If you have to sacrifice a bit of drunken revelry in order to succeed, then so be it.

The only exception concerns the radio operator's course, where it is necessary to effectively learn Morse code. Many are unable to master the complexities in translating little dots and dashes of sound into comprehensible text and vice versa. This is just barely understood and acknowledged by the Legion command authority, so those failing the tests are allowed to renege on their obligations to attain a passing grade. This impotence in learning Morse is normally unearthed within the first few days of the course. Anyone not at an admissible level within a month is usually sent packing back to their regiment. It is possible to pretend that you are unable to learn Morse by purposely failing the tests if you discover you aren't interested in it or if your regiment sent you on the course against your wishes. You can thus remove yourself from this course without fear of rebuke, but make sure you do a good job in faking your slowness of mind. If you show even a slight aptitude for learning Morse code, it will be cultivated until you bear fruit. I knew one fellow who had completed the whole four month course only to fail the final testing. He returned to his regiment and was immediately sent back on the next course for another four months.

There is enough material to learn on these courses that you receive a full eight hours of instruction during the day, then spend a goodly amount of time in the evening studying and reviewing those lessons. You're not overwhelmed with academic responsibilities, but an appropriate amount of devotion is necessary.

The main crux of the administrative course is to teach its students the skills in handling a keyboard using all ten fingers and thumbs on both hands without having to look at the keys. The two-finger poke-and-hunt is therefore enhanced by a speedier and more efficient method of using office machines. Students are slowly trained and brought up to speed and depart the course able typists. They are also taught how to draft letters and other documents, use filing systems, and are instructed in the administrative procedures particular to the Legion. The advent of the modern computer and their unlimited capabilities has also spawned a training curriculum for their use. Someone who completes this course may find that there isn't an immediate opening for them to ply their trade once they return to their combat company. Each company only needs two or three men trained in this area, so a recent graduate may be allocated back to their old combat status indefinitely. Eventually though, positions do become available, even if it means a transfer to Headquarters Company.

For the cook's course, candidates are trained in the monumental assignment of cooking and preparing meals for hundreds of hungry mouths twice daily. I can't really count breakfast as a meal in the Legion since heating up huge vats of coffee and putting some bread out is not the same as preparing full-scale dinners. Training not only involves the cooking aspect of the course, but also includes the logistical planning essential to keeping a unit of any size properly fed. A company that goes overseas frequently has only one person trained as a cook, and he has to know what he is doing to keep 150 men well nourished. Food is probably the biggest factor that affects morale in any army. Being a cook is arguably the most difficult day to day job anyone can have. Slaving in a kitchen readying food for the table is a hot and unglamorous occupation, but one that's not without its perks. A friend of mine who took the course said that as part of their final exam they had to bake a Black Forest cake then subject it to a careful series of scrutinizing taste tests.

The mechanic's course teaches its pupils everything they'll need to know about inspecting, repairing, and maintaining the variety of vehicles used by all units in the French army. Further training on vehicles that are unique to some regiments takes place in that regiment itself.

Many people who pursue this course already have a great deal of experience as mechanics from their civilian life, but they still go through the lengthy training agenda as if they've never seen a piston or carburetor before. This approach is standard for all courses. Every regiment in the Legion has a motorized capability, be it large or small, so there is an endless demand for the skills acquired on this course. Where circumstances permit, each *section* in a company will have one or two men trained as mechanics to look after that *section*'s vehicles.

Those that take the medical course are trained as medics to handle the health care needs of their combat *section*. They learn everything from applying bandages and taking X-rays, to giving shots and sewing stitches. Once a year they assist in supervising the medical check-up of all the men in their unit. They even go as far as to diagnose illnesses and administer medication. I once remarked to our *section*'s medic that I thought it was somewhat unusual for them to be diagnosing medical disorders and recommending medication after a rather short training period of roughly four months. He replied, "I know, it's like we're a bunch of guinea pigs." Don't be alarmed. Medics regularly consult a higher authority for any matter thought to be serious. Your average Legionnaire might be a fairly tough individual but he isn't used for degenerate experiments.

There are times, however, when a medic will have to make important decisions on his own. I remember a march in Djibouti where one fellow was close to exhaustion and could barely walk. We had to climb a steep hill out of a deep ravine to finish our hike, and he was in no condition to do so. Our medic sat him down and gave him an injection of what I believe was a glucose solution. It revived him enough to finish the march. Without the medic's intervention it would have been a lengthy struggle getting him out of there.

Disciples of the radio operator's course, of which I was a devotee, are instructed in the sending and receiving of messages by voice and Morse code in both clear and coded formats and are taught to use all equipment and material related to this task. The bulk of the course is spent on the significant undertaking of sending and receiving Morse at speed. I had always thought Morse code had gone by way of the dinosaur until coming to the Legion, but it is still extensively used by the French Armed Forces. You have to reach a speed of 14 words or groups per minute for the final exam. A word/group is considered to be an average string of five letters, numbers, punctuation marks, or a combination of each. The

The *REP* maintains an isolated villa in the Corsican highlands known as the *Chalet de Vergio*. It is used as a stopover for training in the mountains and becomes a ski lodge when the snow falls. There are usually four Legionnaires stationed here year round that rotate up from the regiment, one of whom is a radio operator responsible for sustaining a link with the regiment if the phones ever go down. This duty can be a nice break from the travails of the regiment but does get rather monotonous after being here for weeks and even months at a time. The regiment is not always quick to send replacements especially if it's involved in operations elsewhere.

French measure this speed in words/groups per hour which translates into 840 groups per hour. You will spend at least two hours every day listening to and deciphering Morse into legible text and at least one hour a day tapping it out. Many people get cassette tape recordings to practice with after hours. There's no real trick to learning Morse other than intense concentration. After awhile you'll notice that it's almost like a form of music, and patterns such as a radio check can be interpreted without having to focus on the individual letters. Those who become exceptionally accomplished at Morse barely have to write it down to comprehend the message. There are a few disadvantages to taking this course that you might want to think over before volunteering for it. The main drawback is that you will henceforth carry a radio in addition to your normal gear anytime you do a march. This adds at least 20 pounds to the load you lug

Specialist Certificate.

around. It can also be extremely difficult to send and receive messages in French if you still have trouble speaking and understanding it. A final point to consider is that you can't use much of what you learn on this course to benefit you in civilian life, unlike the other specialties. As of this writing I have learned that the use of Morse may have been rendered obsolete and is no longer in use. Unfortunately, I am unable to confirm this for you but it wouldn't surprise me since they were introducing high-watt radio sets into the Legion just before the end of my contract.

After the successful completion of your course, you are given a certificate recognizing your accomplishment. Each specialty also has an advanced training program that complements what you've already learned and allows you to delve deeper into your calling. The people who take the advanced training are usually those who will renew their contracts beyond the initial five years. Another trip back to Castel will be necessary to complete any advanced training.

Other courses are available that may not necessarily be considered core specialties but which still have an important function in the regiments.

There are driving courses that train people to operate tractor trailers, buses, and forklifts. Dog handlers are trained to manage the K-9 units many regiments use for guard and patrol duties. Some people are able to get themselves working in wood and machine shops or gravitate to areas like weapons or electrical and technical repair. Once you settle into your regiment you can sniff out the alternatives and start working towards any objective you choose.

If you're a real go-getter, you can inquire into becoming a member of the Legion's elite Deep Reconnaissance Commandos. There is only one unit of this type in the Legion and it is attached to the *REP*. Some regular French army parachute regiments have similar units. To belong to this outfit you have to be at least a *caporal* and pass a series of demanding physical tests. I don't know most of the requirements but I remember them having to do things like climb a rope while carrying a rucksack. The grand-daddy of all tests that they ardently employ, as much to test physical ability as desire, is a 30 kilometer run with a rucksack that has to be completed in three and a half hours. This alone is enough to make most people shy away from a career in the Recon Commandos but, if you've got the urge to be all you can be, go for it.

To be in the Recon Commandos you not only have to be in good physical shape, you have to be in great physical shape. Most people in the Legion can get away with just a daily morning jog with their unit followed by a few push-ups and sit-ups but the men in the Recon Commandos have to extend themselves far beyond these minimum standards. When they do field training they typically carry special rucksacks that are much larger than those used by everyone else. They march around with loads easily in excess of 100 pounds. Their mission statement usually involves them operating deep behind enemy lines in an effort to gather intelligence on enemy forces. They have to have the physical prowess to get themselves in and out as expediently as possible. Their training includes sky-diving, as they are normally inserted into enemy territory by jumping from extreme altitudes. The men in the Recon Commandos are trained on anything and everything that involves being a soldier. They are highly motivated and devoted to being the best they can be.

Before the end of your five year contract you are almost guaranteed to be sent back to Castel to take your *caporal*'s course. I can't think of a single case where someone wasn't sent on this course before their first five years were finished. Some people have the opportunity to take this course with as little as two year's service, but for most they will be sent after having been in a bit longer.

The course is about 10 weeks long and trains you in becoming a junior NCO. You cover everything you've learned as a *légionnaire* up to this point, but are shown it with a view to becoming much more adept at everything. Once you've completed the course, you will subsequently be in charge of unseasoned *légionnaires* who will be looking to you for guidance. Material such as drill and tactical maneuvers has to be learned so that you can, in turn, practically make use of these tools when you have *légionnaires* under your wing. The course places a lot of emphasis on physical conditioning as well, since you can't expect to effectively lead a body of men if you aren't able to keep up to them.

This course doesn't do much to promote or teach leadership, but only instructs its students on how to give orders to subordinates, which is something any half-wit can learn. The Legion doesn't place much stock in tutoring in the subtleties that make a person a capable leader deserving of the highest respect, which helps explain where corporal punishment originates from. If someone in authority has to hit a subordinate to get his point across, there is a weak link in the chain somewhere. You can call it discipline all you want, but there's no denying that a leader such as this is a failing of the system that engendered him.

While on this course it became all too evident how fortunate I would be if I never went into combat with the Foreign Legion. Like most armies engaged in maneuvering their troops in the field, whether on patrol or advancing on an enemy, the French follow an orders procedure to move a body of men, and expect them to act in a regulated manner based on the commands given. A systematic execution of these orders might pass muster when they are given slowly and without duress, but rapidly dissolve into a parody of mayhem when the shit hits the fan. I felt their method of giving orders to be clumsy and stilted, which the ever-present language barrier did not facilitate in the slightest. Commands of this nature are necessary in that they provide a basis from which to work, but wouldn't have much practical use in a live situation. For example, being expected to commence a lengthy dialogue on how many rounds each of your men should fire at an enemy that has just ambushed you may sound like controlled fire discipline, but isn't of much use if everyone is dead before you're finished stuttering out your orders. It's unsettling to think that your life could end while awaiting instructions in a situation that calls for immediate, decisive, instinctive action from everyone involved. I saw enough of what could result under actual circumstances to make me extremely circumspect in accepting as final what I was taught here.

Holidays

The Legion celebrates holidays the same as anyone could be expected to. Holidays like Christmas, New Year's, France's birthday, and those specific to the Legion such as Camerone and regimental patron saint days are all given the special attention they merit.

Christmas is probably the biggest cause for celebration in the Legion and a lot of time and energy is directed toward this festive occasion. In the weeks leading up to it, every *section* in every company in every regiment will construct a bar and serve food and alcohol to anyone in the regiment that pays a visit. Because there can be as many as 20 or 30 drinking establishments that spring up over Christmas, a lot of after hours time is sacrificed in sampling the wares of these impromptu taverns. Each *section* will also build a scene of the Nativity known as a *crèche* or crib, commemorating the birth of Christ and all companies will assemble a major *crèche* on a grander scale than the *sections.* An enormous amount of work goes into these creations which results in some spectacular displays. All are judged by the *Chef de Corps,* and a prize is awarded for the best exhibit.

On Christmas eve a religious mass for those who wish to attend precedes the evening merriment. Once it's complete, each company assembles in parade dress and sits down to what is undoubtedly the finest meal you will enjoy in the course of a year. No expense is spared and you can gorge yourself to the brink of nausea on the wonderful fare that is served. It was at Christmas that I got my first taste of *foie gras* which is a meat paste made from the livers of geese and considered something of a delicacy. It wasn't bad at all.

After the meal everyone in the company is given a Christmas present by their company commander. Presents include things like cameras, watches, Walkmans, and good sunglasses. You can usually choose from about ten different items which are paid for by proceeds from the *foyer.*

After this, everyone enjoys a number of comedy skits put on by members of the company. This is the ultimate time for some sweet revenge. If one of your superiors needs to be shown the folly of his ways, he may become the butt of a burlesque routine. Tastefully done, of course.

Following these jovialities, everybody converges on the bars and continues celebrating until the wee hours of Christmas morning. Those who are married and have families are fully expected to spend this time having Christmas eve dinner with the Legion, and to be absent would be considered AWOL. The Legion is first and foremost in the lives of its men, regardless of whether or not they have families.

The New Year is also a time to make merry, but is somewhat subdued compared to the bash over Christmas. Organized celebrating is actually devoted more to officers and NCOs, but this does not preclude you and your buddies from counting down the seconds to a new year with beer in hand. On New Year's day there is another fine meal served at the mess hall complete with sparkling champagne, but this is the only gala affair that concerns this time of year.

Camerone is one of the major events that the Legion celebrates each year. It commemorates the April 30, 1863 battle of Camerone, Mexico. A Legion company of 65 soldiers opposed a Mexican cavalry and infantry unit of 2,000 men and fought practically to the death of every last man rather than surrendering. The battle immortalized Camerone in the annals of Legion history and bestowed upon the Legion the reputation of an indomitable fighting force in the face of overwhelming odds.

The festivities for Camerone include a ceremonial parade, during which an account of the battle is read aloud by an officer. In Aubagne, the priceless relic of *Capitaine* Danjou's wooden hand is carried from the museum to the *Monument aux Morts* and stands vigil over the proceedings. *Capitaine* Danjou lead the company during the battle and was killed in its course. His hand was lost but later found and returned to the Legion. It is now the most revered artifact the Legion possesses. Activities also involve an opportunity for the general public to come on base and view displays of modern military equipment and Legion history as well as film and video presentations. Depending on the time available, some of these exhibitions can become quite elaborate. While in Abéché, Chad, for one Camerone our company invited several local officials, dignitaries, and missionaries into camp to dine and take part in the celebrations. Of course, having gone to the trouble of preparing a certain amount of pageantry, we'd have looked pretty stupid without an audience with whom we could share it all.

A nice little feature about Camerone is the quaint custom of being served breakfast in bed by your officers and NCOs. In upholding this tradition they bring you coffee, hot chocolate, croissants, bread, and all the trimmings to start your day off right. It's not exactly a continental banquet but it is an agreeable diversion.

France's birthday, known as Bastille Day, falls on July 14, and is celebrated in the usual fashion with a parade, good food, and even better drink. What makes Bastille Day noteworthy for the Legion is its participation in the military parade down the *Champs Élysées* in Paris. This honor rotates each year between the regiments of metropolitan France who send a detachment to represent the Legion. The chosen unit will drill for weeks in advance to get everyone in sync with each other. For the parade itself the detachment is led by the *Musique Principale* who keeps everyone in step by the music they play. The slow, easy gait of the Legion is a sharp contrast from that of the regular army units who participate so the Legion marches down the *Champs Élysées* well apart from the other troop assemblies. This is something I would have loved to have done while in the Legion but had the bad timing of being in Africa when the *REP*'s turn came around. A good friend of mine was lucky enough to have done the march and said it was one of the highlights of his time in the Legion. He even ended up shaking hands with the man who is now President of the Republic, Mr. Jacques Chirac.

In my last summer with the Legion I happened to get some leave that fell on July 14, so I made my way to Paris with the intent of watching the Legion strut their stuff in the parade. I was positioned on the south side of the *Champs Élysées* just to the east of the Franklin D. Roosevelt *Métro* station when the Legion began their march from the *Arc de Triomphe.* Part way into the march they suddenly exited the *Champs Élysées* along a street to the south. I was completely dismayed at having missed this golden opportunity to see the Legion in all its glory and take a few photos of the moment. To this day I don't know why their march terminated so abruptly, but I was not impressed.

Another day that the Legion celebrates throughout the year is for the patron saint of each regiment. Saint Michel is the patron saint of parachutists and is venerated once a year by the *REP.* Festivities mirror those of Camerone and Bastille Day.

For each major holiday every regiment commemorates the occasion with an organized run. Your regiment will assemble in a huge crowd and burst forth along a chosen course once the start signal is given. For these runs everyone in the regiment is given a number, which is recorded once you cross the finish line, with the standings posted later. These runs have differing lengths and the route varies each time they are done. The longest one I ever participated in was at Castel while I was on a course there. For the regimental birthday they organized a run that was no less than a half-marathon, which is to say 21 kilometers (13 miles). I ran it non-stop and finished somewhere in the middle. It may seem odd to celebrate a holiday by running yourself sick, but that's the way the Legion does things. You are fully expected to participate in and complete these types of runs. The Legion loves to stretch its legs, so you'd better get used to the idea that you're going to be doing a lot of it.

I have to relate one story about running. While at Castel for a course, we had the opportunity to take part in a 100 kilometer (62 mile) run if we wanted, that had been organized by a civilian establishment. I gracefully declined the offer since I felt ill-prepared to tackle such a huge distance after being used to running only eight or ten kilometers on a regular basis. I had a friend though who was a fantastic runner and decided to lock horns with this enormous challenge. He completed the course in just over 13 hours of almost continuous running. I was mightily impressed with his feat until I learned of the following.

Our company commander, while we were on course, was an older man of Austrian descent who had climbed his way through the ranks and become an officer in the Legion. He appeared to be well into his 50s, if not his 60s, had gray hair, and looked somewhat frail and feeble. We used to snicker at him because he would do a morning jog at a pace that was just barely more than a shuffle. He apparently completed that 100 kilometer run in a little over seven hours. I was utterly dumbstruck when I heard this. They told us about it during a morning *rassemblement* and we gave him a huge round of applause. Absolutely incredible. I find it almost impossible to believe, yet I don't question the truthfulness of it. He would have had to have run the course without stopping, averaging about 14 kilometers (8.6 miles) per hour, which is amazing for someone his age.

Peacekeeping

In late 1992, several units from the *REC, REG,* and *REI* were sent to Cambodia as part of the United Nations force recently established in that country. In January of 1993, the *REP* provided its 1st and 4th companies with a headquarters detachment from the *CCS* for peacekeeping duties in the embattled city of Sarajevo in the former Yugoslavia. These

United Nations badge.

deployments marked the first time the French Foreign Legion had ever worn the blue beret of the United Nations, notwithstanding its involvement with an international peacekeeping operation in Lebanon in the early 1980s, its alliance with an international coalition during the Gulf War in 1991, and its participation in a UN peacekeeping operation in Somalia in December of 1992. The use of the Legion in these ways has betokened a shift in convention for a fighting force heretofore consigned to combative ends at the discretion of the French government, and has paved the way for what can only be an important part of its future.

Sarajevo in January of 1993 was a very dangerous place to be. The civil war that had reached a flash point in 1992 was in full swing and Sarajevo was the focal point of much of the fighting in progress. We had been routed into this quagmire of ethnic turmoil from Calvi via Bastia, Vienna, and Zagreb before touching down on the besieged runway of Sarajevo with an undeniable amount of foreboding. In previous months we'd become aware of the situation in Sarajevo, and its correlation to the Legion's historic conflict at Dien Bien Phu, where a garrison was encircled and shelled from the surrounding high ground in a similar fashion was not lost on us. A glimpse out the window of the Russian transport that ferried us in was all it took to start the stomach churning with butterflies. Sarajevo was a city in ruins from weeks of relentless bombardment at the hands of the Serbs, and the destruction it had endured was easily visible from the air.

Our first 24 hours on the ground was full of unease due to the continual sounds of artillery and machine gun fire all around us, mere hundreds of meters away. For most of us this was our first experience with war, so it was only natural to feel a little off balance from being set down in the middle of one, even though the fighting was not directed at us. This did not prevent anyone from being quietly fascinated with the whole scenario. Most of us spent some time peeking over the sandbags that protected our installations in order to watch and listen to the artillery rounds detonating in residential areas a few blocks away.

France shared the duties in Sarajevo with the Egyptians and Ukrainians, and was assigned the airport as its zone of responsibility. After settling in we were able to have a good look at the terrible consequences of a people's inability to resolve their disputes in a peaceful, civilized manner. The areas directly adjacent to the airport were completely shot to pieces, and all houses and buildings were forever scarred by the bombing and shooting. Trips deeper into the city exposed the extent of the devastation wrought by the fighting. Nothing lay untouched by small-arms and artillery fire and everywhere you looked were burnt, gutted, bombed out buildings and vehicles perforated with holes. There was one part of the city, called Stup, where I don't think the buildings had so much as a square meter of siding not riddled with bullet holes. Throughout the city were road barriers, barbed wire, trenches, sand bag revetments, and other makeshift defense fortifications, all indicators of a city at war. People were still largely visible and did what they could to secure food and water for themselves and their families but often put their lives at risk in doing so. Crowds of inhabitants had to converge in water and food lineups, which exposed them to random attacks. Artillery could rain down on them at any moment and snipers in concealed hideaways were a constant threat. They had no misgivings about picking off little old ladies, children, or anyone else who strayed into their line of fire. Just after leaving Sarajevo, we heard on the news that an artillery round had fallen in a busy market place killing dozens of locals — tragic testament to the dangers they faced. It was hard to believe that Sarajevo had once hosted the 1984 Winter Olympics, a tribute to world peace and goodwill, only to become a symbol of the infirmities and failings of humanity.

We soon fell into a daily routine of guard and observation duties, convoy escort, filling sandbags, shoring up our defenses, and generally trying to make ourselves as safe and comfortable as possible. Our company was crammed into a cement building that had probably served as a warehouse before the war and was just large enough to house everyone. Privacy was what you made of it. We were mostly confined to these living quarters when not on duty since there wasn't really anywhere to go. Anytime you ventured outside you had to wear a flak vest and helmet. You definitely couldn't go for a stroll outside the airport compound. Physical exercise was, if not impossible, impractical. No one was able to jog outside in the middle of a war zone for the six months we were there. Crude gymnasiums were established using metal vehicle parts as weights, which was some help in retarding the effects of our prolonged sloth.

Legionnaires stand outside a sandbagged building at the Sarajevo airport wearing helmets and flak jackets. Wearing these protective items was not only mandatory but just made good common sense due to the constant threat of stray bits of flying metal entering the airport zone from the nearby fighting. The helmets are not regular steel pots but are made of a sturdy, reinforced, ballistic material capable of withstanding severe impacts such as from that of a bullet. The flak jackets are somewhat less reliable and would never be able to stop a bullet from seriously injuring or killing someone. The French did utilize a heavier vest that had bullet proof plates inserted over the chest and back areas to protect the user but these were only given to officers, NCOs, and guards manning the perimeter observation posts.

Units that had arrived before us had made a good start in fortifying our buildings. They had sandbagged windows and entrances to keep bullets from entering and ricocheting around, but there was still a lot to be done. We piled sandbags from floor to ceiling against every wall that an artillery or tank round could penetrate. Exterior defenses were improved and reinforced as much as possible. Engineers had been busy bulldozing earthen walls into position all over the airport, so we had some protection in moving from place to place. In spite of this constant effort, we were still vulnerable to attack should either side choose to mount any kind of offensive against us. Everybody's weapon was within easy reach and we were each supplied with 100 rounds of ammunition. However, this would not have done much to save our hides in the event of a coordinated strike. We had no bunkers in which to take cover from an artillery bombardment, and if anyone had leveled their guns at us we would have suffered scores of casualties. Neither did we possess weaponry heavier than anti-tank missiles and 20 mm cannons for repelling an attack. They could have blown our defenses to matchsticks without any trouble at all. This was clearly demonstrated to us three weeks into our tour.

One afternoon, upon returning from a short mission to Butmir just south of the airport, our small convoy arrived back at our barracks in time to catch the last few morsels of lunch. After taking care of my vehicle, I had gone indoors while a few other guys were still finishing up in the parking lot. From inside we heard an artillery round explode a fair distance away but thought nothing of it. A short time later another round went off much closer than the last, and I remember thinking how it seemed like someone was walking their rounds towards us. Moments after that, a deafening blast shattered our peace and quiet along with any sense of security we had about being a neutral UN force.

A mortar round had struck one of our armored vehicles in the parking lot, blown the welded gas cover off leaving a hole in the vehicle, and sprayed shrapnel all over, hitting two of our *légionnaires* as well as injuring a third still inside the vehicle. One of the *légionnaires* had been standing less than ten feet from the explosion and was knocked unconscious when the round detonated at the same height as his head. The other had been standing several meters away but was hit by a piece of metal that cut a jagged gash high on the inside of his left thigh. The *légionnaire* inside the vehicle was luckiest but still had some metal blown into his hand. Two of our medics and a few others hurried outside and got them out of harm's way. They were rushed to a better equipped medical facility in Sarajevo. To everyone's shock the *légionnaire* that had been knocked out by the blast did not regain consciousness and died the next morning. He had been from Slovakia. The *légionnaire* hit in the leg was later evacuated to France for emergency treatment but had his leg amputated almost at the hip when doctors found that they had no other option. That news was a severe blow to everyone as this *légionnaire* was a big, strong, Polish fellow who had been one of the best runners in the regiment. The third *légionnaire* was from France and made a full recovery, completing his tour in Sarajevo.

It was later learned that the mortar round had been deliberately fired at us by the Muslims we had just returned from assisting that day. I never did learn what sort of ill will triggered such an attack, but I believe it may have been motivated by our requirement to prevent them from crossing the airport at night. Whatever their pitiful gripes may have been, they had no legitimate reason for this aggression.

The March 15, 1993 issue of *Newsweek* magazine carried a picture of this incident on page 20, but claimed that the *légionnaire* we lost was killed by sniper fire rather than a mortar round. I don't know why that bothers me but it does. The French publication of *Paris Match* also ran a series of photos of the occurrence which were much more graphic.

A week later, exactly to the hour of the previous attack, our lunch was rocked by another thunderous explosion when a round went off right beside our building. This time, luckily, everyone was inside eating and no one was hurt. This was indeed providential, since the round exploded against an observation post and disintegrated a wall of sandbags. Anyone manning the post at the time would surely have been killed. I don't know who fired this round or why, but the attacks stopped after that.

Our regiment initiated a procedure whereby we kept a running tally of the number of artillery rounds falling on the areas adjoining the airport. A common grid was used by all observation posts and radio centers to plot the areas under fire. When the observation posts saw a round explode they radioed the information to the radio room where we recorded the data by marking red Xs on a map. There were days when the shelling was heavy enough in some areas that grid squares were completely blotted out in red. On some days our units were reporting in excess of 1,000 rounds falling on Sarajevo and its outskirts. If the bombing became too intense or crept too close to our positions, everyone was ordered inside and waited it out with helmets and flak vests on.

Every morning our company commander was tasked with maintaining a cooperative relationship with the Muslim enclave located south of the airport in Butmir and with other villages further south. Being one of the radio operators in our company, I often accompanied him on a rotating basis to ensure he had constant radio contact with the company and regiment. We would take a local translator with us in our armored jeep and cross through both Serb and Muslim checkpoints to reach Butmir. We never had any trouble getting through the checkpoints, but there was always a moment of apprehension when passing between groups of armed soldiers who were squared off a couple of hundred meters from each other. Arriving in Butmir our commander went about his business

A radio operator logs incoming reports from observation posts surrounding the Sarajevo airport. During intensified periods of fighting the messages coming over the radio continued in uninterrupted streams for hours at a time. The sandbags piled in front of the window of the radio room were eventually improved on by sandbagging the entire interior wall.

of political discussion with the regional leaders, leaving me to chat with the locals and get the most mileage out of a half-dozen phrases as possible — but you can only make so much conversation out of "yes, no, today, tomorrow, hello, and goodbye."

As in Africa, once we stopped anywhere, crowds of people began to gather round looking for handouts. This would never have occurred if it hadn't been for the war, but desperation leads people to do things they otherwise wouldn't. One thing I couldn't help but notice about the majority of the population was the rotten state of their teeth. Almost everyone over twelve had one or more teeth in various stages of decay, if they had any teeth at all. It couldn't have been the war that was responsible for this and they must have lacked fluoride in their water or toothpaste or both. I felt a bit guilty about giving candy to the kids after seeing this.

It was always sad to see the children caught up in the insanity of a war that was none of their doing. I remember seeing a trio of young girls, who appeared to be sisters, walking around holding hands as if in a daze from the events that had gone on around them. Having repeatedly visited their village and given them candy, the oldest brought me a bunch of strawberries one day as a heartwarming gesture of thanks. We'd all heard tales of soldiers overrunning villages then proceeding to exterminate whatever ethnic presence was contrary to their own, and I couldn't help but feel for these kids. Sickening accounts of children having their throats cut by invading marauders filtered through to us and inflamed our indignations, but there was nothing we could do. A lot of our people vowed to open fire on anyone they saw committing such an act, but it's just as well this never happened or it would have caused a stink as putrid as that already being generated by the atrocities going on. We had explicit instructions to open fire only if under attack ourselves, even if this meant standing by and watching civilians being butchered.

We awoke one morning to a fierce rolling artillery barrage directed at Butmir south of the airport. We'd heard artillery before but never with such a concentrated violence. The Serbs had decided to make a stab at Butmir and were pounding it with all their might after warning the UN to stay out of the way. After the bombardment, they attempted a ground offensive which was repulsed, leaving Butmir still in Muslim control. I was with our company commander who visited the village soon after the attack and was able to see the latest damage produced by the shelling. I never heard the casualty figures for this little battle but what struck me the most was seeing fresh bomb craters in the areas where children had played. It really turns your stomach to see something like that. As far as I know none of them were hurt, and I saw the same kids I always had on later visits.

Escorting convoys carrying aid to areas cut off from the outside world was one of our functions while in Sarajevo. Places like Gorazde, Zepa, and Srebrenica had been left to fend for themselves in the wake of fighting that swirled around them and severed any possibility of supplies reaching them. Truck convoys organized by the United Nations High Commissioner for Refugees (UNHCR) were sent into areas like these to deliver food and other basic essentials necessary for these people to survive. We provided an element of protection for these convoys but I doubt we'd have been able stop a hijacking if anyone had been determined to plunder our goods. As it was, these convoys did not always reach their destinations as planned. We were constantly being harassed and harried by Serb forces unconcerned with whether or not their sworn enemies starved to death.

I went on escort missions to Tuzla and Zepa, which was a nice break from the stale rhythm at the airport. We never did make it through to Tuzla, though, and turned around before arriving. I can't recall why we stopped, but I think we were supposed to rendezvous with the convoy at a specified location then escort it to Tuzla, and it either hadn't shown up or had already proceeded to Tuzla without us. Our trip to Zepa did succeed as intended, and we spent a couple of nights in its deep valley. Similar convoys were in constant motion and we regularly provided a measure of safety for them.

Most escort missions were uneventful, but things did get a little tense at times, not so much because of the Serbs interested in prohibiting our passage, but because of the same folks we were trying to help. Many times our vehicles would be completely inundated with people clamoring for supplies before we could unload them. They would climb onto the vehicles to grab whatever they could, even vehicles not carrying commodities. We couldn't leave tools or jerry cans strapped on the outside of the vehicles or they quickly vanished. One of our officers made the mistake of leaving his hatch open when he stepped out of his vehicle and had his camera, GPS, and briefcase stolen.

Many of the places we escorted convoys to were later declared safe areas by the United Nations and were supposed to have been disengaged from threat of attack. Long after we'd left Sarajevo I heard that Srebrenica and Zepa had been invaded and thousands of civilians massacred. It was spooky having been in Zepa then hearing that most of the people we'd seen there were probably now dead.

The main function of UN forces was to provide a conduit for humanitarian aid to reach civilian populations displaced by the war, and keeping the airport operational was of primary importance. The airport was a lifeline for thousands of people depending on the supplies, and its security was one of our biggest jobs.

Since the airport was considered to be territory under UN control this meant keeping it neutral in the face of the opposing factions surrounding it. The airport was located to the south west of Sarajevo and inadvertently acted as a barrier between two Muslim-held areas. Muslims held Sarajevo itself, north of the airport, and land south of the airport around the village of Butmir and beyond. The Serbs had encroached to both the eastern and western ends of the airport, which therefore placed it squarely in the heart of hostilities. This led to one of the most detestable

Some of the vehicles utilized by UN forces at the Sarajevo airport. The photo was taken from the window of 1st Company's living quarters. The neighborhood in the background was known as Dobrinja and was a constant target of shelling and machine gun fire.

obligations ever imposed on a peacekeeping force since the inception of the United Nations.

Because the airport stood in the way of the two Muslim regions, anyone wanting to cross back and forth between Sarajevo and Butmir was forced to traverse the airport, since skirting it would have taken them through Serb territory. Most of these crossings took place under cover of darkness, at the eastern end of the airport, where the distance from Sarajevo to Butmir was shortest. These crossings were undertaken by civilian and military persons alike and, in order to counter this enemy movement, the Serbs set up machine gun positions to the east of the airport and happily gunned down anyone they saw moving through the airport zone.

In order to maintain its posture of neutrality the UN was required to prevent anyone from using the airport to transit between the two Muslim sectors. To do this we had armored personnel carriers positioned at intervals along the airport tarmac at night which were directed to intercept anyone crossing it. Anyone caught crossing the airport was frisked, all weapons and ammunition were confiscated, then they were returned to whichever side they had started from. So, these people would brave machine gun fire in an effort to cross the airport only to be stopped by the UN who had to take them back to their starting point. This happened every single night from sunset to sunrise for the six months we were there and

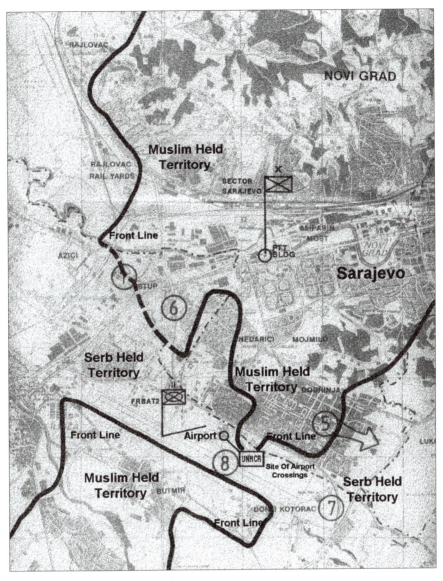

Map of Sarajevo, March 1993.

continued for an indefinite period after our tour was up. Evidently, they eventually succeeded in digging a tunnel under the airport which safely linked the two sides but this was long after we had left.

This tarmac duty, as we referred to it, was a considerable part of what we did in Sarajevo, and a lot of our time and resources was geared towards this single task. Most people I knew were disgusted at having to interfere with a populace struggling to survive this senseless war. Stopping soldiers from crossing was one thing, but blocking people trying to bring food and other materials to their families was quite another. Some of our troops, after witnessing women and children, the elderly, people carrying babies in their arms, and any civilian trying to cross the airport being indiscriminately shot at by Serb gunners, occasionally overstepped their bounds and deposited people on the side of the airport they wished to go to through some carefully devised chicanery. Most of the time, though, our men complied with what was asked of them, even amid the wails and screams of those they had to stop. We did have one *caporal* who refused to continue performing this assignment but was swiftly made an example of by our *Chef de Corps* and sent back to Calvi to spend time in the lockup. He later deserted.

In some respects our presence on the tarmac was beneficial to those trying to cross, especially when a civilian was wounded or pinned down by machine gun fire. We recovered dozens of people who had been shot and otherwise left for dead and ferried them to our dispensary at the airport, then later to the hospital in Sarajevo if necessary. Countless other lives were undoubtedly saved when we intervened with our armored vehicles to pick up people immobilized by ruthless gunfire. We also had the gruesome task of retrieving the bodies of those who didn't make it across the airport before being shot dead.

A friend of mine who worked in the infirmary told me many stories of the cases he assisted in. One person had been shot sideways through the head where his jaws hinged together, but was still conscious and able to talk when they brought him in. Another person had been shot sideways through his abdomen and moaned in agony all night long, keeping our entire barracks awake, since it was attached to the infirmary. I didn't envy any of our medical personnel their jobs, but had to applaud their efforts wholeheartedly.

I was fortunate enough to have been a radio operator throughout this tour and so spent a lot of time bunkered into a reasonably safe radio room. This was not the case for our troops who manned observation posts during the day or went out on the tarmac at night. They were not immune to the impulses of trigger-happy zealots who weren't the least bit impressed with UN soldiers in their midst. One of our men was shot squarely in the chest while in an observation post but was saved by the bullet proof vest

The back of a *VAB* clearly shows where it was hit by machine gun fire from Serb gunners after a night on the tarmac. Our troops continually risked serious injury or death in trying to keep the airport a neutral sector in the midst of hostile forces unconcerned with whoever got in front of their weapons.

he was wearing. Another was shot on two separate occasions in his hand and shoulder but was not seriously hurt and finished the tour. Many of our men were similarly hurt when they got in the way of a bullet or other flying bits of metal. A friend of mine was nearly killed when a bullet just missed his head while he was working in his office. They figure a sniper had a bead on him and only missed because my friend happened to turn his head just before the bullet entered the office.

Tarmac duty was especially hazardous business and I have nothing but the highest regard for those who did this job ungrudgingly night after night. Our vehicles were regularly shot at by the Serbs as we went around picking up civilians, and they repeatedly returned in the morning with bullet-sized chips in the paint and half-inflated tires. The few times I was on the tarmac was an unnerving experience. Stepping out of an armored vehicle only emphasized how naked and vulnerable a person was. The crack of a bullet as it whizzes past you is a very uncomfortable feeling.

One night after driving my company commander out to the tarmac and parking on the runway facing Serb positions to the east, we saw two civilians dash across in front of us then hunker down in a ditch. Seconds later two tracers came streaking from the Serb position towards these civilians and past where we sat. The absolute velocity of those bullets and the suddenness with which they reached their target was terrifying. We were able to prevent the two civilians from being shot and got them safely out of there.

One day a report came in from one of our observation posts that a person on a bicycle had gotten into the airport zone and was riding around on the runway and taxiways, obviously unmindful of the situation he'd stumbled into. He was quickly rounded up and turned out to be an Irish correspondent seeking to cover the events of the war. I never did hear the full story about this episode, but I can't imagine how this guy got where he was or what he was thinking by cycling through the middle of battle zones, completely oblivious to the dangers surrounding him. He could easily have been gunned down by the Serbs.

Our worst incident on the tarmac occurred with roughly a month left in Sarajevo. One of our armored vehicles had been in the process of picking up a group of civilians and when the vehicle commander stepped out onto the ground the Serbs intentionally opened fire on him. I guess they got tired of us getting in the way of their turkey shoot. He was hit in his calf, thigh, and buttock but managed to crawl around the other side of the vehicle to safety. Because he hadn't had time to close his side hatch, a bullet entered the cab of the vehicle, struck the driver in the head, penetrated his helmet, pierced his skull, and touched his brain which left him unable to move but miraculously still alive. Luckily for him we'd been issued a type of ballistic helmet instead of a regular steel pot or he probably would have been killed. The helmet took enough force out of the bullet or deflected it enough so that the damage wasn't fatal.

Because of our adherence to a chickenshit policy on not returning fire when fired upon, the Serbs had gunned down two of our men at their leisure without thinking twice about it. When we finally got the order to rattle off a few rounds in their direction as a laughable display of outrage during this incident, it was too little, too late. Both men were evacuated without further harm being done and made full recoveries. The *légionnaire* shot in the head was partially paralyzed but regained his motor functions after a few months of therapy. The *caporal* shot in the legs and buttock was up and around in no time.

In all, we had 25 people injured and one person killed while in Sarajevo. We can thank our lucky stars it wasn't worse than that. Considering that we couldn't please either side involved in the conflict, and were targeted by both groups of dissidents at one time or another, we left there in as good a shape as could be expected.

In Sarajevo we had five accidental weapon discharges that I know of, and I can think of at least four other occasions of weapons being unintentionally fired while I was in the Legion. From all of these incidents one person had the top of his head blown off in Chad and another was injured in Sarajevo when the bullet punched a hole through the angle iron on a bed and blew some metal fragments into his stomach.

When handling weapons and live ammunition, unwavering diligence is necessary to prevent a careless accident from snuffing out someone's life. Everybody knows this and understands what a lapse in concentration can mean. Yet, they are not nearly as attentive as they should be. Most armies around the world pay lip service to the issue of weapons safety but do not emphasize the importance of taking painstaking care when weapons are used. I learned more from a civilian rifle club as a kid than I did in a total of nine years in the military. The military might tell you to keep your weapon pointed in a safe direction but I couldn't begin to count the number of times I've seen rifle muzzles pass across the bodies of other men, loaded or not. Complacency kills. For all of its professionalism, the Legion is a big culprit of this sort of negligence and fails miserably to underscore this point.

Most of these mishaps involved a *FAMAS*. On two occasions someone had a round in the chamber, then tapped the butt on the ground hard enough to discharge the round. The majority of accidents happen while unloading it or checking to see if it's loaded when someone is tired, but that's no excuse. Don't allow yourself any lassitude when handling a weapon, the stakes are much too high.

During our six month stay in Sarajevo, everyone was accorded a week's leave and rotated in small groups to neighboring Croatia, where arrangements had been made for us to be lodged in a hotel in Primosten. From there we could amuse ourselves in nearby Split or Trogir or just relax where we were. Croatia was in the midst of its own war of independence, and we had been cautioned to steer clear of potentially dangerous areas, such as Sibenik to the northeast, where heavy shelling had been reported.

We had lots of money, and food and drink were agreeably cheap, so we spent most of our time engaged in a rollicking drunkfest. We drank hard liquor every day of the week and, when our flight back to Sarajevo was delayed for three days, we drank some more. When we got back to Sarajevo everyone thought I'd acquired a sun tan but the only time I'd been outside was when walking between bars. My sun tan was the rosy flush of alcohol still in my system. As fun as it was to get away from the demands of Sarajevo and let our hair down a bit, a few minor situations developed during our stay that could have rained heavily on our parade.

One afternoon, four of us hopped on a bus fully besotted with drink, expecting it to take us to Split, where we planned to find a nightclub and continue our debauchery. Once the bus was underway, a fellow came around to issue us our tickets and collect the fare. We couldn't speak in a mutual tongue, but we indicated we wanted to go to Split. He shook his head and said Sibenik. We'd gotten on the wrong bus and were now heading toward a battle zone. This also explained why the bus was half full of Croatian soldiers. The bus didn't stop, and we couldn't make it stop, until it arrived at the edge of Sibenik, where we disembarked and found ourselves stranded. Luckily all was quiet and no shelling was in progress. We instantly turned tail and started walking back to Primosten. We were later able to flag down a taxi which removed us from the danger area around Sibenik.

On several occasions, we found some members of the populace largely unappreciative of the UN interjecting itself in their affairs. One time, we were pleasantly benumbed with alcohol in a bar in Primosten, when one of our guys started talking with a local who spoke English. When the conversation became somewhat heated, the local flashed a handgun he was carrying as a warning signal to us. We left the bar soon after without further altercation. What made this incident alarming was the frontier mentality this individual had championed. He felt that because his country was at war, he could carry a gun around to use if and when he felt it necessary, with limited risk of prosecution. War can breed lawlessness, and there will always be those ready to take full advantage of rifts in legal authority when a social infrastructure crumbles.

On another night, a large group of us had gathered in a bar in Primosten, when a tussle started between two of our men. One of them punched the other fully in the face which dropped him like a sack of potatoes, leaving him in a partial coma. We weren't able to rouse him from his stupor, and had to drag him back to the hotel and dump him into bed. It was only the next morning that it dawned on us to check on his condition. The punch could have caused more damage than we'd originally thought, or were able to think at the time. If he'd somehow died in the night, we'd have been up the creek without a paddle. Luckily for everyone concerned, he was okay and only had a swollen kisser as a reminder of his sparring match. The funny part of it all was that he couldn't remember what had happened or who had hit him. He'd clearly seen his attacker before he was assaulted, but was unable to explain his black eyes when confronted by an officer.

We made it back safely to Sarajevo having thoroughly sated our energies, but in retrospect I don't know if six months in Sarajevo was any more dangerous than this week of leave. Things can get pretty wild when weeks of pent-up tension and stress are suddenly released with full intensity. Our group wasn't the only one involved in events that went slightly awry.

Probably the biggest snafu that occurred during our tour of Sarajevo happened not during one of the leave rotations, but in the course of a convoy escort. A detachment of vehicles from our company had gone out and completed a regular mission but, just before they concluded their duties, they radioed back that they could not return as scheduled. Two or three *légionnaires* had gone missing. Apparently they had either been allowed out on the town for a few beers, or had snuck off without authorization. In either case, they weren't present when the convoy was due to return, and nobody knew what had happened to them. It didn't seem likely that they would attempt desertion in the middle of a war torn country, but stranger things can and do happen. If it had been positively known that they had deserted, they may have been left behind but, because no one was sure, the convoy was obligated to mount a search. For four whole days their whereabouts remained a mystery, until they were finally reunited with the convoy — exactly how I don't know.

The particulars of what had happened were kept quiet to avoid further embarrassment, but a few fragments of the story leaked out. From what I heard these *légionnaires* had been drunk, and had become embroiled in a quarrel with some of the local citizenry. Things escalated from exchanging insults, to the *légionnaires* being overpowered by knife wielding locals. Somehow they managed to extricate themselves from this predicament, but they couldn't immediately find their way back to the convoy.

Of course, their account of what happened could have just been a fabrication to cover up a desertion attempt. Whatever the actual details were, they had no genuine excuse for being absent, and after returning to Sarajevo, spent all of their spare time filling sandbags.

The dangers of Sarajevo presented many occasions for people to be recognized as having performed above and beyond the call of duty. Even though our presence was neutral, and the countries that deployed UN troops to the region were only trying to contribute in some way to world peace, our men repeatedly put their safety at risk to do the thankless jobs that were placed in their hands.

Several incidents arose that were considered worthy of the bestowal of medals. After returning to Calvi, it seemed as though half of the men that served in Sarajevo were awarded various medals in addition to the UN medal that everyone received. There was a notebook in our radio room that we jokingly referred to as the medal book, where anyone could leave a brief account of an incident or action they felt was deserving of higher commendation. Unfortunately, this led to many entries of instances that, while completely entitled to a clap on the back for a job well done, did not necessarily qualify for a medal. It's only natural to want it known when you have risked personal injury or worse to the benefit of others, but to give out medals with little regard to merit, seriously cheapens their value.

About a dozen men and I were awarded the *Croix De La Valeur Militaire Avec Étoile D'Argent* (Military Cross Of Valor With Silver Star) after recovering two wounded civilians from a convoy that had been attacked just as it was entering the airport. We had been required to leave the relative safety of the airport briefly to bring these civilians back on stretchers, and were exposed to possible fire for 10 to 15 minutes. I don't feel such an honor was entirely justified because, in reality, we didn't do anything extraordinary to earn it. Before we'd been allowed to leave the confines of the airport, our commanders had probably spent an hour arranging for the Serb and Muslim sides to comply with a cease fire while we evacuated the injured victims. Any potential danger had thus been removed from the equation. It was a simple task of putting two people on stretchers and carrying them back to the airport.

Numerous similar incidents were unmistakably deserving of acclaim but, when nearly half the men and almost all the officers serving in Sarajevo were given medals of valor, one has to question the validity of those accolades. There were only a couple of instances where this type of medal had been justly earned, the most notable being when the group of men ran out to recover the *légionnaires* hit by the mortar round, not knowing if another shell was about to hit them. This exemplifies the ultimate act of selfless bravery, entirely deserving of the esteemed medal of valor.

Regardless of whether or not a medal was appropriate in most incidents, I cannot detract from the sterling efforts of our men in the performance of their responsibilities while in Sarajevo. Everyone did their duty to the utmost, and each played a part in helping to reestablish order to this part of the world.

As deplorable a circumstance as war is, it was nevertheless extremely interesting to witness first-hand the dreadful aftermath that results when the inability to live in harmony spirals out of control. From the comparatively safe disposition of an impartial onlooker, being in Sarajevo was a lot like having front row seats at a sporting event. One is dissociated from happenings on the playing field, but still close enough to the action to experience the impetus of the affair when the contest spills into the crowd. Having been so directly immersed in this upheaval lent credence to the American Civil War General, William Tecumseh Sherman's, adroit phrase "war is hell." He clearly knew what he was talking about. There is nothing glamorous about war. It produces naught but agony and distress for those that it touches, serving only to remind us of how defective civilization can be.

It is difficult to comprehend the factors that produce the kind of enmity that leads to the cataclysm of war. The peoples of Yugoslavia had been living peacefully together for years, but regressed to primeval animal instincts and began slaughtering their neighbors when Communism was displaced. I don't know enough of the history of Yugoslavia to accurately comment on how it became such a hotbed of antagonism, but it is a shame that it was found necessary to revert to primitive impulses in order to settle their differences.

It could be forever debated whether or not the intervention of foreign troops to pursue the elusive ideal of peace is worth the life of even one of those soldiers — who often shoulder the burden of unclear, inconsistent, and impossible orders. In recent years, international intrusions into countries like Rwanda and Somalia have achieved little in spite of the best of intentions. UN soldiers have repeatedly fallen prey to the very people they help. In spite of the problems and regrettable loss of life that can only be expected in complex international imbroglios, the UN will continue to spearhead any effort that promotes peace, with the Legion assisting when and where called upon.

The winged dagger insignia is widely recognized as the symbol of the mercenary soldier. The *REP* is the only Legion unit that wears it on their berets but it is also worn on the red berets of regular French paratroopers. The *REP* and the regular French parachute regiments comprise France's 11th parachute division.

The French Foreign Legion has revealed itself to be entirely suited for the demands of peacekeeping, relying on its intrinsic wealth of experience in foreign arenas, motivation of volunteer soldiers, and extensive training to rise to the occasion and advance the noble cause of goodwill in the world. The Legion has only just begun a new journey in its long and illustrious evolution, progressing from a crude machine of war to a versatile instrument of peace. As the French Minister of Defense Leotard stated in an address to our regiment after returning from Sarajevo:

"Gentlemen, it was already known that a Legionnaire was at the same time a military man and a builder. The world has learned that you, exceptional professionals of war, were formidable soldiers of peace."

I often saw the Legion to be a shining example of how people from a wide diversity of cultures can come together and work productively toward a common goal. Disregarding the gray areas of its past, its future lies in the pursuit of world peace.

The Mercenary Question

One weekend afternoon a few friends and I were strolling along the quay in Calvi wearing our uniforms, minding our own business, and just enjoying the beautiful day. Two women passed us going in the opposite direction and, after doing so, one of them hissed to the other in an unmistakable British accent, "God, they're nothing but a bunch of bloody mercenaries." Admittedly, this invective was a slap in the face, but it got me thinking about the distinct situation in which those serving in the Foreign Legion find themselves.

The question I was prompted to examine was: Is someone in the Foreign Legion a mercenary? I had thought about this question before joining, but never gave it an undue amount of consideration. I basically shrugged it off as being a contingent effect or conditional consequence of joining the Legion. Someone in the Legion could easily be seen as, and for all intents and purposes is, a mercenary. The dictionary definition of mercenary is: motivated by reasons of gain; obtained by hire: said only of soldiers serving a foreign state — which is definitely true of anyone in the Legion. Legionnaires are hired to serve a foreign state, and an enlistee does stand to gain, in that he can find succor for whatever ails him, though monetary compensation could hardly be the sole influence in someone's decision to join. Unfortunately, the term mercenary has developed a bad reputation and has become synonymous with the darker side of human nature.

The objective of most who join the Legion is undeniably self-serving. No one joins to elevate the interests of France, even if this is a by-product of such an action. People join the Legion to improve their own standing, or fulfill a personal need. Even though France has dominion over the Legion, the Legion comes first in the eyes of its men with France holding a distant second place, giving rise to its motto, *Legio Patria Nostra* (The Legion Is Our Fatherland).

Neither can anyone expect to walk away from the Legion a rich man. A Legionnaire's pay is modest reward for his sacrifices. The familiar view of a mercenary is of a soldier of fortune who receives a large cash settlement for a dangerous operation in a foreign land. The Legion pays its men regularly in small doses, and any money a Legionnaire manages to accumulate has been rightly earned.

While I had to concede that someone who serves in the Foreign Legion is by definition a mercenary, I never considered us to be mercenaries as they are commonly depicted. The popular impression of a mercenary is that of a cold-blooded, scum-sucking, killer-for-hire, bereft of the slightest regard for the sanctity of human life, who rampages through defenseless villages leaving wholesale slaughter in his wake. Or something like that. A killer mind-set does not permeate the Legion, but this notion, combined with the image of it being a diseased infestation of wretched criminality, only makes it understandable why someone could think ill of the Legion.

The Legion still tends to suffer from contestable repute, and I won't pretend for a moment that it is a paragon of piety. Even with its choosy selection process, there are plenty of men in the Legion who are less than angelic. I knew many who had killed other people or committed any manner of crime before joining. Nor can I defend the actions of men from days gone by who may have been involved in less than honorable deeds while serving in the Legion. In spite of any such error, large or small, questionable attitudes or conduct from the past do not resonate in the general temperament of the Legion today. Sardonically branding a Legionnaire as a mercenary is as ambiguous as it is vilifying.

A Legionnaire is simply a soldier who just happens to be serving in a foreign country. The presence of the Legion has often been a soothing balm in areas of the world in need of a helping hand. It has repeatedly been used to build and produce rather than destroy.

However, there's no escaping the fact that the business of being a soldier involves matters of life and death. There are questions of morality that arise when soldiers from a foreign land are involved in wars and kill on behalf of a country that is not their own. This moral dilemma is magnified when someone joins, not out of necessity, so much as a sense of adventure. I joined with an exuberance for thrilling escapade born of the impulses of youth, not to escape an impoverished existence or criminal past. The fact that I could have been involved in a war, and may have had to kill for another country, was always in the back of my mind, but I didn't think about it as much as I should have. As it turned out I was never required to do that, and remain eternally grateful. It would not have been unlawful to have killed an avowed enemy of France, but I would be remiss in minimizing the implications of pulling the trigger for another country.

This is a serious issue and I implore you to think long and hard about the potential consequences of killing for another country. Could you live with having shot someone to death if you genuinely had no rationale for being in a situation that required you to do so? Where would your allegiance lie if France were to declare war or take hostile actions against your country of origin or vice versa? Many countries in the world prohibit their citizens from joining a foreign army if there is any possibility of the two sides warring against each other. You'd best settle these questions with yourself long before you are thrust into such circumstances.

If you do find that the advantages of joining the Legion outweigh its potential side effects, you couldn't go to a better place. The Legion takes a back seat to no one. There is no other mercenary-type body on the planet today that can compare to the French Foreign Legion. There exists a handful of affiliations besides the Legion that are associated with

A procession of vehicles driven by the Foreign Legion pulls off the road during an operation in Chad.

mercenary activity such as the Swiss Guards of the Vatican, the Spanish Legion, and the Gurkhas of Nepal who act as an arm of the British Armed Forces. The Swiss Guards serve more of a decorative function than any practical purpose, and only accept Swiss nationals into its ranks. The Spanish Legion no longer accepts volunteers from outside its borders, due to numerous problems with foreign recruits. I knew a few ex-Spanish Legionnaires in the Foreign Legion and, from what I was able to surmise, the Spanish Legion was a place of brutality in the extreme. The Gurkhas rival the Legion in mercenary practices, but they come solely from Nepal.

In recent years, mercenary activity around the world can be traced mainly to a few nations in Africa where mercenary forces fought in the Congo, Angola, Zimbabwe, Mozambique, and other locales through the '60s, '70s, and into the '80s but had relatively short life spans. The most current example of mercenary operations was in the former Yugoslavia with the creation of the International Brigade. Men were enlisted to serve the fragmented remnants of a nation in disarray at the enticement of exhilarating adventure and the prospect of making a few dollars. Unfortunately, when backing some half-assed regime, the dollars may never materialize and disconsolate recruits can find themselves high and dry with no way out of some very dire straits.

I would strongly advise against enlisting in a shadowy mercenary association that does not have a solid administrative and organizational foundation. If something in you feels compelled to join an outfit involved in ventures of a mercenary nature, I can only suggest the Foreign Legion. The Legion pays you regularly and on time, takes care of your medical needs, allows you vacation leave, provides you with adequate food and shelter, grants you a pension if you serve long enough, and generally takes pretty good care of you.

The *légionnaire* who was killed in Sarajevo was given a ceremonial funeral at Aubagne, with his father in attendance. The casket was later shipped back to his home country, escorted by the *légionnaire*'s former *section* commander, to be laid to rest. The *légionnaire* who lost his leg was offered ample compensation and could have remained in the Legion as long as he liked, although he chose to leave. The *légionnaire* shot in the head, and the *caporal* shot in the legs while on the tarmac, were both nursed back to health. The *légionnaire* with the head wound later received considerable financial requital and was released from his contract early at his request. A dear friend of mine, for whom this book is dedicated, was diagnosed with liver cancer while in the Legion. The Legion paid for his family to visit him in a hospital in Paris and later covered the expenses to send him and his family home, where he spent his final days. They even sent representatives from the Legion to attend his funeral.

One night in Sarajevo our troops picked up two men of British origin who were attempting to cross the tarmac. They said they were mercenaries. From what I gathered, they were just roaming around looking for some way of getting themselves out of a situation that had gone sour. I vaguely knew a fellow from the *REP* who had finished his contract then volunteered for the International Brigade in Yugoslavia. Some time later he was slightly wounded by a rocket blast, for which he did not receive anything for the damages he suffered. He could hardly have expected any sort of indemnity though, since he was hardly being paid for regular service. If you ever subject yourself to the vagaries of an unstable government, remember, you could very well be putting your life in extreme jeopardy.

One of the most tragic aftereffects of being in Yugoslavia occurred months after we'd left. A French fellow, who had been in the Deep Recon Commandos, deserted from the *REP* and went back there with the determination of putting his training to practical use for whatever side he supported. A few weeks later, word filtered back that he'd been killed, and his body was being sent back to France. Those of us who knew him were stunned. He was one of the sharpest soldiers you could ever hope to find, and a hell of a good guy. It was such a waste of life but, in truth, not entirely unanticipated. Trouble has a way of finding those who go looking for it.

If you have any doubts as to the reverberations of joining an organization with mercenary overtones, I can only advise that you do not. You could probably find a better way to make a living. If you do decide to forge ahead and join the Foreign Legion, be prepared to be chastised by those who don't know anything about it. It goes with the territory.

Final Days

After having been in the Legion for over four years, I suddenly received a notice advising me that I owed the French government thousands of francs in taxes. You can understand the shock I felt. I had naively assumed that paying taxes somehow did not apply to members of the Foreign Legion, and since I'd never received any indication that it was required, I had no reason to believe otherwise. I may have also presumed that applicable taxes were being automatically deducted before we received our monthly pay. Having to pay taxes did not bother me so much as did being told of a four year backlog. The French system of imposing taxes proved to be a far cry from what I was used to. They didn't even account for taxes on an annual basis let alone monthly.

This may have been due to the nagging problem of desertion. Because there are so many people that flee their obligations to the Legion, there may be a minimum time requirement before taxes are imposed. I don't see why taxes aren't processed at least annually though. I asked others who had served longer than five years about it. They said that they too had been taxed for the first time just before the end of their initial contract. In the end all I was able to reason was that their tax system was pathetically incapable of doing its job. I asked several people for advice, including our company's head administrator, who all said not to pay, since I was not going to extend my contract. I gladly followed these recommendations and ignored all appeals for payment from the taxation bureau. I completed my contract and returned home without paying.

About a year after I'd settled into a comfortable life back in my homeland, I received a letter from the French embassy requesting payment of those bloody taxes, along with the inevitable penalties for late payment. On leaving the Legion I'd left an obvious paper trail for them to follow and they didn't have too much trouble in tracking me down. I realized this was a problem that was not going to go away and, after receiving some wise council from my father, paid what was owing.

The insight I'm trying to impart here is to be prepared to have a substantial debt materialize from nowhere toward the end of your contract. You can otherwise inquire about paying it annually and save yourself a great deal of trouble.

A few short months before the end of your contract you will be summoned in front of your company commander. He will ask you if there are any more years of your life you'd like to sign away. By the time this happens, you should have a pretty clear idea of whether or not you want to continue in the Legion. I knew within the first year of my contract that I would not be signing an extension, but if you have found the Legion to be a blessing, the best of luck to you. If you have no plans of re-signing, try to have a reasonable explanation as to why you're not interested in order to avert any attempt to make you change your mind. In the course of leaving the Legion, you will be talking with several officers who all have a vested interest in having you stay. The Legion doesn't like to lose good people, any more than would a civilian corporation, so they do chat with you to find out what your plans are. If you say something like you're planning on going back to school to further your education, which is a reasonable possibility if you've been frugal with your money, you won't meet with too much opposition. If you hem and haw, shuffle your feet, and can't really say why you want out of the Legion, you can expect to be continually extolled on the Legion's unending virtues.

You can re-sign for durations of as little as six months or as long as five years, or anything in between. You don't have to sign for five whole years again if this doesn't fit in with your plans. Staying in the Legion for 15 years will qualify you for a modest pension. If you stay in the Legion for at least eight years, you won't receive a pension, but they do pay out a substantial one-time sum in lieu of any type of annuity. A friend of mine, who stayed for a total of nine years reached the rank of *sergent* and was paid 24 times his monthly wage on leaving. This worked out to over 200,000 francs. Very handy to help reestablish your footing in civilian life.

If you're firm in your decision to leave, you can begin inquiries about how to obtain French citizenship and get the paperwork started. You can initiate this procedure after three years of service if you think you want to become a French citizen. If you've put in five good years with the

Legion without having caused too much trouble, acquiring citizenship should be just a simple formality. I did not seek it for myself, so I don't know all the requirements or how long it takes.

Before leaving your regiment and returning to Aubagne for the final clearance phase of your departure from the Legion, you will have to turn in all the material that was issued to you and obtain medical and administrative documents by visiting all pertinent offices in your regiment. There is a significant amount of documentation that is supposed to be given to you to take to the head office in Aubagne. I wasn't given these documents when I left Calvi, and nearly had to wait another week in Aubagne for them to be sent, so make sure you get them.

If you've accumulated a lot of memorabilia you may want to send a few parcels to yourself before leaving. You can only cart around so much luggage when moving from place to place, and you won't be able to store excessive amounts of gear while in Aubagne. It can get rather costly to send even small packages half way around the world, but it does lighten the load. I only mailed three or four boxes, but it cost me between two and three thousand francs to do so. I left the Legion with only a duffel bag and a small knapsack to show for five years there.

At the end of my contract I still had some vacation leave to take and was released 26 days early. I thought this was a pretty good deal since, by the time my contract was almost at an end, I had zero interest in performing my daily duties and was chomping at the bit to get out of there. Even after I'd gone through the formalities at Aubagne and officially been released, I was still technically under the Legion's umbrella for almost a month, and had a leave pass covering me until my projected release date. This was just for the sake of keeping the paperwork squared away though, because once I was finished at Aubagne, I would not have returned come hell or high water.

Any time someone bids farewell to their unit, whether it be to change *sections* within a company, change companies within a regiment, be posted to another regiment, or when leaving the Legion at the end of a contract, their *section* has a going away party known as a *pot* (poh). Everyone gets together and has a few beers, munches on snacks, and shoots the breeze. The person leaving is given a small gift as a souvenir of their time spent with that particular unit. I have three such keepsakes from the moving around I did, and consider them valued momentos of my days in the Legion. The Legion is quite meticulous about acknowledging the departure of one of its brothers-in-arms, and makes every effort to do so, whether he be a *légionnaire* in his first year of service or an *adjudant-chef* with 20 years or more.

On the day you leave you will have to pass by the *chef de poste* at the main gate to let him know you're leaving for civilian life. Not that he'll be interested, other than wondering why you're strolling out of camp in the middle of the day. Don't expect any fancy mode of transport to have been arranged. Your transportation off the island will be via the cheapest route possible, meaning a ferry crossing. When I left I was required to take the tourist train that runs beside the camp at Calvi to get to Ajaccio in order to cross to Marseille. Then, after spending four or five hours on the train, I had to wait about nine hours for the ferry to leave that evening. I had considered buying a plane ticket, even though I wouldn't have been reimbursed for it. I believe I left on a Friday and showed up in Aubagne on Saturday. If I'd have known better at the time I could have stayed in a hotel in Marseille all weekend and arrived in Aubagne Sunday night or Monday morning, but I was so anxious to be gone from the Legion that I wanted to get things over and done with as soon as possible.

Chapter 6

FIN DE CONTRAT

—

You will spend one final week in Aubagne completing the process of departing the Legion. The whole procedure could really be done in one day, but it drags on unnecessarily. This week will probably be the longest time you ever spend waiting at anything. Each day, you may do one or two things related to your departure, then try and find a place to hide for the rest of the day so you don't get nabbed for *corvée*. Believe it or not you'll be doing *corvée* right up until you leave. If they could they'd probably have you take out the trash as you walked out the gates for the last time.

I hinted at not showing up at Aubagne until the last moment possible for a good reason. Having arrived on a Saturday I found myself on a truck bound for Puyloubier to pick grapes on Sunday. I was unbelievably galled at being sent on this detail on a Sunday with less than a week on my contract. I kicked myself all day for having arrived too early. I did have the good fortune of avoiding other major *corvée* duties for the rest of the week though. Puyloubier serves the Legion in a couple of ways. Its main functions are to act as a retirement home for ex-Legionnaires, and to maintain vineyards from which the Legion creates its own varieties of wine. The residents here also produce art and craftwork to sell as souvenirs. Most of the inhabitants fought in Algeria, Indochina, and possibly World War II, and bear the regrettable scars of those battles. Many are amputees and can only move around with the help of wheelchairs or prostheses.

It is highly commendable of the Legion to provide this facility for its veterans who may have no where else to go in their old age. The Legion does an admirable job of taking care of its own. It seemed like an awfully sad and forlorn place to end up, though it was a salvation for some. I couldn't help but notice one unfortunate soul, not much older than 45 who appeared resigned to a life there.

The housing quarters contain amenities commensurate with the needs of the inhabitants. The vets each have a room that they share with at least one other person. They all take meals together in a large dining hall and commence with singing *Le Boudin.* You can take the man out of the Legion, but you can't take the Legion out of the man. Mealtime can get quite rowdy, with people slinging food and insults at each other, after which some fill empty mineral water bottles with wine to take back to their rooms. Groups that arrive from Aubagne to work eat in the same mess hall.

I'm not sure if the Legion assesses a stipend from the residents or whether it provides room and board free of charge. From what I was able to tell the residents are not required to work or participate in daily activities, such as making pottery, unless they want to. Many aren't even able to do simple chores for themselves, so they wouldn't be obliged to accomplish anything from day to day. Neither do I know what qualifies a person to become a resident there, whether the completion of a simple five year contract is enough, or whether you have to serve longer, be drawing a pension, be a minimum age, have fought in a battle for France, or have been wounded. I believe that the *légionnaire* who lost his leg in Sarajevo could find sanctuary here but, as for the rest of us, I don't know. There is only room for about 200 residents.

If you find yourself on hard times in your old age after leaving the Legion, inquire by contacting Aubagne or getting the details before you leave. Puyloubier isn't anything to look forward to in life, but unexpected circumstances can befall a person, and having a room here would beat living under a bridge somewhere.

The final aspects of your stay in Aubagne include wrapping up various administrative details. Your passport will be returned to you if it hasn't been already. If it has expired, you will have to renew it at your consulate in Marseille, Paris, or Nice before you can return home.

If you were never previously *rectified,* they will do all they can to see that you are before you leave. I had never bothered with this process since I was able to get a new passport in Spain, so they hurriedly got this done for me. I kept my real identity all through my time in the Legion,

so there was nothing to be gained by being *rectified* a couple of days before I left. I guess it was just to keep their paperwork in order. It may
have been necessary to do this to verify that the name on the records I
was given to keep coincided with my actual identity. For example, if I'd
had my named changed upon joining and later done a mechanic course,
I wouldn't be able to claim credit for it in civilian life without being
rectified. I would have been released even if I hadn't been *rectified,* but I
may not have been able to show a civilian employer any documentation
of qualifications I had earned in the Legion.

If you attained a military driver's license while in the Legion, they
will take steps to turn it into its civilian equivalent. This is more useful if
you're French or plan to reside in France afterward, but may be helpful
in getting you a new license when you return to your homeland. They
were not able to complete my paperwork on this before I left, but said
they would forward the license to me at my residence. Two or three
months later they wrote and said they still needed a couple of photos of
me. I ended up taking the tests at home to get a license.

They will give you a number of documents as proof of your having
been in the Legion. You'll receive a vaccination booklet, a chronology of
all your activities and courses, records of medals and certificates, and the
final rank you acquired. You may never have use for any of it, but it can
help to corroborate where you've been if you ever have a need to prove it.

You'll be given a final medical examination in Aubagne or at your
regiment, and your departure may be delayed if any serious problems
are found. The Legion will want to correct any health issue, before you
leave, that may result in a liability claim. If you break your leg two weeks
before your release date, they may keep you until they're satisfied it has
properly healed.

Remaining earnings will be paid to you inclusive of the last day of
your contract. If you depart the Legion as early as I did they won't be
able to pay you in advance of an actual payday, but will forward any out-
standing payment. For this, you will need to provide your new address.
I received a check for a tidy sum after I'd returned home.

They will issue you a free train ticket to anywhere in France. They
can punch it up on a computer to give you as soon as you ask for it. I had
planned on visiting Oktoberfest in Munich before going home, so I asked
for a ticket to Strasbourg. From there I headed east into Germany. It was
only after I'd left the Legion that I realized I should have inquired about a

ticket all the way to Munich. They may not have been able to do this, or I may have had to pay the fare between Strasbourg and Munich, but it might have saved me some time and effort. You've got nothing to lose by asking for a ticket to a destination outside of France. If you're flying home, you may only need a ticket to Marseille or Nice, where you can catch a flight. You can ask at Aubagne if they handle plane reservations, but don't expect much, and definitely don't count on them paying for it.

You will have to clear out of Aubagne in a similar fashion as you did when you left your regiment — by visiting various offices around the base. You will have to turn in your good, tailored, dress uniform just before you leave, and won't be able to keep it as a souvenir. I couldn't believe that the Legion was cheap enough to deny someone the privilege of keeping their uniform, especially when it had been tailored to fit. Who else was going to wear it afterward? The way around this is to acquire a second uniform while still in your regiment, and turn that one in when it's time to leave. You are given a clothing allowance in your regiment and are allowed to order a certain number of items each year.

You will speak with a few officers before departing. They will go over the dossier you have compiled and discuss its components with you. Again, they will be trying to determine what your plans are, and if you are really clear in your decision to leave. If you're not sure what your plans are, they may try to lure you back to the Legion with offers of promotion, courses, or a desired posting. This inclination to want to keep you can work to your advantage. A friend of mine was willing to re-sign, but he wanted to be posted to a mainland regiment from the *REP,* and negotiated long and hard before they consented. If they hadn't complied he would have terminated his contract. It took nine weeks of debate to get what he wanted.

During these discussions, one officer mentioned that if I ever wanted to return to the Legion, I should first contact Aubagne. He said that the Legion was so inundated with volunteers that there was no guarantee they would take me back. Considering that I would do almost anything before returning to the Legion, this had little meaning for me, but it did reveal the situation regarding enlistees.

Before leaving, I was on guard duty one day and was called to escort a deserter to the lockup. It turned out to be someone I'd gone through basic training with, who had ended up in another regiment. He was a Croatian who had deserted to fight for his country at the outbreak of the war in Yugoslavia. I only spoke with him for a few minutes, but asked him how it had been in Croatia. He just said, "terrible, terrible." I never learned if the Legion accepted him back after being gone for two or three years, but he may have had a reasonable chance, due to the extenuating circumstances surrounding his desertion. This encounter plainly demonstrated just how tenuous the ties are that bind someone to the Legion. The Legion may have a characteristic appeal and offer a certain amount of solace, but any Legionnaire, no matter how loyal, would desert in certain instances. A short stay in the Legion doesn't negate a lifetime of attachment to the people, places, things, or events that had a hand in your upbringing.

Your last hurrah will be when you are addressed by the Commandant of the Legion. He is a general who reigns supreme over the entire French Foreign Legion. Part of the reason your last days in Aubagne go on so long is to accommodate this ceremony with the general. He takes the time once each week to say goodbye to the men leaving the Legion.

There will likely be several of you who are departing at the same time, so you will be assembled in a line to await him. When he arrives, he looks over your dossier, speaks with each person individually for a moment, then presents you with a *Certificat Des Services Militaires* (Certificate of Military Service) recognizing your stay in the Legion. If you haven't previously been able to articulate why you want to leave the Legion, it will become a topic of conversation between yourself and the Commandant. I remember two people who had vague plans for their future and were given one minute each to change their minds. Both declined.

It is here I have to blow my own horn a bit and share why this occasion was a memorable one for myself. The Commandant briefly read my dossier and asked, "Do you know what your commanding officer from the *REP* said about you?" I replied, "No sir." He proceeded to read aloud a few lines from the document he was holding, and finished by saying, "*Caporal* [E.M.] has decided to depart the ranks of the Foreign Legion … it's too bad for the Legion." I've never received a greater compliment. To have gone through five years in the French Foreign Legion and have someone say that to me just as I was leaving was incredible.

Once this ceremony is complete you are free of the Legion at long last. The next hour or so is spent changing your clothes, turning in your uniform, and wrapping up any last minute administrative details. Before leaving be sure and get a list of addresses and phone numbers to contact the Legion. Being able to stay in touch with the Legion may be the furthest thing from your mind, but it could be of some benefit in the future. When these remaining trivialities have concluded, all that's left is to stroll out the gate one final time, and enjoy the profound sense of satisfaction at having made it through five years in the Foreign Legion.

Legion memorabilia including: a *képi blanc,* a beret with the winged dagger insignia, medals, plaques, badges, insignias, photos, postcards, certificates, African currency, a Legion songbook, a Zippo lighter, a music cassette from the *Musique Principale,* and a couple of art prints bought from the museum in Aubagne. The knife, engraved with my name, is not standard issue but a gift from my *section* in 1st Company.

IN CONCLUSION

~

I've often been asked if I was glad I had been in the Legion. My stock answer is that while I have no regrets, I am very happy it's all behind me now. It was the best of times, it was the worst of times. I cannot say that for all the bad there was an equal amount of good, but it was nevertheless the experience of a lifetime. *Je ne regrette rien.* I could have regretted my decision to join, especially if I'd been seriously maimed or shipped home in a wooden box, but events turned out favorably for me. I would have regretted it more had I not gone and spent the rest of my life wishing I had. I always felt I would come through the whole experience in one piece, which I did, but this isn't something every Legionnaire can say.

If I have any regret, it was when I returned home after being away for five years and saw gray hair on my mother's head for the first time. When I left to join, her hair was jet black. I'll never know if this was partly due to my having been in the Legion, or just the natural aging process, but I suspect being in the Legion, and consequently in places like Sarajevo at the height of a war, were contributing factors. We each have our own life to live, and we can't live it through the hopes and desires of someone else, but our actions invariably have an effect on those around us.

Rarely do I talk about my time in the Legion. It's not that I have anything to hide, but I have found that mentioning it makes many people uncomfortable. A lot of people experience disquietude in the presence of

193

someone who has stepped beyond the pale so I have seldom discussed it with anybody. Neither am I interested in hearing snide remarks from self-righteous buffoons who rail against the Legion without knowing anything about it. You may find that the only empathy you receive from having been in the Legion is just being secure in the knowledge that you were there. Don't be surprised if prospective employers shy away from you at the sight of French Foreign Legion on your resume. It's only natural for people to be apprehensive about something they don't understand. Never forget that a stereotype of the Legion will always precede you, erroneous though it may be. This is part of the price you pay for having joined the Legion. Readjusting to life as a civilian can be almost as difficult as life in the Legion.

One side effect of having been in the Legion is that I still have aggravating dreams about it. No cold sweats or screams in the dark, but enough recall to be bothersome. The dream that recurs the most is one where I've signed an extension of my contract for some inexplicable reason. I can't believe that I did such a thing and am overwrought with a sense of claustrophobia as I slowly count away the days until this second contract expires. When I finally wake up, I let out a huge sigh of relief, and thank the heavens it was just a dream. It merely illustrates how anxious I was to be done with the Legion.

I have declined from mentioning or making reference to the names of people I knew in deference to the inviolable right of anonymity enjoyed by each member of the Legion. You often never learn the secret reasons that propelled someone to the Legion's fold, and to betray this confidence would fracture the sacrosanct integrity regarding privacy expected of everyone who has ever served there. I remember being shown a video in Fort de Nogent of exactly what I mean about the privilege of remaining anonymous. Even though it was in French, and most of us couldn't speak it at the time, we all got the message when it satired one Legionnaire killing another because of the violation of this code. Most people I met didn't have a deep, dark, mysterious past, but a host of names would do little to enhance the credibility of all I've related to you.

I trust I've been able to provide enough information about what the Legion is like and what you can expect of it to aid you in your decision. I know I developed a number of biases both for and against the Legion, but I don't think they've cast so much of a shadow that the facts have been obscured. Still, I hope that you will not entertain any plans to join. If you were sitting on the fence, I've given you ample incentive not to.

At the very least, I hope I've given you enough reasons to stop and think before you act. If you're currently a soldier in another army, or have military experience, you may want to consider remaining where you are, or find another outlet for your interest in military endeavors. Ex-soldiers, more than anybody else, are disappointed and even disgusted by much of what they discover in the Legion.

My wish has been to dispense a few words of wisdom, not to fuel the imaginations of romanticists. We used to have a little saying that went, "It's not an adventure when you're living it." The Legion might attract men from all walks of life, but it does take a certain type of individual to follow through and prevail as a Legionnaire, and only a small percentage of determined men manage to do this.

I remember philosophizing with a fellow Legionnaire. We both agreed that to come to the Legion and go through all it throws at you, sets a person apart from others like little else can. This may sound like I'm vaunting my own exploits, which is partially true, but I hope I've made you distinctly aware of how sincerely dedicated you must be to make it as a Legionnaire. The Legion is definitely not for everyone, and I shudder to think of someone joining on impulse due to a rousing influence from this or any other form of media.

Please take your time and think about what you're doing before making a decision that could turn out to be the sorriest course of action you ever take. I spent six long years weighing the potential consequences of joining the Legion. Even if I'd had this information, I probably still would have joined. I wanted to experience the Legion, and nothing could have stopped me. I fully understand what it's like to be fixated on a goal and rendered myopic by an all-consuming passion, so be wary of the one great danger you face in any resolutions you make to join; yourself. You are ultimately the cause for the effects that result from your decision.

I've given you the facts as I knew them to be as of October, 1994. Things are continually changing, so you may find that your experiences are a marked departure from what I've related to you here. For the handful of you who do venture forth to join the French Foreign Legion, I can only wish you the very best of luck and a safe return. Be careful out there.

My Favorite Moment

Before we part ways I would like to share with you a small event that I regard as my most gratifying moment in the Legion.

We stopped at a small game farm north of N'Djamena one day, and spent some time looking at the wildlife. Just before we were ready to leave, I was standing watch over our vehicles when I noticed a group of local children approach to within about 30 meters. One of the kids appeared to be carrying a small animal, but I couldn't quite see what he had because of the distance. He stood there for a moment talking before dropping it carelessly on the grass. The kids ran off to play somewhere, and I stood watching this thing they had left behind expecting it to move. A minute or two passed and when this creature still hadn't moved, curiosity got the better of me. I strolled over to where it was.

I thought I knew what I was looking at, and these suspicions were confirmed as I got closer. Sitting upright with its head slumped forward on its chest was a baby monkey. I approached it as quietly as I could, not wanting to scare it away. I got within a couple of feet before stopping. For some reason it did not seem to be aware of how near I was and remained sitting there with its head bent over. I began to wonder if it was even alive, so I picked up a stick and gently nudged its side. I heard a soft whimper, and saw its tiny diaphragm moving up and down, but it was still unresponsive to my presence. I then noticed how dirty and matted its fur was and began to realize that it was probably sick. Since a group of kids had been carrying it around, it may not have had a mother to care for it.

At that point I wondered if it might be in need of a drink of water so I took my canteen, filled the cap, and bent down to hold it under its nose. As soon as I did it suddenly came to life, grasped both sides of the cap with its little hands, and began sipping at the water. It coughed quietly a few times as it drank but it never let go until the cap was empty. I refilled it three or four times and let the monkey keep drinking. Even after it was done it continued to clutch the cap as if afraid to let it go for fear of not being able to drink again. The water seemed to rejuvenate it and it looked at me several times with almost human-like acknowledgment.

The rest of our *section* noticed what I was doing and came over to see what was happening. Someone produced a camera and took a couple of pictures, but to my everlasting regret I was never able to secure a photo for myself. The kids showed up again not long after and took possession of it as we departed, hopefully in slightly better condition.

Being able to help this poor little monkey was an especially pleasant interlude, and the incident made my day. I was smiling for a long time thereafter, and still do whenever I think of it.

LEGION SONGS

———

Here are just a few of the songs you will have to learn in the Legion. If you take the time to translate them and teach yourself some French you will see that there is an unsettling theme of death and defeat running through many of them. The final song is in German, evidence of the strong presence of German nationals in the Legion after World War II.

Le Boudin – The Sausage [Equivocal translation]

Sous Le Soleil Brûlant D'Afrique – Under the Burning Sun of Africa

Eugénie – Eugenie

La Lune Est Claire – The Moon Is Clear

Képi Blanc – White Képi

Contre Les Viets – Against the Viets [Vietnamese]

En Algérie – In Algeria

La Petite Piste – The Little Trail

Soldats De La Légion Étrangerè – Soldiers of the Foreign Legion

La Légion Marche – The Legion Marches

En Afrique, Malgré Le Vent, La Pluie – In Africa, in Spite of
the Wind, the Rain

Schwarze Rose – Black Rose

Le Boudin

Translated in Chapter 4.

Sous Le Soleil Brûlant D'Afrique

Refrain:

Vive la Légion étrangère
Et quand défilent les képis blancs
Si leur allure n'est pas légère,
Ils portent tous tête haute et fière,
Et s'élançant dans la fournaise,
Le coeur joyeux, jamais tremblant,
Au son de notre Marseillaise,
Savent combattre les képis blancs.

1.

Sous le soleil brûlant d'Afrique,
Cochinchine, Madagascar,
Une phalange magnifique,
A fait flotter nos étendards,
Sa devise Honneur et Vaillance,
Forme des soldats valereux,
Son drapeau, celui de la France,
Est un emblème des plus glorieux.

2.

C'est une chose d'importance,
La discipline de la Legion,
L'amour du chef, l'obéissance,
Sont de plus pure tradition,
Et pour notre France chérie,
Tous ces étrangers bravement,
Viennent défendre la patrie,
Avec honneur et dévouement.

Eugénie

Eugénie les larmes aux yeux
Nous venons te dire adieu
Nous partons de bon matin
Par un ciel des plus sereins
Nous partons pour le Mexique
Nous partons la voile au vent
Adieu donc belle Eugénie,
Nous reviendrons dans un an.

Ce n'est pas commode du tout
Que de penser a l'amour
Surtout quand il fait grand vent
Par dessus l'gaillard d'avant
Nous partons pour le Mexique
Nous partons la voile au vent
Adieu donc belle Eugénie
Nous reviendrons dans un an.

La Lune Est Claire

La lune est claire, la ville dort,
J'ai rendez-vous avec celle que j'adore.
Mais la Légion s'en va,
Oui s'en va,
Part au baroud, baroud,
Jeannine je reviendrai
Sans aucun doute.

Mais la mitraille autour de moi,
Elle ne respecte pas la loi.
Les légionnaires les plus vaillants
Tombent sous le feu, le feu
Mais ton amour Jeannine m'a protégé.

Képi Blanc

Puisqu'il nous faut vivre et lutter dans la souffrance
Le jour est venu où nous imposerons au front
La force de nos âmes
La force de nos coeurs et de nos bras
Foulant la boue sombre
Vont les képis blancs.

La rue appartient à celui qui y descend
La rue appartient au drapeau des képis blancs
Autour de nous la haine
Autour de nous les dogmes que l'on abat
Foulant la boue sombre
Vont les képis blancs.

Combiens sont tombés au hasard d'un clair matin
De nos camarades qui souriaient au destin
Nous tomberons en route
Nous tomberons ou vaincrons au combat
Foulant la boue sombre
Vont les képis blancs.

La vie ne sourit qu'aux plus forts, aux plus vaillants
L'ardeur, la fierté, la jeunesse sont dans nos rangs,
Pour nos combats, nos luttes
Honneur, Fidélité sur nos drapeaux
Foulant la boue sombre
Vont les képis blancs.

Contre Les Viets

Refrain:
O légionnaires, le combat qui commence,
Met dans nos âmes, enthousiasme et vaillance,
Peuvent pleuvoir grenades et gravates,
Notre victoire en aura plus d'éclat.

1.
Contre les Viets, contre l'ennemi,
Partout où le devoir fait signe,
Soldats de France, soldats du pays,
Nous remonterons vers les lignes.

2.
Et si la mort frappe en chemin,
Si nos doigts sanglants se crispent au sol,
Un dernier rêve: adieu à demain,
Nous souhaiterons faire école.

3.
Malgré les balles, malgré les obus,
Sous les rafales ou sous les bombes,
Nous avançons vers le même but,
Dédaignant l'appel de la tombe.

En Algérie

En Algérie, dans le djebel,
Un légionnaire monte la garde
Auprès de son camarade,
Touché à mort par une balle rebelle.

Camarade, toi mon pays,
Je vous quitte sans regret,
Volontaire, j'ai bien servi,
Avec honneur et fidélité.

Un légionnaire quand il tombe,
Quand il a fermé les yeux,
Il repose en Algérie,
Dans le djebel une croix le dit.

La Petite Piste

Refrain:

O porteur
Et Askari
Aillo, Aillo-Ay Safari.

1.
Combien d'fois a-t'on parcouru
Cette petite piste
Traversant la lande herbue
Lorsque le jour se lève
En écoutant le rythme
De la chanson intime.

2.
Et quand un jour nous partirons
Pour le dernier voyage
Chante-nous cette chanson
Comme un dernier hommage
Et s'il ne pleure personne
Que Dieu nous le pardonne.

Soldats De La Légion Étrangère

Soldats de la Légion Étrangère
Se sont battus
Partout en Algérie;
Beaucoup sont tombés, de braves légionnaires
Pour la Légion, qui est notre Patrie.

Comme nos anciens
Nous défendrons l'Algérie
Contre le diable
Et contre les fellaghas
Avec notre drapeaux, Honneur, Fidélité
Nous tomberons ou vaincrons au combat.

La Légion Marche

Refrain:
Nous sommes les hommes des troupes d'assaut,
Soldats de la vieille Légion,
Demain brandissant nos drapeaux,
En vainqueurs nous défilerons,
Nous n'avons pas seulement des armes,
Mais le diable marche avec nous,
Ha, ha, ha, ha, ha, ha, car nos aînés de la Légion,
Se battant là-bas, nous emboîtons le pas.

1.
La Légion marche vers le front,
En chantant nous suivons,
Héritiers de ses traditions,
Nous sommes avec elle.

2.
Pour ce destin de chevalier,
Honneur, Fidélité,
Nous sommes fiers d'appartenir au
2ème R.E.P.

En Afrique, Malgré Le Vent, La Pluie

Refrain:

Dans le ciel brille l'étoile qui lui rappelle son enfance
Adieu mon pays, adieu mon pays, jamais je ne t'oublierai
Heili, Heilo Heili Heilo, Hei tralalalala la la
Heili, Heilo Heili Heilo, Hei tralalalala
Dans le ciel brille l'étoile qui lui rappelle son enfance
Adieu mon pays jamais je ne t'oublierai.

1.

En Afrique, malgré le vent , la pluie,
Guette la sentinelle sur le piton,
Mais son coeur est au pays chéri,
Quitté pour voir des horizons lointains,
Ses yeux ont aperçu l'ennemi, (qui s'approche), (bis)
L'alerte est sonnée, les souvenirs s'envolent
Maintenant au combat.

Schwarze Rose

Im hafen kehren die Legionäre
Bei der schwarzen rose ein
Sie pfeiffen auf geld und ruhm und ehre
Denn schon bald kann alles anders sein.

Refrain:

Schwarze rose von Oran
Küss noch einmal deinen Legionär
Schwarze rose von Oran
Vielleicht siehst du ihn nicht mehr
Schwarze rose schwarze rose
Küss noch einmal deinen Legionar
Schwarze rose schwarze rose
Vielleicht siehst du ihn nicht mehr.

Dein leben gehört den Legionären
Denn du kennst den grossen schmerz
Du weisst dass sie niemals wiederkehren
Darum schenkst du dem jungen auch dein herz.

GLOSSARY

—

T he following is a list of a few words and phrases you are likely to encounter along with their meanings. Many of the words are Legion slang, not readily spoken among French citizens. All italicized text throughout the book denotes a word or phrase in a language other than English. The term "Legionnaire" has not been italicized. I've also included a few profanities since everyone wants to know how to swear in a foreign language.

acte d'engagement: the contract you sign at the recruiting center. Not binding until you've passed a six month probationary period.

affectation: the administrative process whereby you are assigned to one of the regiments.

AK47: Russian manufactured assault rifle.

anciens: ex-Legionnaires. Usually elderly war veterans.

anonymat: anonymous.

appel: roll call.

a priori: "it would seem as if," "it seems as though." It took me forever to figure out what this meant. I finally found a definition of it in an English dictionary of all places. It refers "to a mode of reasoning by which we proceed from the cause to the effect; applied to knowledge independent of or prior to all experience." In layman's terms, this means to assume something about a person or situation without having all the facts. For example, if a *sergent,* who doesn't know you, sees you walking around with your beret on backwards, he might say *"A priori t'es une brelle"* (It would appear as though you're an idiot).

bâche: a plastic tarp used in the field as a makeshift tent.

baguette du pain: an elongated loaf of bread with a nearly impervious shell-like crust.

baiser: to have sexual intercourse.

bakshish: Arabic term for a present or gratuity of money. Usually voiced as a supplication for alms.

balai: broom. A word you'll become all too familiar with.

banane: a mistake or error. It's also a banana.

béret: a soft cap worn with your combat uniform that displays your unit's insignia. The Legion is the only unit in the French army that wears a green beret other than the *Commandos Marines,* a regular unit.

binôme: a French speaking partner who is assigned to you during basic training to assist you in speaking French, and to help you understand what is going on at any given moment. You may also have a *binôme* in your combat regiment, but his role is usually more as someone who watches your back in combat situations than as a tutor.

bite: penis.

bordel: a mess. Untidiness or confusion.

boudin: literally means black pudding, but refers to blood sausage that is a part of the Legion's traditional menu. A disgusting meal that most people don't even eat. The inside of the sausage does resemble a grainy, meaty, black pudding.

bouffe: food, nourishment.

boy: a local worker hired to wash and iron your laundry and keep your living quarters clean. I only heard the term applied to black Africans, and could never be sure whether or not the French realized it was a derogatory expression in English.

brelage: combat web gear. The model in use in 1994 being poorly designed and out of date.

brelle: an incredibly stupid person. An idiot.

brevet: a badge indicating your regimental designation or that displays the courses you've successfully completed. For example, passing a parachute course would earn you a *brevet parachutiste.*

cadeau: gift or present. African locals will yell this at you hoping you'll part with something of value. Also refers to the gift each Legion member receives at Christmas.

cadre: the upper echelon on the rank scale. The Legion considers anyone who is a *sergent* and above to be *cadre.*

caporal du jour: caporal of the day. A duty that rotates between *section caporals.* He is in charge of all details regarding roll call, *corvée,* organizing the activities of the *section,* and ensuring that orders pertaining to the *section* as issued by the *cadre* are carried out.

caporal de semaine: caporal of the week. A duty that rotates between company *caporals.* He is in charge of blowing a whistle at specified times of the day to coordinate company level activities.

capote: condom. An essential item to have before you can go out on the town in Africa.

casse croûte: snack. Because the French don't eat a heavy breakfast, *casse croûte* is usually eaten after morning sports activity around 9:00 A.M. It normally consists of a piece of bread torn off of a *baguette* and filled with *pâté,* sardines, ham, or other type of meat.

c'est pas la peine: "it's not worth it," "there's no point in doing that," "don't bother," "leave well enough alone." A phrase you will frequently hear and be able to distinguish, due to its rhythmic tempo, from the babble of French you won't understand as a new recruit.

cheche: a long cloth scarf worn as a turban, face cover, or around the neck. Not a part of your regular issued gear, but is distributed for use in Africa. Hot to wear if you're not used to it.

chef de chambre: the person in charge of a sleeping and living quarters. Usually a *caporal* but can be a *caporal-chef.*

Chef de Corps: the commanding officer of your regiment. A *colonel.*

chef de poste: the person in charge of the regiment's main guard house and all the activities associated with it for a 24 hour period. Almost always a *sergent.*

chiasse: diarrhea. A guaranteed occurrence within your first week in Africa.

chiote: I could never figure out if this meant a toilet or feces. The only way I ever heard it used was as *corvée chiote* which meant to either clean the toilets or whatever mess was left inside them.

clochard: a vagabond. Refers to someone whose attire or living space is dirty or untidy.

compagnie: company. A regimental company will have 150 men when departing overseas.

compte rendu: an administrative procedure where a commentary is written by hand in triplicate for any matter requiring clarification. It is most commonly used to account for incidents of theft or broken, damaged, or lost equipment. It can be used as a mild form of punishment due to the meticulous effort needed to write it properly.

con: stupid.

connard: a person who is stupid.

corvée: chore or work detail.

coubaya: (I'm not sure of the spelling). A large cooler filled with ice to keep perishables from spoiling while in the field. Normally used only in Africa.

couilles: balls, testicles. If someone says *"J'en ai pleins de couilles"* it literally means — I have full balls — but really means you have one severely pissed-off individual on your hands.

cul: ass, bum, rectum. When you're being counted in a line-up you often hear the order *"bite au cul"* which means for everybody to squeeze together, with everyone's *bite* approaching uncomfortably close to the *cul* in front of them.

dégage: "get out of here." Usually spoken in a rude manner. Synonymous to the English use of "fuck off."

dégueulasse: gross, disgusting. The French think ketchup is *dégueulasse* if you can believe it. To me it is one of the world's finest gourmet sauces, so I could never quite understand their point of view. Neither did I appreciate having to pay for it anytime I had a Big Mac and fries at a French McDonald's.

démerder: to make do with available resources. A hallmark the Legion prides itself on. It likes to think of itself as having the ingenuity to do anything from tunneling through mountains with only picks and shovels to mopping floors with a wet towel thrown around a broom head.

demi-tour droite: drill command meaning "About turn!"

doucement: softly or gently. Usually spoken to mean "take it easy."

élève: student. On your *caporal*'s course you are known as an *élève caporal*.

engagé gamelle: mess tin recruit. Someone who joins the Legion more out of an interest in food than in being a soldier. Usually refers disparagingly to men from eastern bloc countries or less than affluent nations.

engagé volontaire: volunteer recruit.

épervier: sparrowhawk. Refers to the name of the ongoing French military operation in Chad.

étrangère: foreign.

extinction des feux: lights out. Whistled at 10:30 P.M.

fait foutre: loosely means to go fuck yourself. Usually said as *"vas te faire foutre."* *Foutre* refers to semen, so *"va te faire foutre"* translates closely as "go make semen on yourself." You may also hear *"tu ma fouts la gueule ou quoi?"* which means "are you kidding me or what?" but since *gueule* refers to a person's face, you can infer the literal meaning. You could probably survive without these little gems of wisdom. Just make sure you never say them to someone who outranks you.

fait gaffe: "watch yourself," "watch your step." Used either in a menacing tone to indicate that someone is very displeased with you, or simply to alert you to a hazard.

FAMAS: acronym referring to the standard-issue assault rifle of the French army. It stands for *Fusil Automatique Manufacture d'Armes de St. Etienne.*

fin de contrat: end of contract. Expiration of the contract you sign with the Legion.

footing: Legion slang for a jog or run. I suspect this word is an adaptation of the English word "foot" which was somehow transmuted into Legion vernacular.

foot-foot: (I'm not sure of the spelling). Refers to someone who assumes the tentative rank of *caporal* after a mere four months of basic training. He is required to remain in Castel for the duration of several basic training courses. He will be a member of the training staff in return for an accelerated promotion to full *caporal.*

foulard: triangular, colored piece of cloth worn on the left shoulder of your combat uniform to identify a regimental company when in the field.

fouragère: braided piece of colored cord worn on the left shoulder as decoration with your dress uniform that indicates which regiment you belong to. Not all regiments wear a *fouragère.*

foyer: common lounge area found on all bases. It will have a bar and small store where you can purchase things like a new *képi,* portable camp stoves, cassette tapes, walkmans, watches, cameras, articles of clothing, food, beer, magazines, and a variety of other items. It is one of the few places you can relax on base after a workday, but closes at 9:00 P.M.

fusil: rifle.

galon: rank insignia worn on the center of your combat vest. It is a Velcroed piece of cloth that can be removed and replaced depending on the situation. Usually anytime the *brelage* is worn, your *galon* and name tag, which is also Velcroed, are removed from your uniform.

gamelle: cooking pot, mess tin.

garde à vous: drill command meaning "Attention!"

gendarme: French civilian police officer.

GPS: English abbreviation for Global Positioning System. A hand held receiver is used to acquire signals from a satellite system that calculates your position to within 10 meters and displays the coordinates on the receiver — an invaluable device to have especially in the middle of Africa's trackless wastelands.

grade: rank.

groupe: a formation of seven to ten men within a company's *section.*

gueule: a person's mouth or face. You will hear this most often as *"ta gueule"* or *"ferme ta gueule"* which both mean shut your mouth. You will never hear *"ferme ta bouche"* as an order to shut your mouth even though *bouche* is the well known form of mouth.

housse: a covering with a Velcro seam that protects your weapon from water and dirt.

infirmerie: infirmary, sick room.

infirmier: medic.

interdit: forbidden, prohibited.

je ne regrette rien: "I regret nothing." A tenet affirmed by many Legionnaires as their stance on having joined the Legion.

jumelles: binoculars. Not to be confused with *gamelles.*

képi blanc: traditional white peaked cap recognized as a symbol of the Foreign Legion throughout the world. *Képi blanc* also refers to the monthly magazine about the Legion published in Aubagne.

Legio Patria Nostra: "The Legion is our Fatherland." Motto of the Foreign Legion.

légionnaire: a member of the Foreign Legion with the equivalent rank of "private."

Legionnaire: any member of the Foreign Legion.

linge: laundry.

matricule: your personal six-digit serial number issued to you in Aubagne. It must be memorized and recited aloud in French before departing for basic training. Never forget it.

mec: guy, man.

mégot: cigarette butt.

merde: shit.

Métro: subway system.

Métropole: mother country, mainland France. In the Legion the term also refers to the regiments that are located in France itself, including the *REP,* which is on the island of Corsica.

mission profonde: literally "deep mission." Refers to the prolonged excursions into the jungles of French Guiana undertaken by the *3ᵉ REI.*

Monument aux Morts: Monument to the Dead. Located on the parade square at Aubagne, the monument is a huge globe on a marble pedestal guarded on its four corners by bronze statues of Legionnaires.

moustiquaire: mosquito net. Issued when operating in areas where the possibility of contracting malaria is heightened, such as Africa or French Guiana.

moustique: mosquito.

Musique Principale: the main band of the Foreign Legion. The regiments often have their own musical accompaniment made up of volunteers within the regiment, but they aren't normally as skilled as the *Musique Principale,* who play music for their bread and butter. The *Musique Principale* spends a lot of its time practicing, visiting the regiments on special occasions, and traveling around the world putting on shows. You can volunteer to become a member when you're asked which regiment you prefer to join, or when you return to Aubagne after basic training.

NCO: English abbreviation for non-commissioned officer. It includes the French ranks from *sergent* to *major. Major* in the French army is not the rank of an officer, but is as high as one can go without becoming an officer. NCO translates into *sous-officier* or "under-officer" which is what the ranks from *sergent* to *major* are known as.

niveau général: general level. Refers to a score out of 20 that measures your basic abilities and aptitudes. The score is extracted from the results of the tests you take at Aubagne as a raw recruit, and follows you throughout your time in the Legion.

on s'en fou: "who cares?"

on y va: "let's go." "Away we go."

outre mer: overseas.

paludisme: malaria. Also called *palu* for short.

Paludrine: anti-malarial tablets taken with your noon meal while in Africa or other high risk malaria zones.

paquetage: the military gear that is issued to you at Aubagne before you depart for basic training.

passe partout: literally means "go everywhere." Refers to the piece of paper you have to have signed by all administrative offices in a regiment anytime you arrive as a new member of that regiment, anytime you depart one regiment to be posted to another regiment, or when leaving the Legion at the end of your contract.

passe rapport: to be called up in front of your *section* or company commander for the purpose of input and feedback with them. Everybody is summoned to *"passe rapport"* at least once a year, whereupon your performance is evaluated and the needs and concerns of yourself and your superiors are addressed. You can request to *passe rapport* any time you feel the need.

pâté: meat paste. Normally comes in a small tin and is commonly found in ration packs.

permission: vacation leave of various durations.

permissionnaire: someone on vacation leave.

peter: to fart.

piaule: room, living quarters.

pif: Legion slang for wine.

PMs: *police militaire.* The Legion's internal policing force that maintains order among its own troops and upholds the rules of decorum particular to the Legion.

popote: refers to a drinking mess and lounge area. Officers, NCOs, and *caporal-chefs* each have their own *popote* which is separate from common areas like the company club or *foyer.* You either have to be the corresponding rank to frequent a *popote* or be invited as a guest.

popotier: someone who works in a *popote* handling all the bartending, cleaning, and serving duties. Usually a *légionnaire* but can be a *caporal.* It also refers to someone who serves the *cadre* and cleans up after them while in the field. You will be led to believe that it is somehow an honor to perform these duties, but it is a despised chore to be avoided at all costs.

pot: a small get-together to say goodbye to anyone who is departing a unit, irrespective of rank or time served with that unit. Usually only done at a *section* level. Beer and party snacks are consumed and a small gift given to the person(s) leaving.

poussière: dust.

promotion: *promo* for short. Refers to the parachute course taken immediately upon arrival in the *2e REP.*

putain: a whore but uttered as an expression of disgust.

pute: also a whore.

Puyloubier: location of the retirement home for Legion veterans and the vineyards from which the Legion produces its own wine.

quart: metal canteen cup.

quartier: quarter, neighborhood, immediate vicinity.

rabiot: leftovers. Shouted by the cooks in the mess hall once everyone has been served, often resulting in a fevered scramble for the serving counter — especially at Castel.

raid marche: route march. A lengthy march often lasting several days, used for both training and endurance conditioning. You will do this type of march at the end of basic training, at the end of your *caporal*'s course, any time you complete a commando course, and on other occasions determined appropriate throughout your training in the Legion.

ramasser: to pick something up, such as pieces of garbage or cigarette butts. It also has another meaning that you might not immediately interpret. If someone is pointing a finger or shaking a fist at you and says in a threatening tone *"Fait gaffe mec ou tu vas ramasser"* it doesn't mean "watch it or you're going to pick something up" but rather "you'd better watch yourself or you're going to get it!" "It" referring to a punch in the face or something equally unpleasant.

Rangers: the combat boots worn by the French army that have a distinctive leather flap and two buckles in addition to the laces. You will notice that the French tend to refer to many items by their brand names rather than what an item actually is. Combat boots are never called *bottes de combats* but rather, *Rangers.* Another example is calling a truck by its manufacturer's name such as *Simca* and *Marmon* instead of *camion,* which is what it actually is.

RAS: *"rien a signaler."* "Nothing to signal or report," "everything's normal or OK." You will hear this all the time as both a question and a response and is spoken either as one word (*rass*) or as individual letters (*air ah ess*).

rassemblement: assembly. It is both the command to assemble (*rassemblement!*) and what the actual assembly is known as. A company *rassemblement* takes place twice daily at 7:30 a.m. and 2:00 p.m. and any other time necessary, such as when organizing for a parachute jump.

rempez les rangs: drill command for "dismissed." When I first heard this order it sounded like *"rompeleron"* and I couldn't understand it. When this happens, just try and blend into the crowd and follow what everyone else is doing.

rendre compte: literally means to give back the count. Report back.

REP man: a French phrase using the English word "man" to describe someone (a man) serving in the *REP.*

repos: drill command for "stand at ease."

réveille: wake up. Whistled at 5:00 A.M.

sac à dos: rucksack.

seau: pail, bucket.

section: a formation of 30 men within a company. A company departing on *tour-nante* will have a total of 5 *sections*: 4 combat *sections* and a headquarters *section* totalling 150 men. *Section* strengths in a company within a regiment constantly fluctuate for any number of reasons; desertions, people on course or vacation, etc.

séjour: sojourn, stay. Refers to a tour overseas as in a *séjour outre mer.*

semaine: a week. Also refers to the office that coordinates activities within a company. This office is known as the *semaine* due to the length of time the duty here lasts, which is to say one week.

sergent de semaine: the *sergent* in charge of the duties of the *semaine.* This task may also be given to a *caporal-chef.*

serpillière: a towel that is soaked in water then wrapped around a broom head to serve as an improvised mop.

sieste: a nap. In Africa the Legion incorporates a four hour *sieste* into its work day between noon and 4:00 P.M. to wait out the overpowering afternoon heat.

sketch: charade, farce, useless or annoying activity serving no practical purpose. For example, being required to assemble then march to the mess hall while singing every day for the noon meal usually elicits several disgusted grumbles of *"quel sketch!"* May be an English adaptation of the same word. Also refers to the skits that are put on every Christmas for entertainment.

solde: your monthly pay disbursed to you in cash.

sortie en ville: a night out on the town.

sortie terrain: field excursion for training and adapting to local conditions.

sous-officier: a non-commissioned officer. Includes the ranks from *sergent* to *major.*

stage: training course.

tarif militaire: military rate. Your regiment provides you with a card that grants you a 75 percent reduction on all train travel within France.

taule: the lockup located at the main guard house.

tchatcher: it's slang, meaning to chatter.

tête de noeud: knot head. Said as an insult.

titre de permission: a slip of paper you must fill out and have signed by your *section* commander if you want to leave base for the night and stay out past *appel.*

tournante: a rotating tour overseas. Usually of a four month duration.

VAB: véhicule de l'avant blindé. Front line armored vehicle. France's principal wheeled armored personnel carrier.

VLRA: véhicule léger de reconnaissance et d'appui. Light reconnaissance and support vehicle. Pronounced as one word: *velera.* Oversized pickup truck used for operations in Africa.

zone de saut: literally means "jump zone," but refers to the zone where both parachutists and material can be dropped from an airplane. Drop zone.

This is just a small sampling of the words and phrases you will come in contact with during your daily interactions in the Legion. I haven't even scratched the surface in relating all that you will hear and would have to write a dictionary to give you the full extent. Once again, take the time to learn as much French as you can before attempting to join. Even though most people don't, it can make your life immeasurably easier if you are able to understand and be understood. No matter how smart someone may be, if they can't relate their thoughts clearly and concisely their competency may be in doubt, and others less likely to give them their entire trust and respect.

INDEX

—

213